Teach Yourself VISUAL

Excel® 2013

Visual™

Paul McFedries

WILEY

John Wiley & Sons, Inc.

Teach Yourself VISUALLY™ Excel® 2013

Published by
John Wiley & Sons, Inc.
10475 Crosspoint Boulevard
Indianapolis, IN 46256

www.wiley.com

Published simultaneously in Canada

Library of Congress Control Number: 2012955839

ISBN: 978-1-118-50539-7

Manufactured in the United States of America

10 9 8 7 6 5 4 3 2 1

Trademark Acknowledgments

Contact Us

For general information on our other products and services please contact our Customer Care Department within the U.S. at 877-762-2974, outside the U.S. at 317-572-3993 or fax 317-572-4002.

For technical support please visit www.wiley.com/techsupport.

WILEY **Sales** | Contact Wiley at (877) 762-2974 or fax (317) 572-4002.

Credits

Executive Editor
Jody Lefevere

Project Editor
Lynn Northrup

Technical Editor
Namir Shammas

Copy Editor
Marylouise Wiack

Editorial Director
Robyn Siesky

Business Manager
Amy Knies

Senior Marketing Manager
Sandy Smith

**Vice President and Executive
Group Publisher**
Richard Swadley

**Vice President and Executive
Publisher**
Barry Pruett

Project Coordinator
Sheree Montgomery

Graphics and Production Specialists
Jennifer Henry
Jennifer Mayberry

Quality Control Technician
John Greenough

Proofreading
Cynthia Fields

Indexing
Potomac Indexing, LLC

About the Author

Paul McFedries is a full-time technical writer. He has been authoring computer books since 1991 and has more than 80 books to his credit. Paul's books have sold more than four million copies worldwide. These books include the Wiley titles *Teach Yourself VISUALLY Windows 8, Windows 8 Visual Quick Tips, The Facebook Guide for People Over 50, iPhone 5 Portable Genius,* and *iPad and iPad mini Portable Genius.* Paul is also the proprietor of Word Spy (www.wordspy.com), a website that tracks new words and phrases as they enter the language. Paul invites you to drop by his personal website at www.mcfedries.com or follow him on Twitter @paulmcf and @wordspy.

Author's Acknowledgments

It goes without saying that writers focus on text, and I certainly enjoyed focusing on the text that you will read in this book. However, this book is more than just the usual collection of words and phrases designed to educate and stimulate the mind. A quick thumb through the pages will show you that this book is also chock-full of treats for the eye, including copious screenshots, beautiful colors, and sharp fonts. Those sure make for a beautiful book, and that beauty comes from a lot of hard work by Wiley's immensely talented group of designers and layout artists. They are all listed in the Credits section on the previous page and I thank them for creating another gem. Of course, what you read in this book must also be accurate, logically presented, and free of errors. Ensuring all of this was an excellent group of editors with whom I got to work directly, including project editor Lynn Northrup, copy editor Marylouise Wiack, and technical editor Namir Shammas. Thanks to all of you for your exceptional competence and hard work. Thanks, as well, to Wiley executive editor Jody Lefevere for asking me to write this book.

How to Use This Book

Who This Book Is For

This book is for the reader who has never used this particular technology or software application. It is also for readers who want to expand their knowledge.

The Conventions in This Book

❶ Steps

This book uses a step-by-step format to guide you easily through each task. **Numbered steps** are actions you must do; **bulleted steps** clarify a point, step, or optional feature; and **indented steps** give you the result.

❷ Notes

Notes give additional information — special conditions that may occur during an operation, a situation that you want to avoid, or a cross-reference to a related area of the book.

❸ Icons and Buttons

Icons and buttons show you exactly what you need to click to perform a step.

❹ Tips

Tips offer additional information, including warnings and shortcuts.

❺ Bold

Bold type shows command names or options that you must click or text or numbers you must type.

❻ Italics

Italic type introduces and defines a new term.

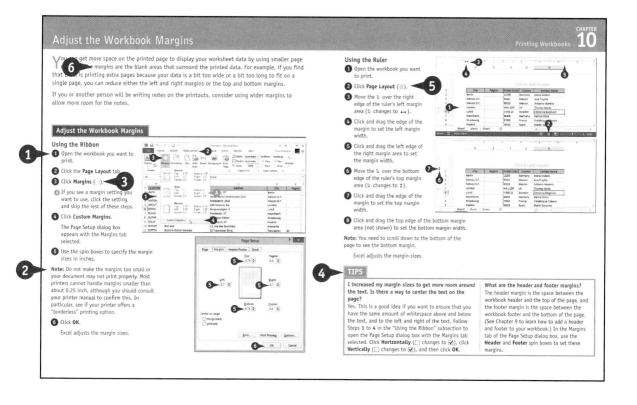

Table of Contents

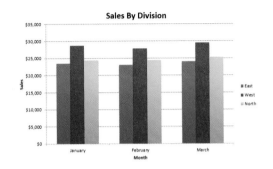

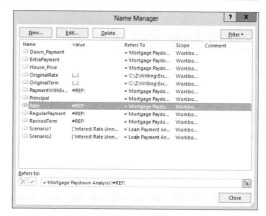

Table of Contents

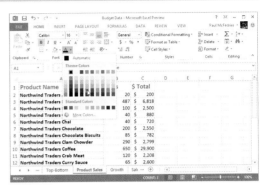

Chapter 7 | Manipulating Worksheets

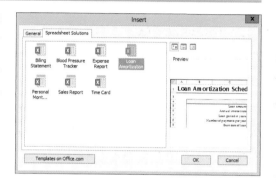

Table of Contents

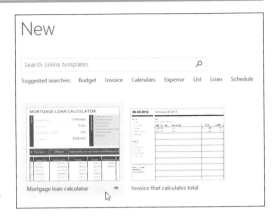

Chapter 10 Printing Workbooks

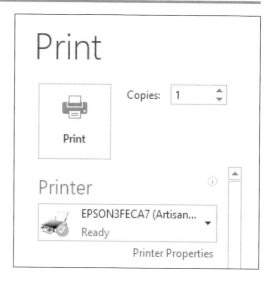

Chapter 11 Working with Tables

Table of Contents

Chapter 12 — Analyzing Data

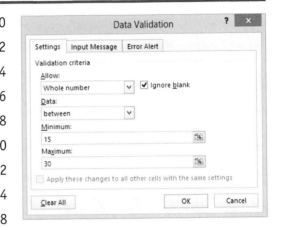

Chapter 13 — Visualizing Data with Charts

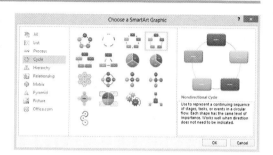

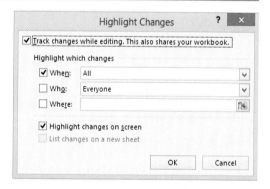

CHAPTER 1

Working with Excel

You use Microsoft Excel to create *spreadsheets*, which are documents that enable you to manipulate numbers and formulas to quickly create powerful mathematical, financial, and statistical models. In this chapter you learn about Excel, take a tour of the program's features, and learn how to customize some aspects of the program.

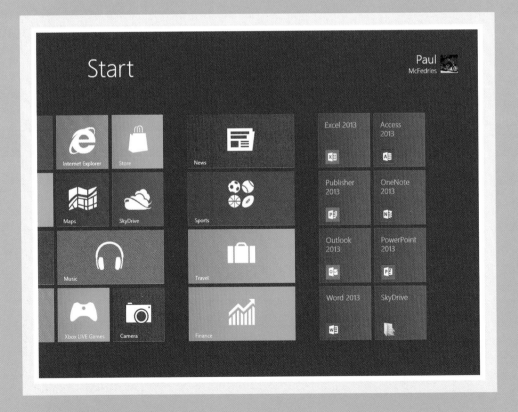

Getting to Know Excel

Working with Excel involves two basic tasks: building a spreadsheet and then manipulating the data on the spreadsheet. Building a spreadsheet involves adding data such as numbers and text, creating formulas that run calculations, and adding functions that perform specific tasks. Manipulating spreadsheet data involves calculating totals, adding data series, organizing data into tables, and visualizing data with charts.

This section just gives you an overview of these tasks. You learn about each task in greater detail as you work through the book.

Build a Spreadsheet

Add Data

You can insert numbers, text, and other characters into any cell in the spreadsheet. Click the cell that you want to work with and then type your data in the formula bar. This is the large text box above the column letters. Your typing appears in the cell that you selected. When you are done, press Enter. To edit existing cell data, click the cell and then edit the text in the formula bar.

	Expense Budget Calculation		
1	**Expense Budget Calculation**		
2			
3	**January**	**February**	**March**
4	**Advertising** 4,600	4,200	5,200
5	**Rent** 2,100	2,100	2,100
6	**Supplies** 1,300	1,200	1,400
7	**Salaries** 16,000	16,000	16,500
8	**Utilities** 500	600	600
9			

Add a Formula

A *formula* is a collection of numbers, cell addresses, and mathematical operators that performs a calculation. In Excel, you enter a formula in a cell by typing an equal sign (=) and then the formula text. For example, the formula =B1-B2 subtracts the value in cell B2 from the value in cell B1.

	Expense Budget Calculation		
1	**Expense Budget Calculation**		
2			
3	**January**	**February**	**March**
4	**Advertising** 4,600	4,200	5,200
5	**Rent** 2,100	2,100	2,100
6	**Supplies** 1,300	1,200	1,400
7	**Salaries** 16,000	16,000	16,500
8	**Utilities** 500	600	600
9	**2012 TOTAL** 24,500	24,100	25,800
10			
11			

Add a Function

A *function* is a predefined formula that performs a specific task. For example, the AVERAGE function calculates the average of a list of numbers, and the PMT function calculates a loan or mortgage payment. You can use functions on their own, preceded by =, or as part of a larger formula. Click **Insert Function** (*fx*) to see a list of the available functions.

Manipulate Data

Calculate Totals Quickly

If you just need a quick sum of a list of numbers, click a cell below the numbers and then click the **Sum** button (Σ), which is available in the Home tab of the Excel Ribbon. You can also select the cells that you want to sum, and their total appears in the status bar.

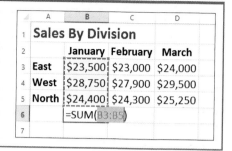

	A	B	C	D
1	**Sales By Division**			
2		**January**	**February**	**March**
3	**East**	$23,500	$23,000	$24,000
4	**West**	$28,750	$27,900	$29,500
5	**North**	$24,400	$24,300	$25,250
6		=SUM(B3:B5)		
7				

Fill a Series

Excel enables you to save time by completing a series of values automatically. For example, if you need to enter the numbers 1 to 100 in consecutive cells, you can enter just the first few numbers, select the cells, and then click and drag the lower-right corner to fill in the rest of the numbers. With Excel you can also fill in dates, as well as the names for weekdays and months.

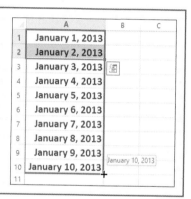

	A	B	C
1	January 1, 2013		
2	January 2, 2013		
3	January 3, 2013		
4	January 4, 2013		
5	January 5, 2013		
6	January 6, 2013		
7	January 7, 2013		
8	January 8, 2013		
9	January 9, 2013	January 10, 2013	
10	January 10, 2013		
11			

Manage Tables

The row-and-column format of a spreadsheet makes Excel suitable for simple databases called *tables*. Each column becomes a field in the table, and each row is a record. You can sort the records, filter the records to show only certain values, and add subtotals.

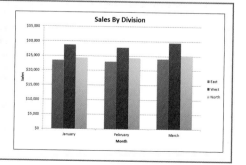

	Account Name	Account Number	Invoice Number	Invoice Amount	Due Date
3					
4	Door Stoppers Ltd.	01-0045	117328	$58.50	2/2/2013
5	Door Stoppers Ltd.	01-0045	117319	$78.85	1/16/2013
6	Door Stoppers Ltd.	01-0045	117324	$101.01	1/26/2013
7	Door Stoppers Ltd.	01-0045	117333	$1,685.74	2/11/2013
8	Chimera Illusions	02-0200	117334	$303.65	2/12/2013
9	Chimera Illusions	02-0200	117350	$456.21	3/15/2013
10	Chimera Illusions	02-0200	117345	$588.88	3/6/2013
11	Chimera Illusions	02-0200	117318	$3,005.14	1/14/2013
12	Renaud & Son	07-0025	117331	$565.77	2/8/2013
13	Renaud & Son	07-0025	117359	$1,125.75	4/9/2013
14	Renaud & Son	07-0025	117335	$3,005.14	2/13/2013

Add a Chart

A *chart* is a graphic representation of spreadsheet data. As the data in the spreadsheet changes, the chart also changes to reflect the new numbers. Excel offers a wide variety of charts, including bar charts, line charts, and pie charts.

Start Excel

Before you can perform tasks such as adding data and building formulas, you must first start Excel. This brings the Excel window onto the Windows desktop, and you can then begin using the program. How you start Excel depends on which version of Windows you are using. In this section, you learn how to start Excel 2013 in Windows 8 and in Windows 7.

This task and the rest of the book assume that you have already installed Excel 2013 on your computer.

Start Excel

Start Excel in Windows 8

1 In the Windows 8 Start screen, click **Excel 2013**.

The Microsoft Excel window appears on the desktop.

Note: Click **Blank workbook** to open a new Excel file.

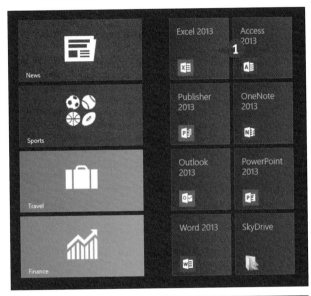

Start Excel in Windows 7

1 Click **Start**.

The Start menu appears.

2 Click **All Programs**.

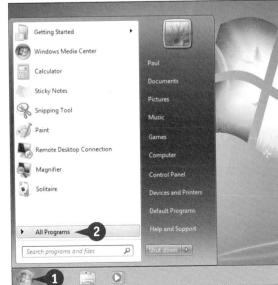

The All Programs menu
appears.

3 Click **Microsoft Office 2013**.

The Microsoft Office menu appears.

4 Click **Excel 2013**.

The Microsoft Excel window appears
on the desktop.

Note: Click **Blank workbook** to open a
new Excel file.

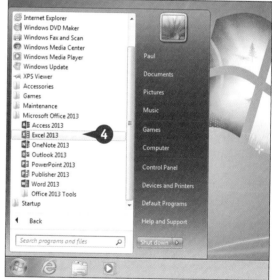

TIP

Are there faster methods I can use to start Excel?

Yes. After you have used Excel a few times in Windows 7, it should appear on the main Start menu in the
list of your most-used programs. If so, you can click that icon to start the program. You can also add the
Excel icon to the Start menu by following Steps **1** to **3** in the "Start Excel in Windows 7" subsection,
right-clicking the **Excel 2013** icon, and then clicking **Pin to Start Menu**. If you are using Windows 8,
you can right-click the **Excel 2013** tile and then click **Pin to Taskbar** to add the Excel icon to the desktop
taskbar.

Tour the Excel Window

To get up to speed quickly with Excel, it helps to understand the various elements of the Excel window. These include standard window elements such as the title bar, window controls, and status bar; Office-specific elements such as the Ribbon, Quick Access Toolbar, and File tab; and Excel-specific elements such as the worksheet.

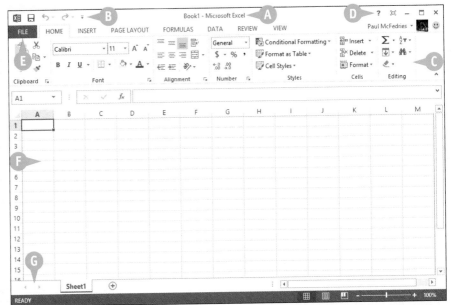

A Title Bar

The title bar displays the name of the current workbook.

B Quick Access Toolbar

This area gives you one-click access to commands that you use often. To learn how to customize this toolbar, see "Customize the Quick Access Toolbar," later in this chapter.

C Ribbon

This area gives you access to all the Excel commands, options, and features. To learn how to use this element, see the following section, "Work with the Excel Ribbon."

D Workbook Window Controls

You use these controls to minimize, maximize, restore, and close the current workbook window.

E File Tab

Click this tab to access file-related commands, such as Save and Open.

F Worksheet

This area displays the current worksheet, and it is where you will do most of your Excel work.

G Status Bar

This area displays messages about the current status of Excel, the results of certain operations, and other information.

Work with the Excel Ribbon

You use the Ribbon element to access all the features, commands, and options in Excel. The Ribbon is organized into various tabs, such as File, Home, and Insert, and each tab contains a collection of controls that are related in some way. For example, the File tab contains controls related to working with files, such as opening, saving, and printing them. Similarly, the Insert tab contains controls related to inserting objects into a worksheet. Each tab usually includes buttons, lists, and check boxes.

There is no menu bar in Excel, so you do not use pull-down menus to access commands.

Work with the Excel Ribbon

1 Click the tab that contains the Excel feature you want to work with.

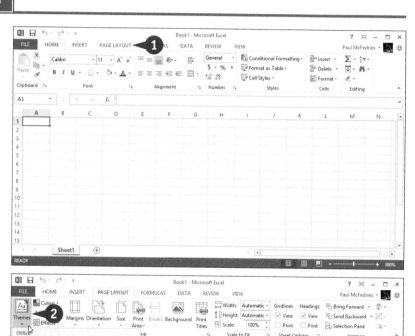

Excel displays the controls in the tab.

A Each tab is organized into groups of related controls, and the group names appear here.

B In many groups you can click the dialog box launcher button (⌐) to display a dialog box that contains group settings.

2 Click the control for the feature.

C If the control displays a list of options, click the option you want.

Excel runs the command or sets the option.

Work with the Excel Galleries

In the Excel Ribbon, a *gallery* is a collection of preset options that you can apply to the selected object in the worksheet. To get the most out of galleries, you need to know how they work.

Although some galleries are available all the time, in most cases you must select an object — such as a range of cells or a clip art image — before you work with a gallery.

Work with the Excel Galleries

Work with a Gallery List

1 If necessary, click the object to which you want to apply an option from the gallery.

2 Click the tab that contains the gallery you want to use.

3 Click the gallery's **More** arrow (▾).

Ⓐ You can also scroll through the gallery by clicking the **Down** (▾) and **Up** (▴) arrows.

Excel displays a list of the gallery's contents.

4 Move the mouse pointer (▷) over a gallery option.

Ⓑ Excel displays a preview of the effect.

5 Click the gallery option you want to use.

Excel applies the gallery option to the selected object.

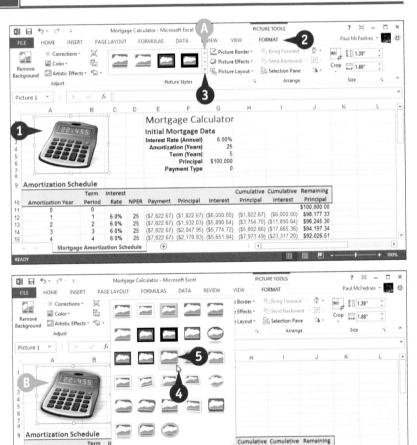

Work with a Drop-Down Gallery

1. If necessary, click the object to which you want to apply an option from the gallery.

2. Click the tab that contains the gallery you want to use.

3. Click the gallery's drop-down arrow (▼).

   Excel displays a list of the gallery's contents.

4. If the gallery contains one or more subgalleries, click the subgallery you want to use.

   Excel displays the subgallery's contents.

C. If a gallery has commands that you can run, those commands appear at the bottom of the gallery menu.

5. Move the mouse ⬚ over a gallery option.

D. Excel displays a preview of the effect.

6. Click the gallery option you want to use.

   Excel applies the gallery option to the selected object.

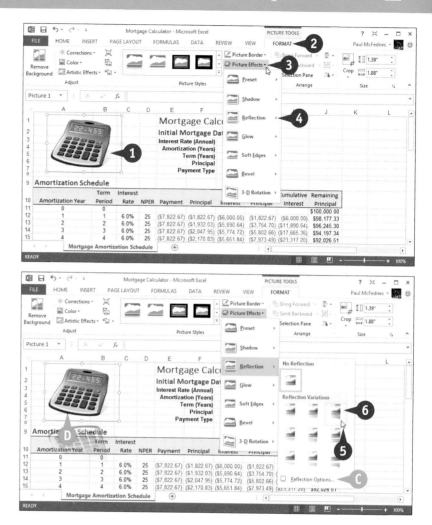

TIP

If I find the gallery preview feature distracting, can I turn it off?

Yes. The Live Preview feature is often handy because it shows you exactly what will happen when you click a gallery option. However, as you move the mouse ⬚ through the gallery, the previews can be distracting. To turn off Live Preview, click the **File** tab, click **Options**, click the **General** tab, click **Enable Live Preview** (☑ changes to ☐), and then click **OK**.

Customize the Quick Access Toolbar

You can make Excel easier to use by customizing the Quick Access Toolbar to include the Excel commands you use most often. You run Quick Access Toolbar commands with a single click, so adding your favorite commands saves time because you no longer have to search for and click a command in the Ribbon. By default, the Quick Access Toolbar contains three buttons: Save, Undo, and Redo. However, with just a couple of clicks, you can also add common commands such as New and Open to the Quick Access Toolbar, as well as hundreds of other Excel commands.

Customize the Quick Access Toolbar

1 Click the **Customize Quick Access Toolbar** button ( ).

A If you see the command you want, click it and skip the rest of the steps in this section.

2 Click **More Commands**.

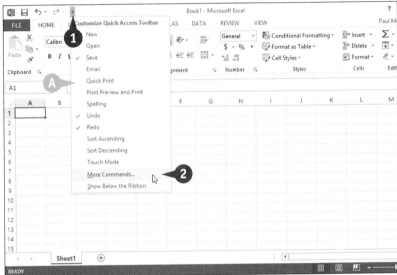

The Excel Options dialog box appears.

B Excel automatically displays the Quick Access Toolbar tab.

3 Click the **Choose commands from** .

4 Click the command category you want to use.

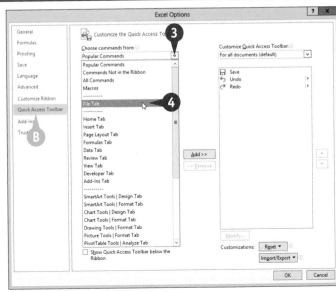

12

5 Click the command you want to add.

6 Click **Add**.

C Excel adds the command.

D To remove a command, click it and then click **Remove**.

7 Click **OK**.

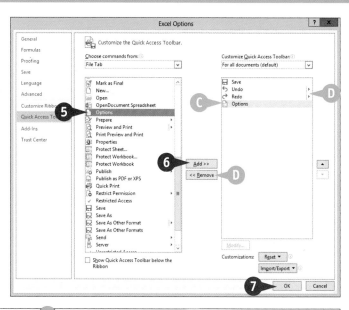

E Excel adds a button for the command to the Quick Access Toolbar.

Note: Another way to remove a command is to right-click the command and then click **Remove from Quick Access Toolbar**.

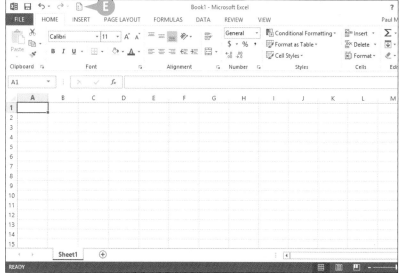

Can I get more room on the Quick Access Toolbar to show more buttons?

Yes, you can increase the space available to the Quick Access Toolbar by moving it below the Ribbon. This gives the toolbar the full width of the Excel window, so you can add many more buttons. Click the **Customize Quick Access Toolbar** button (☰) and then click **Show Below the Ribbon**.

Is there a faster way to add buttons to the Quick Access Toolbar?

Yes. If the command you want to add appears on the Ribbon, you can add a button for the command directly from the Ribbon. Click the Ribbon tab that contains the command, right-click the command, and then click **Add to Quick Access Toolbar**. Excel inserts a button for the command on the Quick Access Toolbar.

13

Customize the Ribbon

Y ou can improve your Excel productivity by customizing the Ribbon with extra commands that you use frequently. The Ribbon is a handy tool because it enables you to run Excel commands with just a few clicks of the mouse. However, the Ribbon does not include every Excel command. If there is a command that you use frequently, you should add it to the Ribbon for easy access.

To add a new command to the Ribbon, you must first create a new tab or a new group within an existing tab, and then add the command to the new tab or group.

Customize the Ribbon

Display the Customize Ribbon Tab

1 Right-click any part of the Ribbon.

2 Click **Customize the Ribbon**.

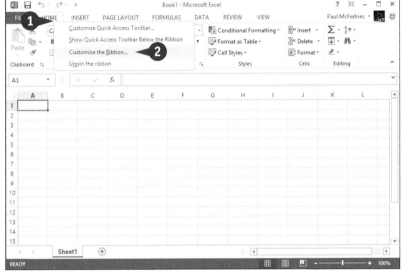

Add a New Tab or Group

The Excel Options dialog box appears.

Ⓐ Excel automatically displays the Customize Ribbon tab.

1 Click the tab you want to customize.

Ⓑ You can also click **New Tab** to create a custom tab.

2 Click **New Group**.

Ⓒ Excel adds the group.

3 Click **Rename**.

4 Type a name for the group.

5 Click **OK**.

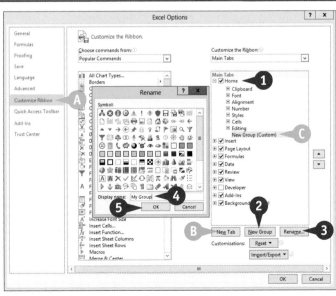

14

Add a Command

1️⃣ Click the **Choose commands from** 🔽.

2️⃣ Click the command category you want to use.

3️⃣ Click the command you want to add.

4️⃣ Click the custom group or tab you want to use.

5️⃣ Click **Add**.

Ⓓ Excel adds the command.

Ⓔ To remove a custom command, click it and then click **Remove**.

6️⃣ Click **OK**.

Ⓕ Excel adds the new group and command to the Ribbon.

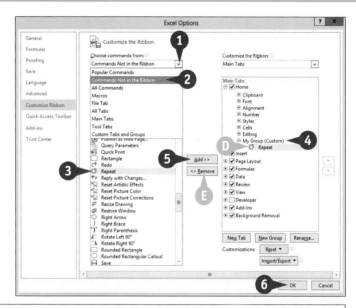

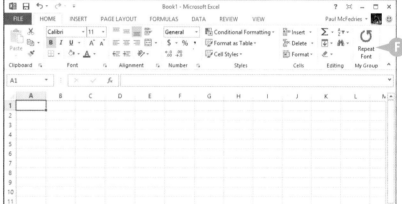

TIPS

Can I customize the tabs that appear only when I select an Excel object?

Yes. Excel calls these *tool tabs*, and you can add custom groups and commands to any tool tab. Right-click any part of the Ribbon and then click Customize the Ribbon to display the Excel Options dialog box with the Customize Ribbon tab displayed. Click the **Customize the Ribbon** 🔽 and then click **Tool Tabs**. Click the tab you want and then follow the steps in this section to customize it.

How do I restore the Ribbon to its default configuration?

Right-click any part of the Ribbon and then click **Customize the Ribbon** to display the Excel Options dialog box with the Customize Ribbon tab displayed. To restore a tab, click the tab, click **Reset**, and then click **Restore only selected Ribbon tab**. To remove all customizations, click **Reset** and then click **Restore all customizations**.

Change the View

You can adjust Excel to suit what you are currently working on by changing the view to match your current task. The view determines how Excel displays your workbook.

Excel offers three different views: Normal, which is useful for building and editing worksheets; Page Layout, which displays worksheets as printed pages; and Page Break Preview, which displays the page breaks as blue lines, as described in the first Tip in this section.

Change the View

Switch to Page Layout View

1. Click the **View** tab.

2. Click **Page Layout**.

Ⓐ You can also click the **Page Layout** button (🗐).

Ⓑ Excel switches to Page Layout view.

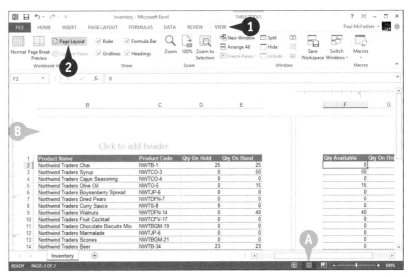

Switch to Page Break Preview

1. Click the **View** tab.

2. Click **Page Break Preview**.

Ⓒ You can also click the **Page Break Preview** button (🗐).

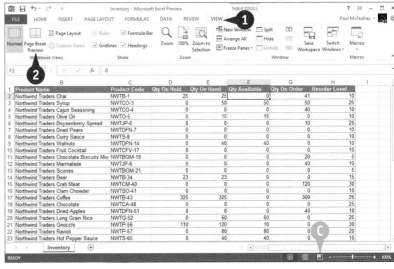

D Excel switches to Page Break Preview.

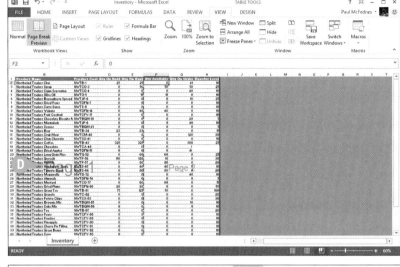

Switch to Normal View

1 Click the **View** tab.

2 Click **Normal**.

E You can also click the **Normal** button (⊞).

Excel switches to Normal view.

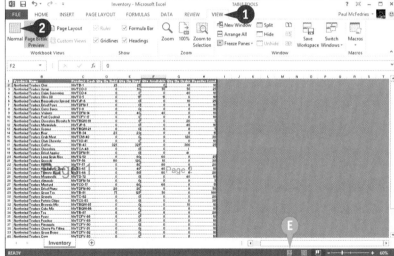

What does Page Break Preview do?

In Excel, a *page break* is a position within a worksheet where a new page begins when you print the worksheet. When you switch to Page Break Preview, Excel displays the page breaks as blue lines. If a page break occurs in a bad position — for example, the page break includes the headings from a range, but not the cells below the headings — you can use your mouse ⇩ to click and drag the page breaks to new positions.

Can I change the view to make my workbook take up the entire screen?

Yes, you can switch the workbook to Full Screen mode by clicking the **Full Screen Mode** icon (⌑) in the upper-right corner of the window. Full Screen mode removes many of the Excel window features, including the Ribbon, Quick Access Toolbar, formula bar, and status bar. To exit Full Screen mode, click the horizontal strip at the top of the screen and then click ⌑.

Configure Excel Options

You can customize Excel to suit the way you work by configuring the Excel options. These options are dialog box controls such as check boxes, option buttons, and lists that enable you to configure many aspects of Excel. To use these options, you must know how to display the Excel Options dialog box. The Excel Options dialog box is divided into several tabs, such as General, Formulas, Save, and Customize Ribbon. Each tab contains a collection of related options.

Configure Excel Options

1 Click the **File** tab.

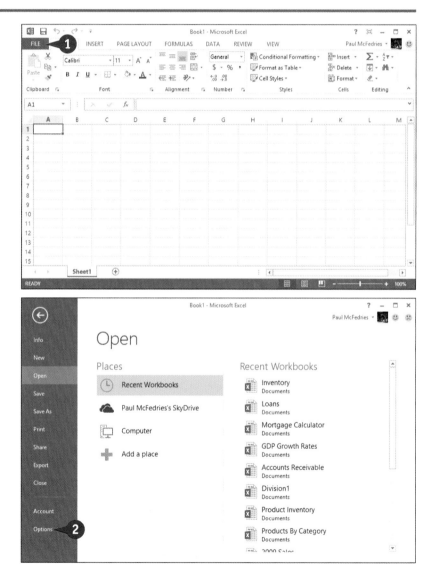

2 Click **Options**.

The Excel Options dialog box appears.

3 Click a tab on the left side of the dialog box to choose the configuration category you want to work with.

A The controls that appear on the right side of the dialog box change according to the tab you select.

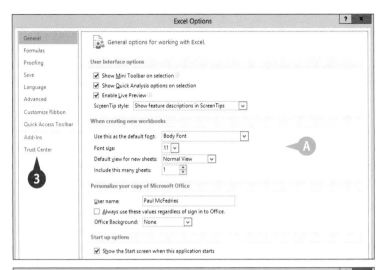

4 Use the controls on the right side of the dialog box to configure the options you want to change.

5 Click **OK**.

Excel puts the new options into effect.

Are there faster methods I can use to open the Excel Options dialog box?

Yes. Some features of the Excel interface offer shortcut methods that get you to the Excel Options dialog box faster. For example, right-click the Ribbon and then click **Customize Ribbon** to open the Excel Options dialog box with the Customize Ribbon tab displayed. From the keyboard, you can open the Excel Options dialog box by pressing **Alt**+**F** and then pressing **T**.

How do I know what each option does?

Excel offers pop-up descriptions of some — but, unfortunately, not all — of the options. If you see a small *i* with a circle around it to the right of the option name, it means pop-up help is available for that option. Hover the mouse over the option and Excel displays a pop-up description of the option after a second or two.

Add Excel to the Windows Taskbar

If you use Excel regularly, you can start the program with just a single mouse click by adding an icon for Excel to the Windows taskbar. When you install Excel, the setup program pins a tile for Excel to the Windows 8 Start screen. However, that is helpful only if you use the Start screen regularly. If you use the desktop more often, you might prefer to have Excel just a single click away. You can achieve this by pinning Excel to the taskbar. The following instructions assume that you are running Excel in Windows 8, but you can also pin Excel to the taskbar if you are using Windows 7.

Add Excel to the Windows Taskbar

1 With Excel running, right-click the Excel icon in the taskbar.

2 Click **Pin this program to taskbar**.

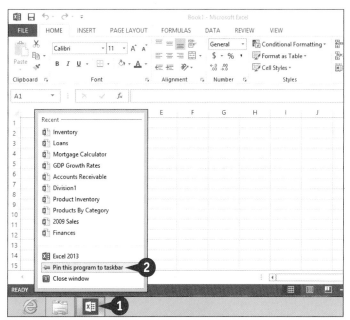

A After you quit Excel, the icon remains on the taskbar, and you can now launch Excel by clicking the icon.

Quit Excel

When you have finished your work with Excel, you should shut down the program. This reduces clutter on the desktop and in the taskbar, and it also conserves memory and other system resources. When you quit Excel, the program checks your open workbooks to see if any of them have unsaved changes. If Excel detects a workbook that has unsaved changes, it prompts you to save the file. This is a very important step because it prevents you from losing work, so be sure to save your changes when Excel prompts you.

Quit Excel

1 Right-click the Excel icon in the taskbar.

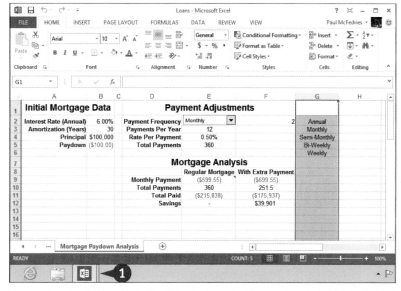

2 Click **Close all windows**.

Note: If you have only one Excel workbook open, click **Close window** instead.

Note: If you have any open documents with unsaved changes, Excel prompts you to save those changes.

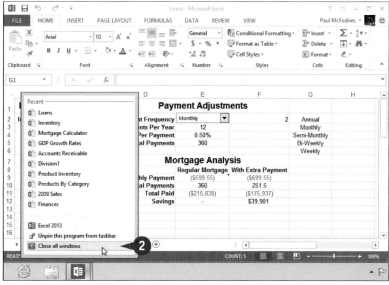

CHAPTER 2

Entering Data

Are you ready to start building a spreadsheet? To create a spreadsheet in Excel, you must know how to enter data into the worksheet cells, and how to edit that data to fix typos, adjust information, and remove data you no longer need.

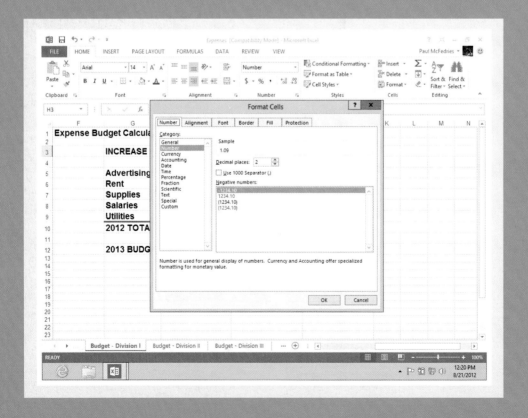

Learning the Layout of a Worksheet

In Excel, a spreadsheet file is called a *workbook*, and each workbook consists of one or more *worksheets*. These worksheets are where you enter your data and formulas, so you need to know the layout of a typical worksheet.

In particular, you need to know that worksheets are laid out in rows and columns, that a cell is the intersection of a row and column that has its own unique address, and that a range is a collection of cells. You also need to be familiar with worksheet tabs and the Excel mouse pointer.

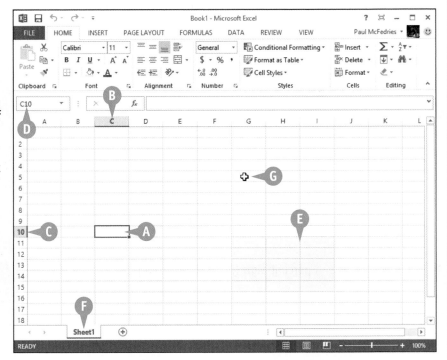

A Cell

A *cell* is a box in which you enter your spreadsheet data.

B Column

A *column* is a vertical line of cells. Each column has a unique letter that identifies it. For example, the leftmost column is A, and the next column is B.

C Row

A *row* is a horizontal line of cells. Each row has a unique number that identifies it. For example, the topmost row is 1, and the next row is 2.

D Cell Address

Each cell has its own *address,* which is determined by the letter and number of the intersecting column and row. For example, the cell at the intersection of column C and row 10 has the address C10.

E Range

A *range* is a rectangular grouping of two or more cells. The range is indicated by the address of the top-left cell and the address of the bottom-right cell. H12:K16 is an example of a range of cells, and it refers to all the cells selected between column H, row 12 and column K, row 16.

F Worksheet Tab

The *worksheet tab* displays the worksheet name. Most workbooks contain multiple worksheets, and you use the tabs to navigate between the worksheets.

G Mouse Pointer

Use the Excel mouse pointer (⊕) to select cells.

You might think that Excel would accept only numeric input, but it is actually much more flexible than that. So, to build a spreadsheet in Excel, it helps to understand the different types of data that Excel accepts. There are three main types of data that you can enter into a cell: text, numbers, and dates and times. Excel places no restrictions on where, how, or how often you can enter these types of data on a worksheet.

Text

Text entries can include any combination of letters, symbols, and numbers. You will mostly use text to describe the contents of your worksheets. This is very important because even a modest-sized spreadsheet can become a confusing jumble of numbers without some kind of text guidelines to keep things straight. Most text entries are usually labels such as *Sales* or *Territory* that make a worksheet easier to read. However, text entries can also be text or number combinations for items such as phone numbers and account codes.

Door Stoppers Ltd.	01-0045
Door Stoppers Ltd.	01-0045
Door Stoppers Ltd.	01-0045
Door Stoppers Ltd.	01-0045
Chimera Illusions	02-0200
Chimera Illusions	02-0200
Chimera Illusions	02-0200
Chimera Illusions	02-0200
Renaud & Son	07-0025
Renaud & Son	07-0025
Renaud & Son	07-0025
Rooter Office Solvents	07-4441
Reston Solicitor Offices	07-4441
Lone Wolf Software	07-4441
Emily's Sports Palace	08-2255
Emily's Sports Palace	08-2255
	Accounts Receivable Data

Numbers

Numbers are the most common type of Excel data. The numbers you enter into a cell can be dollar values, weights, interest rates, temperatures, or any other numerical quantity. In most cases you just type the number that you want to appear in the cell. However, you can also precede a number with a dollar sign ($) or other currency symbol to indicate a monetary value, or follow a number with a percent sign (%) to indicate a percentage value.

GDP, annual growth rate (Sour

Country	2006	2005	2004
Austria	2.5%	1.3%	1.7%
Belgium	2.6%	0.5%	2.5%
Canada	1.7%	1.9%	2.1%
China	10.1%	9.7%	9.4%
Denmark	2.8%	2.8%	1.9%
Finland	5.1%	2.6%	3.4%
France	1.4%	1.1%	1.9%
Germany	2.9%	1.0%	1.3%
Greece	3.9%	3.3%	4.4%
Hungary	4.1%	4.3%	5.0%
Iceland	0.9%	5.5%	6.7%
Ireland	3.0%	3.2%	2.4%
Italy	1.5%	-0.6%	0.2%
Japan	2.2%	1.9%	2.7%
Netherlands	2.7%	1.3%	1.6%

Dates and Times

Date entries appear in spreadsheets that include dated information, such as invoices and sales. You can either type out the full date (such as August 23, 2013) or use either the forward slash (/) or the hyphen (-) as a date separator (such as 8/23/2013 or 8-23-2013). Note that the order you enter the date values depends on your regional settings. For example, in the United States the format is month/day/year. For time values, you use a colon (:) as a time separator, followed by either a.m. or p.m. — such as 9:15 a.m.

	Current Date	20-Mar-13
Due Date	**Date Paid**	**Days Overdue**
2/2/2013		
1/16/2013	1/16/2013	
1/26/2013		
2/11/2013		37
2/12/2013	2/16/2013	
3/15/2013		5
3/6/2013	3/6/2013	
1/14/2013		65
2/8/2013		40
4/9/2013		
2/13/2013		35
2/15/2013	3/2/2013	
3/30/2013	4/14/2013	
1/29/2013	1/24/2013	

Enter Text into a Cell

Your first step when building a spreadsheet is usually to enter the text data that defines the spreadsheet's labels or headings. Most labels appear in the cell to the right or above where the data will appear, while most headings appear at the top of a column of data or to the left of a row of data.

Note, however, that you do not have to use text for just labels and headings. You can also enter text as data, such as a database of book or movie names. You can also write short notes that explain sections of the worksheet, and add reminders to yourself or others about missing data or other worksheet to-do items.

Enter Text into a Cell

1 Click the cell in which you want to enter the text.

A Excel marks the current cell by surrounding it with a thick border.

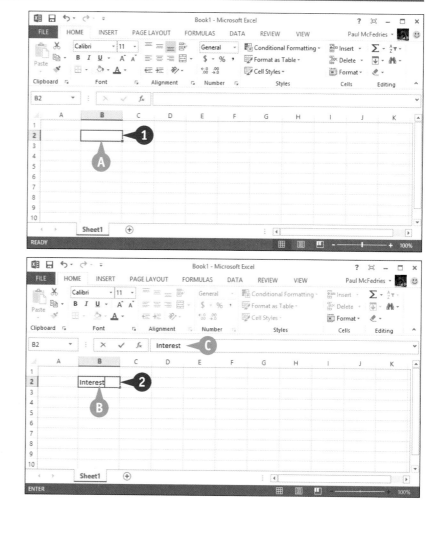

2 Start typing your text.

B Excel opens the cell for editing and displays the text as you type.

C Your typing also appears in the formula bar.

Note: Rather than typing the text directly into the cell, you can also type the text into the formula bar.

③ When your text entry is complete, press **Enter**.

Ⓓ If you do not want Excel to move the selection, click **Enter** (✓) or press **Ctrl** + **Enter** instead.

Ⓔ Excel closes the cell for editing.

Ⓕ If you pressed **Enter**, Excel moves the selection to the cell below.

TIPS

When I press Enter, the selection moves to the next cell down. Can I make the selection move to the right instead?

Yes. When you have finished adding the data to the cell, press ➡. This tells Excel to close the current cell for editing and move the selection to the next cell on the right. If you prefer to move left instead, press ⬅; if you prefer to move up, press ⬆.

When I start typing text into a cell, why does Excel sometimes display the text from another cell?

This is part of an Excel feature called AutoComplete. If the letters you type at the start of a cell match the contents of another cell in the worksheet, Excel fills in the full text from the other cell under the assumption that you are repeating the text in the new cell. If you want to use the text, click ✓ or press **Enter**; otherwise, just keep typing your text.

Enter a Number into a Cell

Excel is all about crunching numbers, so most of your worksheets will include numeric values. Although you will often use numbers by themselves as part of a database or table, many of the numbers you enter will be used as the inputs for the formulas you build, as described in Chapter 6.

You can enter whole numbers (such as 5 or 1,024), decimals (such as 0.25 or 3.14), negative numbers (such as -10 or -6.2), percentages (such as 6% or 25.9%), and currency values (such as $0.25 or $24.99). To get the most out of Excel, you need to know how to enter these numeric values.

Enter a Number into a Cell

1 Click the cell in which you want to enter the number.

A Excel marks the current cell by surrounding it with a thick, black border.

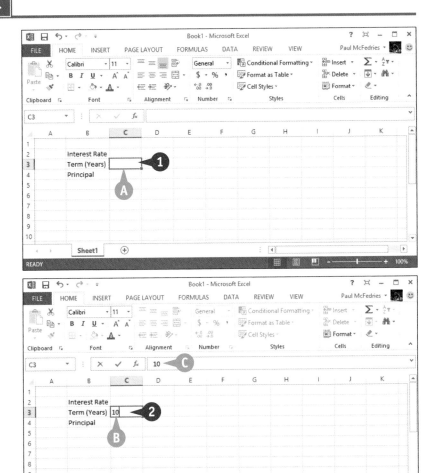

2 Start typing your number.

B Excel opens the cell for editing and displays the number as you type.

C Your typing also appears in the formula bar.

Note: Rather than typing the number directly into the cell, you can also type the number into the formula bar.

3 When your number is complete, press **Enter**.

D If you do not want Excel to move the selection, click **Enter** (✓) or press **Ctrl** + **Enter** instead.

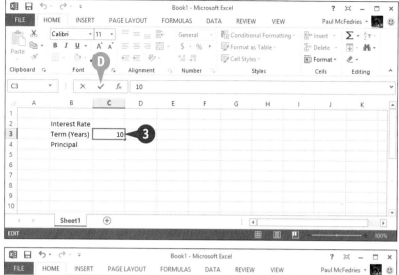

E Excel closes the cell for editing.

F To enter a percentage value, type the number followed by a percent sign (%).

G To enter a currency value, type the dollar sign ($) followed by the number.

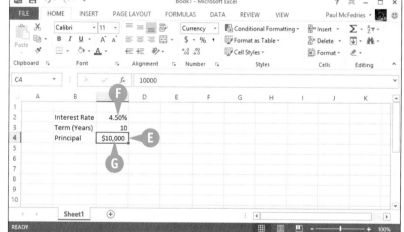

Can I use symbols such as a comma, decimal point, or minus sign when I enter a numeric value?

Yes. If your numeric value is in the thousands, you can include the thousands separator (,) within the number. For example, if you enter **10000**, Excel displays the value as 10000; however, if you enter **10,000**, Excel displays the value as 10,000, which is easier to read. If your numeric value includes one or more decimals, you can include the decimal point (■) when you type the value. If your numeric value is negative, precede the value with a minus sign (■).

Is there a quick way to repeat a number rather than entering the entire number all over again?

Yes. Excel offers a few methods for doing this. The easiest method is to select the cell directly below the value you want to repeat and then press **Ctrl** + ■. Excel adds the value to the cell. For another method, see "Fill a Range with the Same Data" in Chapter 3.

Enter a Date or Time into a Cell

Many Excel worksheets use dates and times either as part of the sheet data or for use in calculations, such as the number of days an invoice is overdue. For these and similar uses, you need to know how to enter date and time values into a cell.

The date format you use depends on your location. In the United States, for example, you can use the month/day/year format (such as 8/23/2013). The time format also depends on your location, but the general format for entering a time is hour:minute:second followed by a.m. or p.m. (such as 3:15:30 p.m.).

Enter a Date or Time into a Cell

Enter a Date

1 Click the cell in which you want to enter the date.

A Excel marks the current cell by surrounding it with a thick, black border.

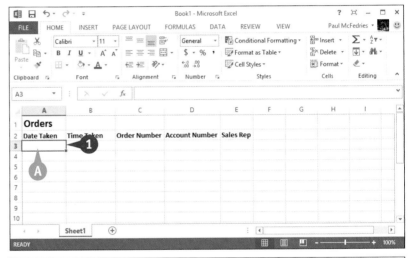

2 Type the date.

Note: See the following Tip to learn which date formats your version of Excel accepts.

3 When your date is complete, press **Enter**.

B If you do not want Excel to move the selection, click **Enter** (✓) or press **Ctrl** + **Enter** instead.

Excel closes the cell for editing.

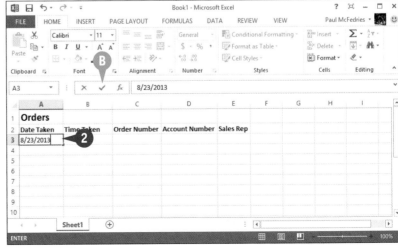

Enter a Time

1 Click the cell in which you want to enter the time.

C Excel marks the current cell by surrounding it with a thick, black border.

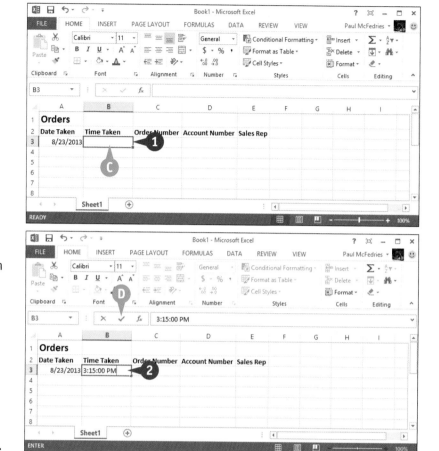

2 Type the time.

Note: See the following Tip to learn which time formats your version of Excel accepts.

3 When your time is complete, press **Enter**.

D If you do not want Excel to move the selection, click **Enter** (✔) or press **Ctrl**+**Enter** instead.

Excel closes the cell for editing.

TIP

How can I tell which date and time formats my version of Excel accepts?

Follow these steps:

1 Click the **Home** tab.

2 Click the dialog box launcher button (⌐) in the bottom-right corner of the **Number** group.

3 Click the **Number** tab.

4 Click **Date**.

5 Click the **Locale (location)** drop-down arrow (⌄) and then click your location.

6 Examine the **Type** list to see the formats you can use to enter dates.

7 Click **Time**.

8 Examine the **Type** list to see the formats you can use to enter times.

9 Click **Cancel**.

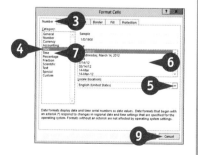

Insert a Symbol

You can make your Excel worksheets more readable and more useful by inserting special symbols that enhance your text. These symbols are special in the sense that they are not available via your keyboard's standard keys.

These special symbols include foreign characters such as ö and é, mathematical symbols such as ° and ∞, financial symbols such as ¢ and ¥, commercial symbols such as © and ®, and many more.

Insert a Symbol

1 Click the cell in which you want the symbol to appear.

2 Type the text that you want to appear before the symbol, if any.

3 Click the **Insert** tab.

4 Click **Symbols**.

5 Click **Symbol**.

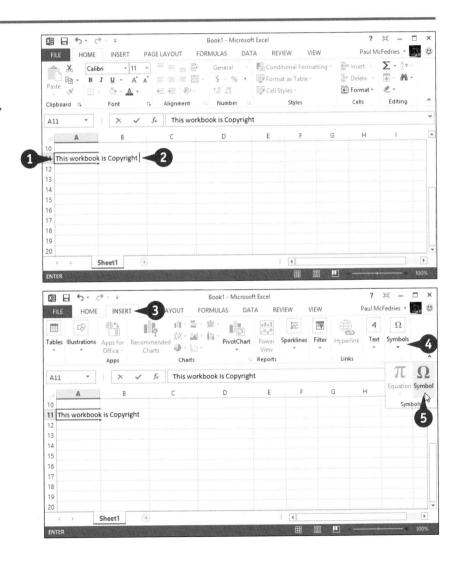

The Symbol dialog box appears.

6 Click the **Symbols** tab.

7 Click the symbol you want to insert.

Note: Many other symbols are available in the Webdings and Wingdings fonts. To see these symbols, click the **Font** ✓, and then click either **Webdings** or **Wingdings**.

8 Click **Insert**.

A Excel inserts the symbol.

9 Repeat Steps **7** and **8** to insert any other symbols you require.

10 Click **Close**.

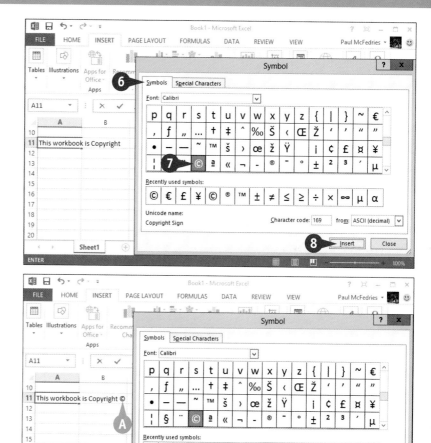

TIP

Are there keyboard shortcuts available for symbols I use frequently?
Yes, in many cases. In the Symbol dialog box, click ✓ in the **from** list and select **ASCII (decimal)**. Click the symbol you want to insert and then examine the number in the Character code text box. This number tells you that you can enter the symbol via the keyboard by holding down **Alt**, pressing **0**, and then typing the number. For example, you can enter the © symbol by pressing **Alt**+**0 1 6 9**. Be sure to type all the numbers using your keyboard's numeric keypad.

Edit Cell Data

The data that you enter into a worksheet cell is not set in stone after you press Enter or click ✓. Whether you entered text, numbers, dates, or times, if the data you typed into a cell has changed or is incorrect, you can edit the data to update or fix the information. You can edit cell data either directly in the cell or by using the formula bar.

Edit Cell Data

1 Click the cell in which you want to edit the text.

2 Press F2.

You can also double-click the cell you want to edit.

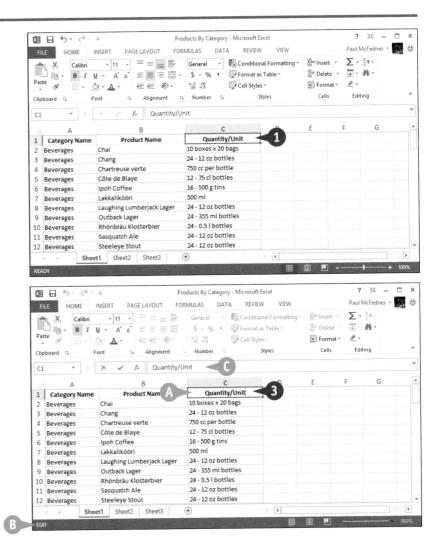

Ⓐ Excel opens the cell for editing and moves the cursor to the end of the existing data.

Ⓑ Excel displays Edit in the status bar.

Ⓒ You can also click inside the formula bar and edit the cell data there.

3 Make your changes to the cell data.

④ When you finish editing the data, press **Enter**.

Ⓓ If you do not want Excel to move the selection, click **Enter** (✓) or press **Ctrl** + **Enter** instead.

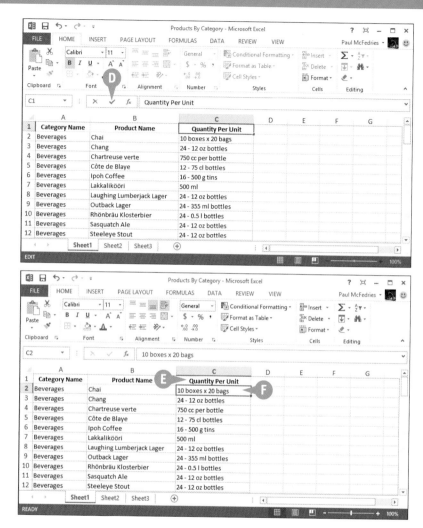

Ⓔ Excel closes the cell for editing.

Ⓕ If you pressed **Enter**, Excel moves the selection to the cell below.

Is there a faster way to open a cell for editing?

Yes. Move the mouse ⊕ over the cell you want to edit, and center the ⊕ over the character where you want to start editing. Double-click the mouse. Excel opens the cell for editing and positions the cursor at the spot where you double-clicked.

I made a mistake when I edited a cell. Do I have to fix the text manually?

Most likely not. If the cell edit was the last action you performed in Excel, press **Ctrl** + **Z** or click the **Undo** button (↺) in the Quick Launch Toolbar. If you have performed other actions in the meantime, click the **Undo** ⌄ and then click the edit in the list that appears. Note, however, that doing this also undoes the other actions you performed after the edit.

Delete Data from a Cell

If your worksheet has a cell that contains data you no longer need, you can delete that data. This helps to reduce worksheet clutter, ensures that your worksheet does not contain erroneous or unnecessary data, and makes your worksheet easier to read.

If you want to delete data from multiple cells, you must first select those cells; see "Select a Range" in Chapter 3. To delete cells and not just the data, see "Delete a Range" in Chapter 3.

Delete Data from a Cell

Delete Cell Data

1 Select the cell that contains the data you want to delete.

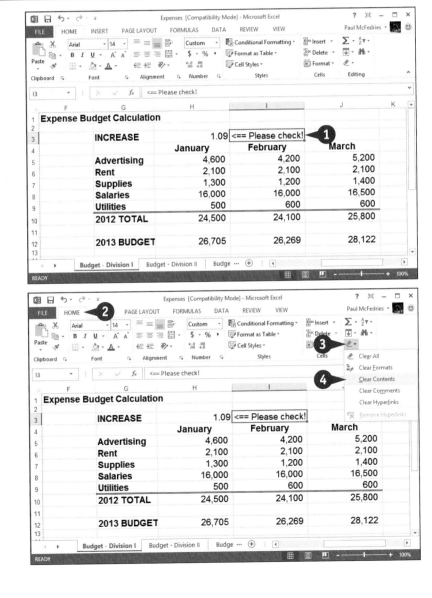

2 Click the **Home** tab.

3 Click **Clear** (✐).

4 Click **Clear Contents**.

Note: You can also delete cell data by pressing `Delete`.

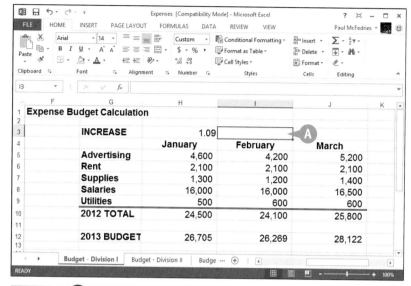

Ⓐ Excel removes the cell data.

Undo Cell Data Deletion

① Click the **Undo** drop-down arrow (⌄).

② Click **Clear**.

Note: If the data deletion was the most recent action you performed, you can undo it by pressing Ctrl+Z or by clicking **Undo** (↺).

Ⓑ Excel restores the data to the cell.

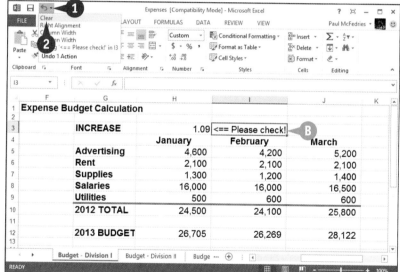

When I delete cell data, Excel keeps the cell formatting intact. Is it possible to delete the data and the formatting?

Yes. Excel offers a command that deletes everything from a cell. First, select the cell with the data and formatting that you want to delete. Click **Home**, click **Clear** (✐), and then click **Clear All**. Excel removes both the data and the formatting from the selected cell.

Is it possible to delete just a cell's formatting?

Yes. Excel offers a command that deletes just the cell formatting while leaving the cell data intact. Select the cell with the formatting that you want to delete. Click **Home**, click **Clear** (✐), and then click **Clear Formats**. Excel removes just the formatting from the selected cell.

CHAPTER 3

Working with Ranges

In Excel, a *range* is a collection of two or more cells that you work with as a group rather than separately. This enables you to fill the range with values, move or copy the range, sort the range data, and insert and delete ranges. You learn these and other range techniques in this chapter.

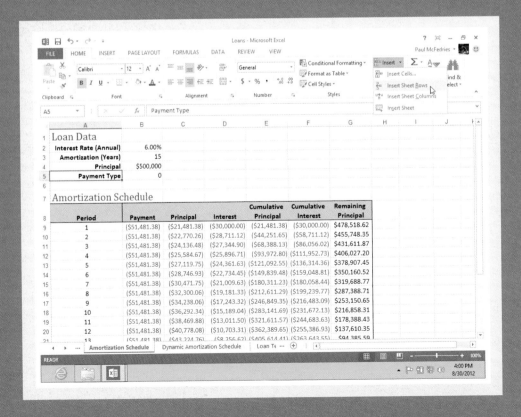

Select a Range

To work with a range in Excel, you must first select the cells that you want to include in the range. After you select the range, you can fill it with data, move it to another part of the worksheet, format the cells, and perform the other range-related tasks that you learn about in this chapter.

You can select a range as a rectangular group of cells, as a collection of individual cells, or as an entire row or column.

Select a Range

Select a Rectangular Range

1. Position the Excel mouse pointer (✛) over the first cell you want to include in the range.

2. Click and drag the ✛ over the cells that you want to include in the range.

   Ⓐ Excel selects the cells.

3. Release the mouse button.

Select a Range of Individual Cells

1. Click in the first cell that you want to include in the range.

2. Hold down Ctrl and click in each of the other cells that you want to include in the range.

   Ⓑ Each time you click in a cell, Excel adds it to the range.

3. Release Ctrl.

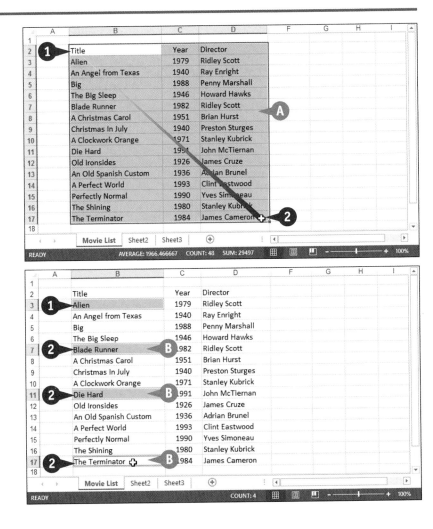

Select an Entire Row

1 Position the mouse ⊕ over the header of the row you want to select (⊕ changes to →).

2 Click the row header.

C Excel selects the entire row.

To select multiple rows, click and drag across the row headers or hold down Ctrl and click each row header.

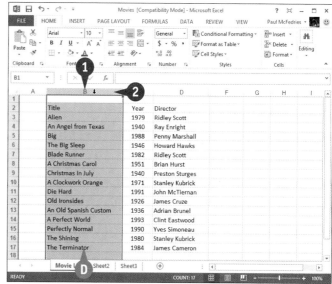

Select an Entire Column

1 Position the mouse ⊕ over the header of the column you want to select (⊕ changes to ↓).

2 Click the column header.

D Excel selects the entire column.

To select multiple columns, click and drag across the column headers, or hold down Ctrl and click each column header.

TIPS

Are there keyboard techniques I can use to select a range?

Yes. To select a rectangular range, navigate to the first cell that you want to include in the range, hold down Shift, and then press ← or ↓ to extend the selection. To select an entire row, navigate to any cell in the row and press Shift + Spacebar. To select an entire column, navigate to any cell in the column and then press Ctrl + Spacebar.

Is there an easy way to select every cell in the worksheet?

Yes. There are two methods you can use. Either press Ctrl + A, or click the **Select All** button (◢) in the upper-left corner of the worksheet (A).

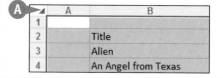

Fill a Range with the Same Data

If you need to fill a range with the same data, you can save time by getting Excel to fill the range for you. The AutoFill feature makes it easy to fill a vertical or horizontal range with the same value, but you can also fill any selected range. This method is much faster than manually entering the same data in each cell.

See the previous section, "Select a Range," to learn how to select a range of cells.

Fill a Range with the Same Data

Fill a Vertical or Horizontal Range

1 In the first cell of the range you want to work with, enter the data you want to fill.

2 Position the mouse ⌖ over the bottom-right corner of the cell (⌖ changes to ✛).

3 Click and drag ✛ down to fill a vertical range or across to fill a horizontal range.

4 Release the mouse button.

A Excel fills the range with the initial cell value.

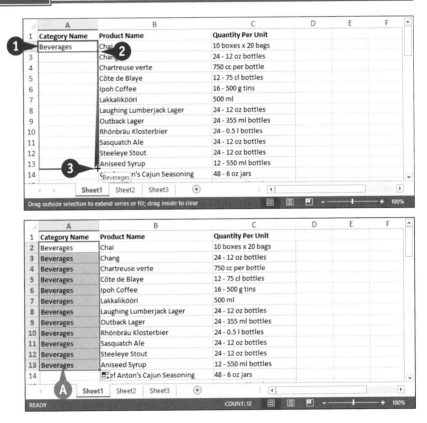

Fill a Selected Range

1. Select the range you want to fill.

2. Type the text, number, or other data.

3. Press Ctrl + Enter.

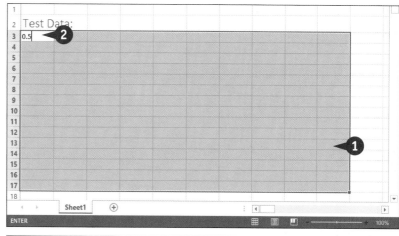

B Excel fills the range with the value you typed.

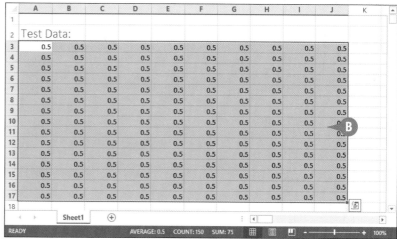

How do I fill a vertical or horizontal range without also copying the formatting of the original cell?
Follow these steps:

1. Perform Steps **1** to **4** to fill the data.

A Excel displays the AutoFill Options smart tag (🖺).

2. Click the AutoFill Options ▼ .

3. Click **Fill Without Formatting**.

Excel removes the original cell's formatting from the copied cells.

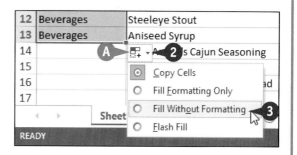

Fill a Range with a Series of Values

If you need to fill a range with a series of values, you can save time by using the AutoFill feature to create the series for you. AutoFill can fill a series of numeric values such as 5, 10, 15, 20, and so on; a series of date values such as January 1, 2013, January 2, 2013, and so on; or a series of alphanumeric values such as Chapter 1, Chapter 2, Chapter 3, and so on.

You can also create your own series with a custom step value, which determines the numeric difference between each item in the series.

Fill a Range with a Series of Values

AutoFill a Series of Numeric, Date, or Alphanumeric Values

1 Click in the first cell and type the first value in the series.

2 Click in an adjacent cell and type the second value in the series.

3 Select the two cells.

4 Position the mouse ⊕ over the bottom-right corner of the second cell (⊕ changes to +).

5 Click and drag + down to fill a vertical range or across to fill a horizontal range.

A As you drag through each cell, Excel displays the series value that it will add to the cell.

6 Release the mouse button.

B Excel fills the range with a series that continues the pattern of the initial two cell values.

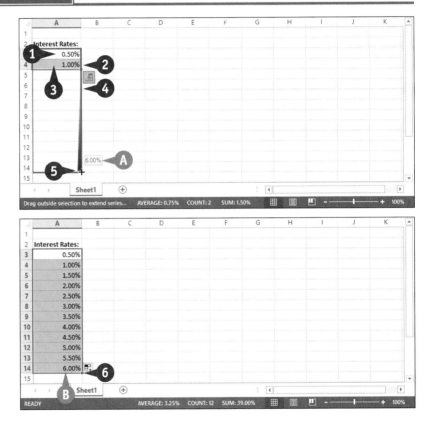

44

Fill a Custom Series of Values

1 Click in the first cell and type the first value in the series.

2 Select the range you want to fill, including the initial value.

3 Click the **Home** tab.

4 Click **Fill** (⬇).

5 Click **Series**.

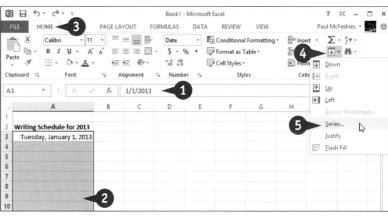

The Series dialog box appears.

6 In the Type group, select the type of series you want to fill (○ changes to ●).

7 If you selected Date in Step **6**, select an option in the Date unit group (○ changes to ●).

8 In the Step value text box, type the value you want to use.

9 Click **OK**.

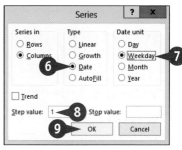

Ⓒ Excel fills the range with the series you created.

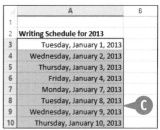

TIP

Can I create my own AutoFill series?
Yes. You can create a *custom list*, which is a series of text values. When you add the first value in your custom list, you can then use AutoFill to fill a range with the rest of the series. Follow these steps:

1 Click the **File tab**.

2 Click **Options**.

The Excel Options dialog box appears.

3 Click **Advanced**.

4 Scroll down to the General section and then click **Edit Custom Lists**.

The Custom Lists dialog box appears.

5 Click **NEW LIST**.

6 In the List entries box, type each item in your list, and press Enter after each item.

7 Click **Add**.

8 Click **OK** to return to the Excel Options dialog box.

9 Click **OK**.

Flash Fill a Range

You can save time and effort by using the Flash Fill feature in Excel to automatically fill a range of data based on a sample pattern that you provide.

Although there are many ways to use Flash Fill, the two most common are flash filling a range with extracted data and flash filling a range with formatted data. For example, if you have a column of full names, you might want to create a new column that includes just the first names extracted from the original column. Similarly, if you have a column of phone numbers in the form 1234567890, you might want a new column that formats the numbers as (123) 456-7890.

Flash Fill a Range

Flash Filling a Range with Extracted Data

1 Make sure the column of original data has a heading.

2 Type a heading for the column of extracted data.

3 Type the first value you want in the new column.

4 Begin typing the second value.

A Excel recognizes the pattern and displays suggestions for the rest of the column.

5 Press Enter.

B Excel flash fills the column with the extracted data.

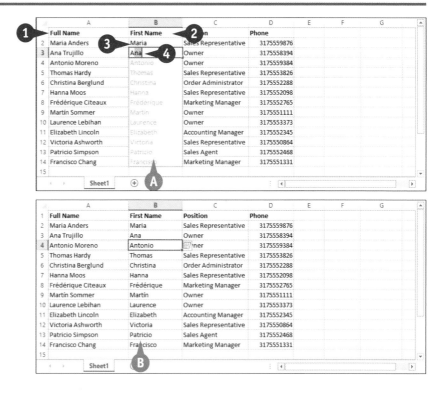

Flash Filling a Range with Formatted Data

1 Make sure the column of original data has a heading.

2 Type a heading for the new column of formatted data.

3 Type the first value you want in the new column.

4 Begin typing the second value.

C Excel recognizes the pattern and displays suggestions for the rest of the column.

5 Press Enter.

D Excel flash fills the column with the formatted data.

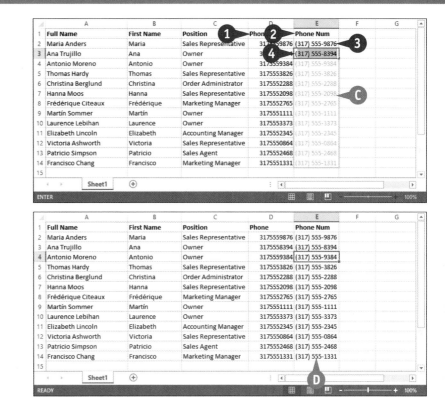

Why do I not see the automatic Flash Fill suggestions when I type the sample data?

For Flash Fill's automatic suggestions to appear, you must have headings at the top of both the column of original data and the column you are using for the filled data. Also, the flash fill column must be adjacent to the original column and the sample entries you make in the fill column must occur one after the other. Finally, note that Flash Fill's automatic suggestions usually only work with text data, not numeric data.

Can I still use Flash Fill even though I do not see the automatic suggestions?

Yes, you can still invoke Flash Fill on any range by running the Ribbon command. In the fill range, type the first value, then select that value and the rest of the fill range. Click the **Data** tab and then click **Flash Fill** (⊞). Excel flash fills the selected range.

Move or Copy a Range

If your worksheet is not set up the way you want, you can restructure or reorganize the worksheet by moving an existing range to a different part of the sheet.

You can also make a copy of a range, which is a useful technique if you require a duplicate of the range elsewhere, or if you require a range that is similar to an existing range. In the latter case, after you copy the range, you can then edit the copied version of the data as needed.

Move or Copy a Range

Move a Range

1 Select the range you want to move.

2 Position the mouse ✛ over any outside border of the range (✛ changes to ⭧).

3 Click and drag the range to the new location (⭧ changes to ⮕).

A Excel displays an outline of the range.

B Excel displays the address of the new location.

4 Release the mouse button.

C Excel moves the range to the new location.

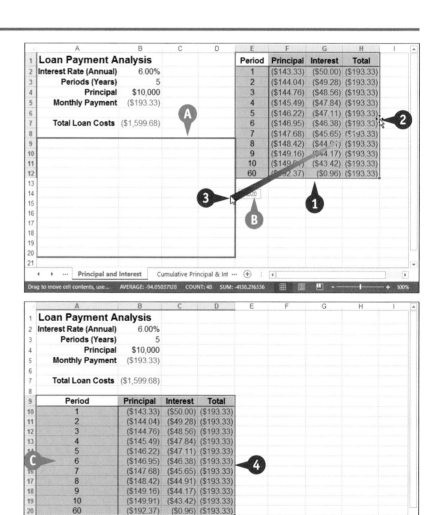

Copy a Range

1 Select the range you want to copy.

2 Press and hold **Ctrl**.

3 Position the mouse ⊕ over any outside border of the range (⊕ changes to ▷).

4 Click and drag the range to the location where you want the copy to appear.

D Excel displays an outline of the range.

E Excel displays the address of the new location.

5 Release the mouse button.

6 Release **Ctrl**.

F Excel creates a copy of the range in the new location.

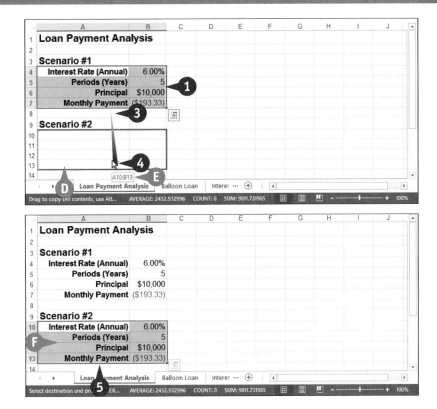

Can I move or copy a range to another worksheet?

Yes. Click and drag the range as described in this section. Remember to hold down **Ctrl** if you are copying the range. Press and hold **Alt** and then drag the mouse pointer over the tab of the sheet you want to use as the destination. Excel displays the worksheet. Release **Alt** and then drop the range on the worksheet.

Can I move or copy a range to another workbook?

Yes. If you can see the other workbook on-screen, click and drag the range as described in this section, and then drop it on the other workbook. Remember to hold down **Ctrl** if you are copying the range. Otherwise, select the range, click the **Home** tab, click **Cut** (✂) to move the range or **Copy** (📄) to copy it, switch to the other workbook, select the cell where you want the range to appear, click **Home**, and then click **Paste** (📋).

Insert a Row or Column

You can insert a row or column into your existing worksheet data to accommodate more information. The easiest way to add more information to a worksheet is to add it to the right or at the bottom of your existing data. However, you will often find that the new information you need to add fits naturally within the existing data. In such cases, you first need to insert a new row or column in your worksheet at the place where you want the new data to appear, and then add the new information in the blank row or column.

Insert a Row or Column

Insert a Row

1. Click any cell in the row below where you want to insert the new row.

2. Click the **Home** tab.

3. Click the **Insert** ▾.

4. Click **Insert Sheet Rows**.

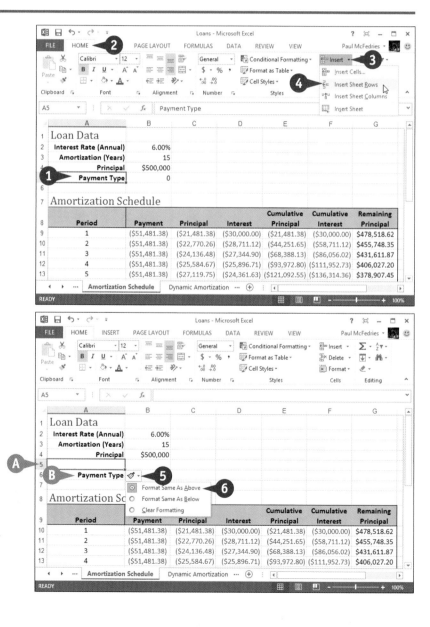

A. Excel inserts the new row.

B. The rows below the new row are shifted down.

5. Click the **Insert Options** smart tag (✸).

6. Select a formatting option for the new row (○ changes to ◉).

Insert a Column

1 Click any cell in the row to the right of where you want to insert the new column.

2 Click the **Home** tab.

3 Click the **Insert** ▼.

4 Click **Insert Sheet Columns**.

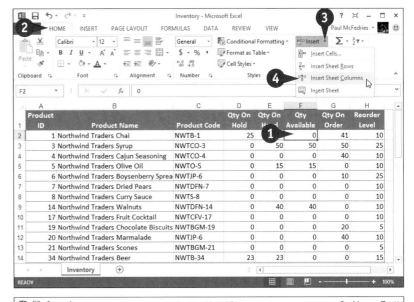

C Excel inserts the new column.

D The columns to the right of the new column are shifted to the right.

5 Click the **Insert Options** smart tag (✐).

6 Select a formatting option for the new column (○ changes to ⦿).

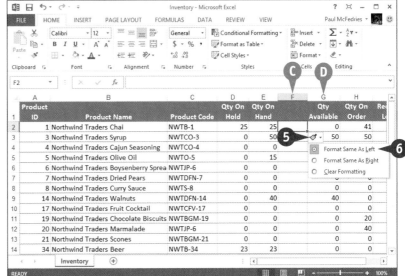

TIP

Can I insert more than one row or column at a time?

Yes. You can insert as many new rows or columns as you need. First, select the same number of rows or columns that you want to insert. (See "Select a Range" earlier in this chapter to learn how to select rows and columns.) For example, if you want to insert four rows, select four existing rows. For rows, be sure to select existing rows below where you want the new rows inserted and then follow Steps **2** to **4** in the "Insert a Row" subsection. For columns, be sure to select existing columns to the right of where you want to insert the new columns and then follow Steps **2** to **4** in the "Insert a Column" subsection.

Insert a Cell or Range

$\mathbf{I}$f you need to add data to an existing range, you can insert a single cell or a range of cells within that range. When you insert a cell or range, Excel shifts the existing data to accommodate the new cells. Although it is often easiest to create room for new data within a range by inserting an entire row or column, as explained in "Insert a Row or Column," earlier in this chapter, this causes problems for some types of worksheet layouts. (See the first Tip in this section to learn more.) You can work around such problems by inserting just a cell or range.

Insert a Cell or Range

1 Select the cell or range where you want the inserted cell or range to appear.

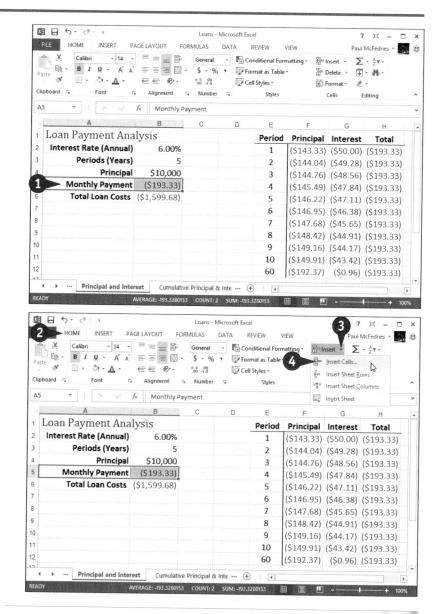

2 Click the **Home** tab.

3 Click the **Insert** ▼.

4 Click **Insert Cells**.

Note: You can also press Ctrl + Shift + =.

The Insert dialog box appears.

5 Select the option that corresponds to how you want Excel to shift the existing cells to accommodate your new cells (○ changes to ◉).

Note: In most cases, if you selected a horizontal range, you should click the **Shift cells down** option; if you selected a vertical range, you should click the **Shift cells right** option.

6 Click **OK**.

Ⓐ Excel inserts the cell or range.

Ⓑ The existing data is shifted down (in this case) or to the right.

7 Click the **Insert Options** smart tag (✔).

8 Select a formatting option for the new row (○ changes to ◉).

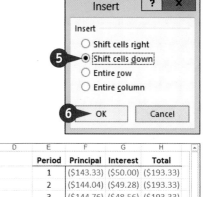

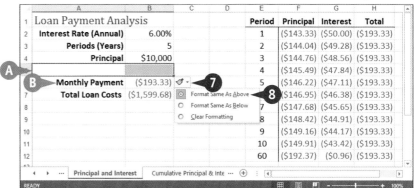

Delete Data from a Range

If your worksheet has a range that contains data you no longer need, you can delete that data. This helps to reduce worksheet clutter and makes your worksheet easier to read.

Note that deleting cell data does not adjust the structure of your worksheet in any way. That is, after you delete the cell data, the rest of your worksheet data remains intact and in the same place that it was before the data deletion. If you want to delete cells and not just the data within the cells, see the following section, "Delete a Range."

Delete Data from a Range

Delete Range Data

1 Select the range that contains the data you want to delete.

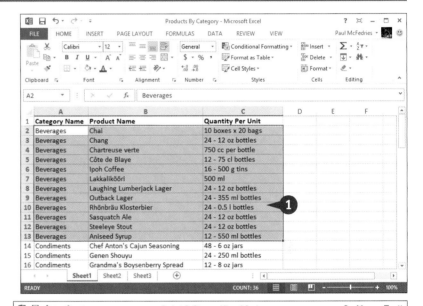

2 Click the **Home** tab.

3 Click **Clear** (🧼).

4 Click **Clear Contents**.

A If you want to delete the range data and its formatting, click **Clear All** instead.

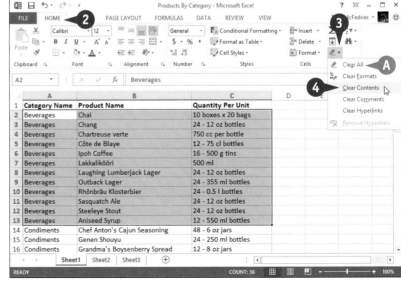

ⓑ Excel removes the range data.

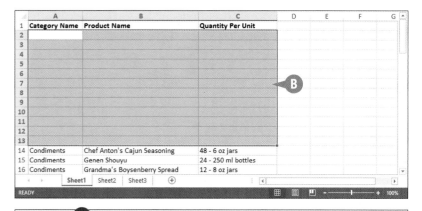

Undo Range Data Deletion

① Click the **Undo** ☑.

② Click **Clear**.

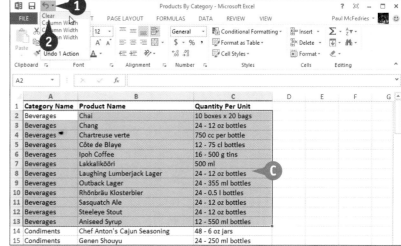

Note: If the data deletion was the most recent action you performed, you can undo it by pressing Ctrl+Z or by clicking **Undo** (↺).

ⓒ Excel restores the data to the range.

Are there faster ways to delete the data from a range?

Yes. Probably the fastest method is to select the range and then press Delete. You can also select the range, right-click any part of the range, and then click **Clear Contents**.

Is it possible to delete a cell's numeric formatting?

Yes. Select the range with the formatting that you want to remove, click **Home**, click 🧼, and then click **Clear Formats**. Excel removes all the formatting from the selected range. If you prefer to delete only the numeric formatting, click **Home**, click the **Number Format** ▼, and then click **General**.

Delete a Range

If your worksheet contains a range that you no longer need, you can delete that range. Note that this is not the same as deleting the data within a cell or range, as described in the previous section, "Delete Data from a Range." When you delete a range, Excel deletes not just the data within the range, but also the range cells. Excel then shifts the remaining worksheet data to replace the deleted range. Excel displays a dialog box that enables you to choose whether the data is shifted up or to the left.

Delete a Range

1 Select the range that you want to delete.

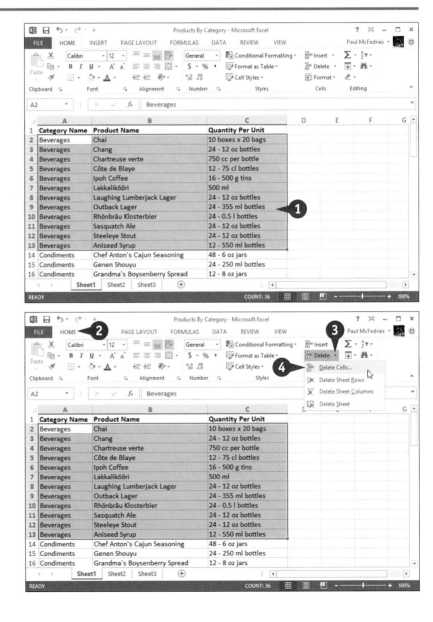

2 Click the **Home** tab.

3 Click the **Delete** ▼.

4 Click **Delete Cells**.

The Delete dialog box appears.

5 Select the option that corresponds to how you want Excel to shift the remaining cells after it deletes the range (○ changes to ◉).

Note: In most cases, if you have data below the selected range, you should click the **Shift cells up** option; if you have data to the right of the selected range, you should click the **Shift cells left** option.

6 Click **OK**.

Ⓐ Excel deletes the range and shifts the remaining data.

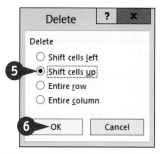

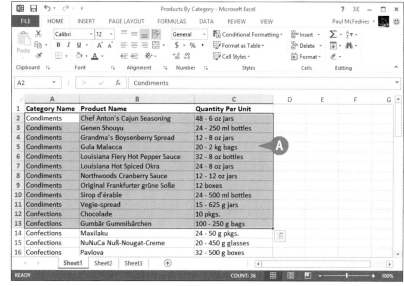

TIPS

Are there faster ways to delete a range?
Yes. Probably the fastest method is to select the range and then press Ctrl+▬. You can also select the range, right-click any part of the range, and then click **Delete**. Both methods display the Delete dialog box.

How do I delete a row or column?
To delete a row, select any cell in the row, click the **Home** tab, click the **Delete** ▾, and then click **Delete Sheet Rows**. To delete a column, select any cell in the column, click the **Home** tab, click the **Delete** ▾, and then click **Delete Sheet Columns**. Note, too, that you can delete multiple rows or columns by selecting at least one cell in each row or column.

Hide a Row or Column

If you do not need to see or work with a row or column temporarily, you can make your worksheet easier to read and to navigate by hiding the row or column. Hiding a row or column is also useful if you are showing someone a worksheet that contains private or sensitive data that you do not want the person to see.

Hiding a row or column does not affect other parts of your worksheet. In particular, formulas that use or rely on data in the hidden rows and columns still display the same results.

Hide a Row or Column

Hide a Row

1 Click in any cell in the row you want to hide.

2 Click the **Home** tab.

3 Click **Format**.

4 Click **Hide & Unhide**.

5 Click **Hide Rows**.

Note: You can also hide a row by pressing Ctrl + 9.

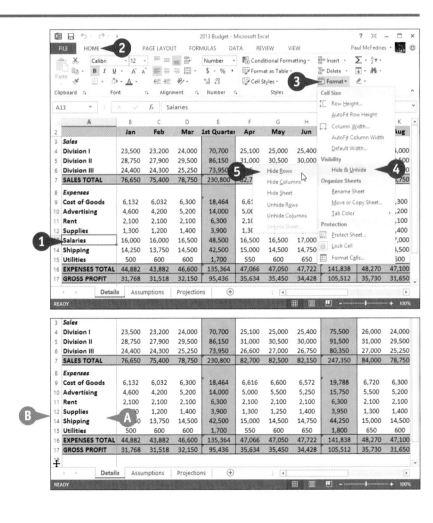

A Excel removes the row from the worksheet display.

B Excel displays a double-line heading border between the surrounding rows to indicate that a hidden row lies between them.

Another way to hide a row is to move the mouse ✛ over the bottom edge of the row heading (✛ changes to ╪), and then click and drag the edge up until the height displays 0.

Hide a Column

1 Click in any cell in the column you want to hide.

2 Click the **Home** tab.

3 Click **Format**.

4 Click **Hide & Unhide**.

5 Click **Hide Columns**.

Note: You can also hide a column by pressing Ctrl + 0.

C Excel removes the column from the worksheet display.

D Excel displays a slightly thicker heading border between the surrounding columns to indicate that a hidden column lies between them.

Another way to hide a column is to move the mouse ⊕ over the right edge of the column heading (⊕ changes to ✛), and then click and drag the edge left until the width displays 0.

TIP

How do I display a hidden row or column?

To display a hidden row, select the row above and the row below the hidden row, click **Home**, click **Format**, click **Hide & Unhide**, and then click **Unhide Rows**. Alternatively, move the mouse ⊕ between the headings of the selected rows (⊕ changes to ✛) and then double-click. To unhide row 1, right-click the top edge of the row 2 header and then click **Unhide**.

To display a hidden column, select the column to the left and the column to the right of the hidden column, click **Home**, click **Format**, click **Hide & Unhide**, and then click **Unhide Columns**. Alternatively, move the ⊕ between the headings of the selected columns (⊕ changes to ✛) and then double-click. To unhide column A, right-click the left edge of the column B header and then click **Unhide**.

Freeze Rows or Columns

You can keep your column labels in view as you scroll the worksheet by freezing the row or rows that contain the labels. This makes it easier to review and add data to the worksheet because you can always see the column labels.

If your worksheet also includes row labels, you can keep those labels in view as you horizontally scroll the worksheet by freezing the column or columns that contain the labels.

Freeze Rows or Columns

Freeze Rows

1 Scroll the worksheet so that the row or rows that you want to freeze are visible.

2 Select the cell in column A that is one row below the last row you want to freeze.

For example, if you want to freeze row 1, select cell A2.

3 Click the **View** tab.

4 Click **Freeze Panes**.

5 Click **Freeze Panes**.

Excel freezes the rows.

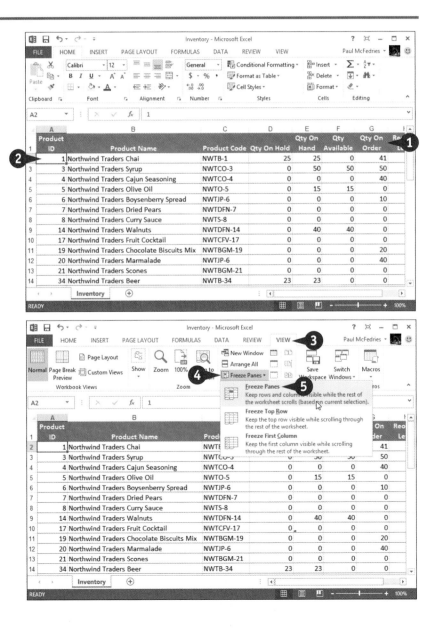

Freeze Columns

1 Scroll the worksheet so that the column or columns that you want to freeze are visible.

2 Select the cell in row 1 that is one row to the right of the last column you want to freeze.

For example, if you want to freeze column A, select cell B1.

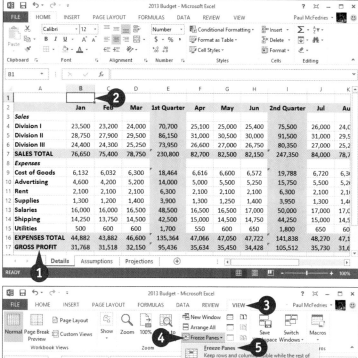

3 Click the **View** tab.

4 Click **Freeze Panes**.

5 Click **Freeze Panes**.

Excel freezes the columns.

Are there easier methods I can use to freeze just the top row or first column?

Yes. To freeze just the top row, click **View**, click **Freeze Panes**, and then click **Freeze Top Row**. To freeze just the first column, click **View**, click **Freeze Panes**, and then click **Freeze First Column**. Note that in both cases you do not need to select a cell in advance.

How do I unfreeze a row or column?

If you no longer require a row or column to be frozen, you can unfreeze it by clicking **View**, clicking **Freeze Panes**, and then clicking **Unfreeze Panes**.

Merge Two or More Cells

You can create a single large cell by merging two or more cells. For example, it is common to merge several cells in the top row to use as a worksheet title.

Another common reason for merging cells is to create a label that applies to multiple columns of data. For example, if you have three columns labeled *January*, *February*, and *March*, you could select the three cells in the row above these labels, merge them, and then use the merged cell to add the label *First Quarter*.

Merge Two or More Cells

1 Select the cells that you want to merge.

2 Click the **Home** tab.

3 Click the **Merge & Center** ▼.

4 Click **Merge Cells**.

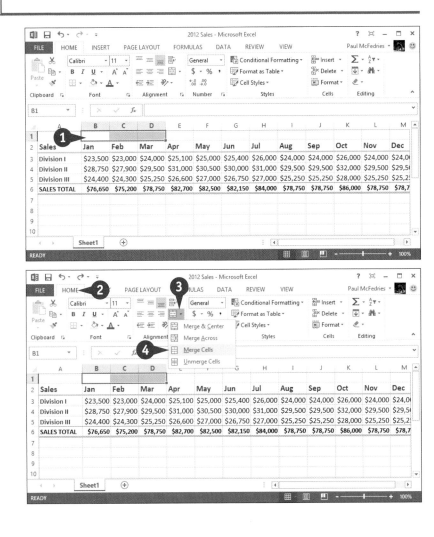

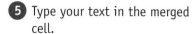 Excel merges the selected cells into a single cell.

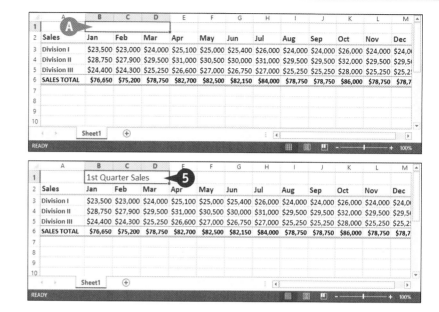

5 Type your text in the merged cell.

How do I center text across multiple columns?
This is a useful technique for your worksheet titles or headings. You can center a title across the entire worksheet, or you can center a heading across the columns that it refers to. Follow Steps **1** to **3** and then click **Merge & Center**. Excel creates the merged cell and formats the cell with the Center alignment option. Any text you enter into the merged cell appears centered within the cell.

Transpose Rows and Columns

You can use the Transpose command in Excel to easily turn a row of data into a column of data, or a column of data into a row of data.

The Transpose command is useful when you enter data into a row (or column) or receive a worksheet from another person that has data in a row (or column), and you decide the data would be better presented as a column (or row). You can also transpose rows and columns together in a single command, which is handy when you need to restructure a worksheet.

Transpose Rows and Columns

1. Select the range that includes the data you want to transpose.

2. Click the **Home** tab.

3. Click **Copy** (📋).

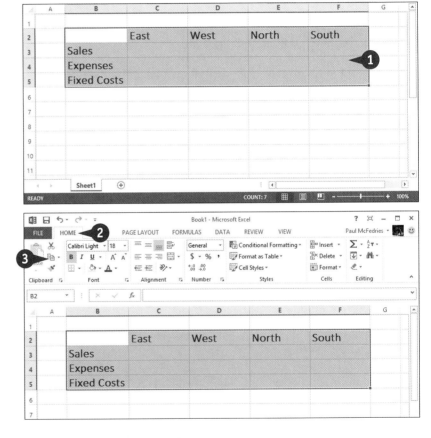

4 Click where you want the transposed range to appear.

5 Click the **Paste** ▼.

6 Click **Transpose** ( ).

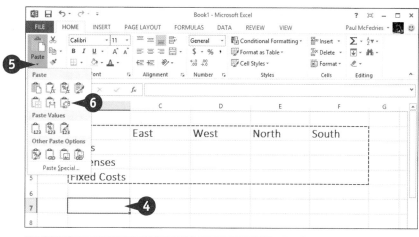

A Excel transposes the data and then pastes it to the worksheet.

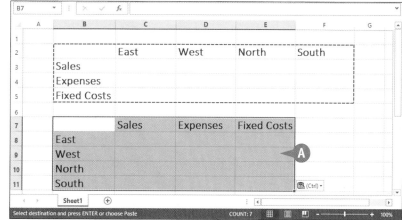

How do I know which cells to select?
The range you select before copying depends on what you want to transpose. If you want to transpose a single horizontal or vertical range of cells, then select just that range. If you want to transpose a horizontal range of cells and a vertical range of cells at the same time, select the range that includes all the cells, as shown in this section's example.

Can I transpose range values as well as range labels?
Yes. The Transpose command works with text, numbers, dates, formulas, and any other data that you can add to a cell. So if you have a rectangular region of data that includes row labels, column labels, and cell values within each row and column, you can select the entire range and transpose it.

CHAPTER 4

Working with Range Names

You can make it easier to navigate Excel worksheets and build Excel formulas by applying names to your ranges. This chapter explains range names and shows you how to define, edit, and use range names.

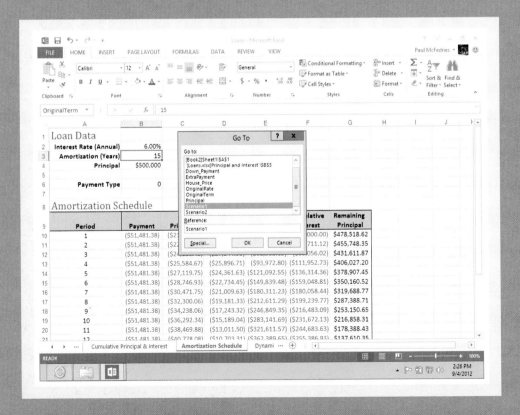

Understanding the Benefits of Using Range Names

A *range name* is a text label that you apply to a single cell or to a range of cells. Once you have defined a name for a range, you can use that name in place of the range coordinates, which has several benefits. These benefits include making your worksheets more intuitive and making your work more accurate. In addition, a range name is easier to remember than range coordinates, it does not change when you move the underlying range, and it makes it easier to navigate your worksheets.

More Intuitive

Range names are more intuitive than range coordinates, particularly in formulas. For example, if you see the range B2:B10 in a formula, the only way to know what the range refers to is to look at the data. However, if you see the name Quarterly_Sales in the formula, then you already know what the range refers to.

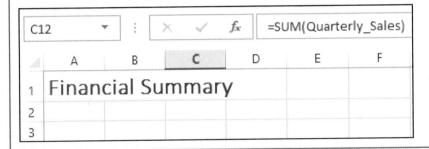

More Accurate

Range names are more accurate than range coordinates. For example, consider the range address A1:B3, which consists of four different pieces of information: the column (A) and row (1) of the cell in the upper-left corner of the range, and the column (B) and row (3) of the cell in the lower-right corner. If you get even one of these values wrong, it can cause errors throughout a spreadsheet. By contrast, with a range name you need only reference the actual name.

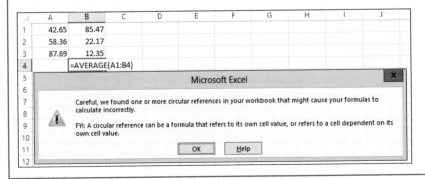

Easier to Remember

Range names are easier to remember than range coordinates. For example, if you want to use a particular range in a formula, but that range is not currently visible, to get the coordinates you must scroll until you can see the range and then determine the range's coordinates. However, if you have already assigned the range an intuitive name such as Project_Expenses, you can add that name directly without having to view the range.

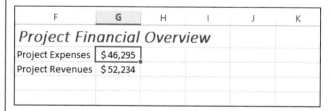

Names Do Not Change

Range names do not change when you adjust the position of a range, as they do with range coordinates. For example, if you move the range A1:B5 to the right by five columns, the range coordinates change to F1:B5. If you have a formula that references that range, Excel updates the formula with the new range coordinates, which could confuse someone examining the worksheet. By contrast, a range name does not change when you move the range.

	F	G	H	I	J	K
	Project Financial Overview					
	Project Expenses	$46,295				
	Project Revenues	$52,234				

Easier Navigation

Range names make it easier to navigate a worksheet. For example, Excel has a Go To command that enables you to choose a range name, and Excel takes you directly to the range. You can also use the Name box to select a range name and navigate to that range. You can also use Go To and the Name box to specify range coordinates, but range coordinates are much more difficult to work with.

Define a Range Name

Before you can use a range name in your formulas or to navigate a worksheet, you must first define the range name. You can define as many names as you need, and you can even define multiple names for the same range.

You can create range names manually, or you can get Excel to create the names for you automatically based on the existing text labels in a worksheet. To do this, see the following section, "Use Worksheet Text to Define a Range Name."

Define a Range Name

1 Select the range you want to name.

2 Click the **Formulas** tab.

3 Click **Define Name**.

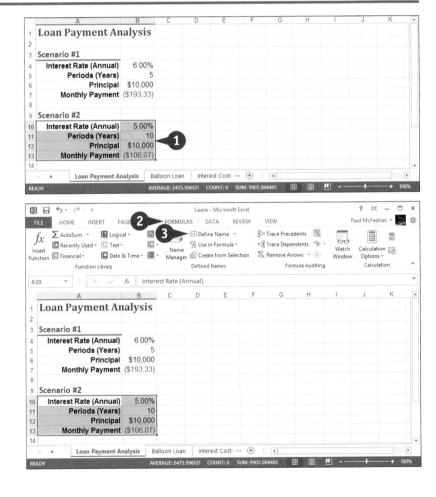

The New Name dialog box appears.

4 Type the name you want to use in the **Name** text box.

Note: The first character of the name must be a letter or an underscore (_). The name cannot include spaces or cell references, and it cannot be any longer than 255 characters.

Note: You can only use a particular range name once in a workbook.

5 Click **OK**.

Excel assigns the name to the range.

A The new name appears in the Name box whenever you select the range.

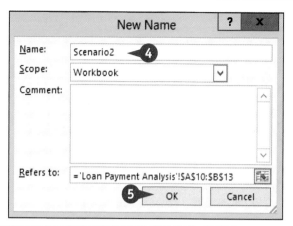

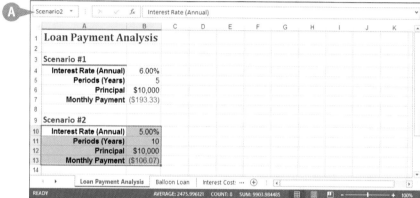

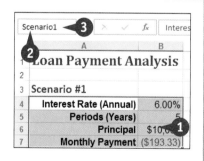

Use Worksheet Text to Define a Range Name

If you have several ranges to name, you can speed up the process by getting Excel to create the names for you automatically based on each range's text labels.

You can create range names from worksheet text when the labels are in the top or bottom row of the range, or the left or right column of the range. For example, if you have a column named Company, using the technique in this section results in that column's data being assigned the range name "Company."

Use Worksheet Text to Define a Range Name

1 Select the range or ranges you want to name.

A Be sure to include the text labels you want to use for the range names.

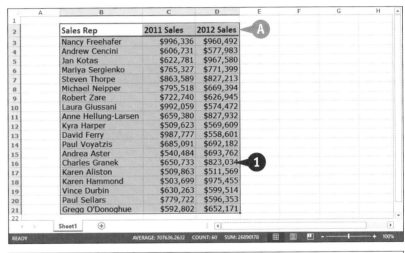

2 Click the **Formulas** tab.

3 Click **Create from Selection**.

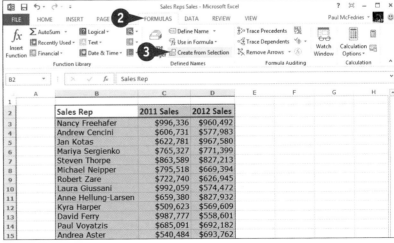

The Create Names from Selection dialog box appears.

④ Select the setting or settings that correspond to where the text labels are located in the selected range (☐ changes to ☑).

If Excel has activated a check box that does not apply to your data, click it (☑ changes to ☐).

⑤ Click **OK**.

Excel assigns the text labels as range names.

Ⓑ When you select one of the ranges, the range name assigned by Excel appears in the Name box.

Note: If the label text contains any illegal characters, such as a space, Excel replaces each of those characters with an underscore (_).

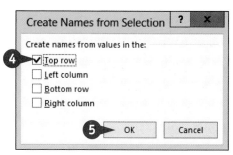

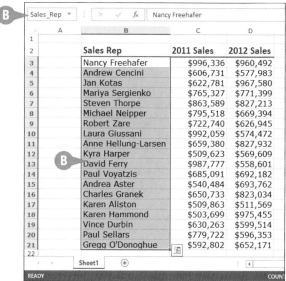

TIPS

Is there a faster way to run the Create from Selection command?
Yes, Excel offers a keyboard shortcut for the command. Select the range or ranges you want to work with and then press Ctrl+Shift+F3. Excel displays the Create Names from Selection dialog box. Follow Steps **4** and **5** to create the range names.

Given a table with labels in the top row and left column, is there a way to automatically assign a name to the table data?
Yes. The table data refers to the range of cells that does not include the table headings in the top row and left column. To assign a name to the data range, type a label in the top-left corner of the table. When you run the Create from Selection command on the entire table, Excel assigns the top-left label to the data range, as shown here.

Navigate a Workbook Using Range Names

One of the big advantages of defining range names is that they make it easier to navigate a workbook. You can choose a range name from a list and Excel automatically selects the associated range. This works even if the named range exists in a different worksheet of the same workbook.

Excel offers two methods for navigating a workbook using range names: the Name box and the Go To command.

Navigate a Workbook Using Range Names

Using the Name Box

1 Open the workbook that contains the range you want to work with.

2 Click the Name box 🔽.

3 Click the name of the range you want to select.

A Excel selects the range.

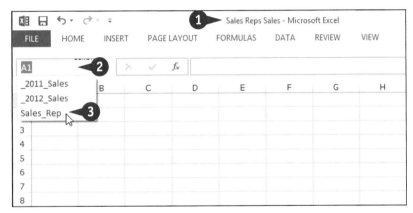

Using the Go To Command

1 Open the workbook that contains the range you want to work with.

2 Click the **Home** tab.

3 Click **Find & Select** (﷼).

4 Click **Go To**.

Note: You can also select the Go To command by pressing `Ctrl`+`G`.

The Go To dialog box appears.

5 Click the name of the range you want to select.

6 Click **OK**.

Ⓑ Excel selects the range.

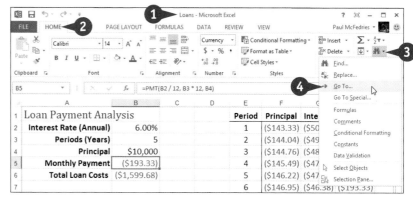

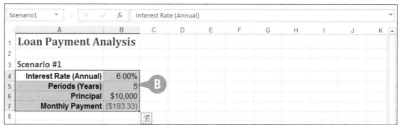

TIP

Is it possible to navigate to a named range in a different workbook?

Yes, but it is not easy or straightforward:

1 Follow Steps **1** to **4** in the "Using the Go To Command" subsection to display the Go To dialog box.

2 In the **Reference** text box, type the following:

'[workbook]worksheet'!name

Replace *workbook* with the filename of the workbook; replace *worksheet* with the name of the worksheet that contains the range; and replace *name* with the range name.

3 Click **OK**.

Change a Range Name

You can change any range name to a more suitable or accurate name. Changing a range name is useful if you are no longer satisfied with the original name you applied to a range or if the existing name no longer accurately reflects the contents of the range. You might also want to change a range name if you do not like the name that Excel generated automatically from the worksheet labels. If you want to change the range coordinates associated with a range name, see the second Tip in this section.

Change a Range Name

1 Open the workbook that contains the range name you want to change.

2 Click the **Formulas** tab.

3 Click **Name Manager**.

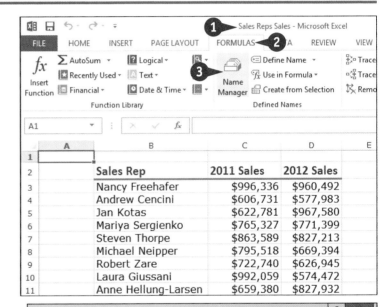

The Name Manager dialog box appears.

4 Click the name you want to change.

5 Click **Edit**.

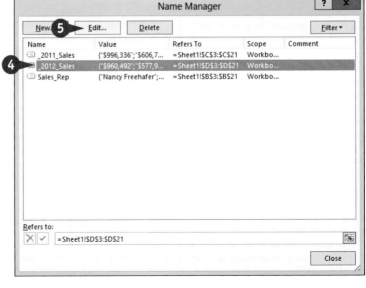

The Edit Name dialog box appears.

6 Use the **Name** text box to edit the name.

7 Click **OK**.

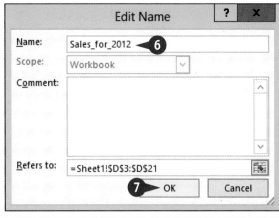

A The new name appears in the Name Manager dialog box.

8 Repeat Steps **4** to **7** to rename other ranges as needed.

9 Click **Close**.

Excel closes the dialog box and returns you to the worksheet.

Is there a faster method I can use to open the Name Manager dialog box?

Yes, Excel offers a shortcut key that enables you to bypass Steps **2** and **3**. Open the workbook that contains the range name you want to change, and then press `Ctrl` + `F3`. Excel opens the Name Manager dialog box.

Can I assign a name to a different range?

Yes. If you add another range to your workbook and you feel that an existing name would be more suited to that range, you can modify the name to refer to the new range. Follow Steps **1** to **5** to open the Edit Name dialog box. Click inside the **Refers to** reference box, click and drag the Excel mouse pointer (✛) on the worksheet to select the new range, and then press `Enter`. Click **Close**.

Delete a Range Name

If you have a range name that you no longer need, you should delete it. This reduces clutter in the Name Manager dialog box, and makes the Name box easier to navigate.

Note, however, that deleting a range name will generate an error in any formula that uses the name. This occurs because when you delete a range name, Excel does not convert the name to its range coordinates in formulas that use the name. Therefore, before deleting a range name, you should convert that name to its range coordinates in every formula that uses the name.

Delete a Range Name

1 Open the workbook that contains the range name you want to delete.

2 Click the **Formulas** tab.

3 Click **Name Manager**.

Note: You can also open the Name Manager dialog box by pressing Ctrl + F3 .

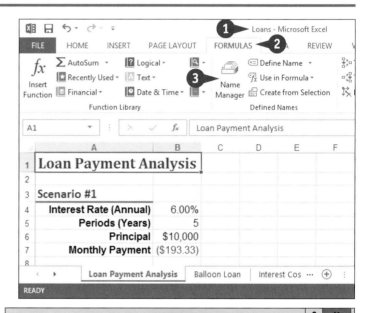

The Name Manager dialog box appears.

4 Click the name you want to delete.

5 Click **Delete**.

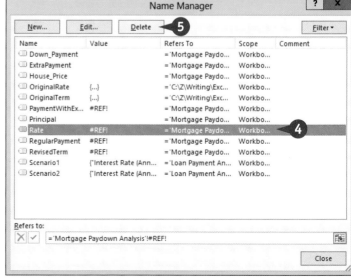

Excel asks you to confirm the deletion.

⑥ Click **OK**.

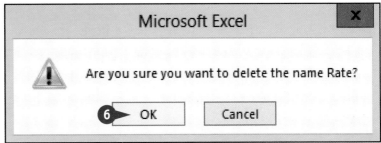

Ⓐ Excel deletes the range name.

⑦ Repeat Steps **4** to **6** to delete other range names as needed.

⑧ Click **Close**.

Excel closes the dialog box and returns you to the worksheet.

Is there a faster way to delete multiple range names?
Yes, you can delete two or more range names at once. First, follow Steps **1** to **3** to display the Name Manager dialog box. Next, select the range names you want to delete: To select consecutive names, click the first name you want to delete, hold down Shift, and then click the last name you want to delete; to select nonconsecutive names, hold down Ctrl and click each name you want to delete. When you have selected the names you want to remove, click **Delete** and then click **OK** when Excel asks you to confirm the deletion. Click **Close** to return to the worksheet.

Paste a List of Range Names

To make your workbook easier to use, particularly for other people who are not familiar with the names you have defined, you can paste a list of the workbook's range names to a worksheet. This is also useful for a workbook you have not used in a while. Examining the list of range names can help you familiarize yourself once again with the workbook's contents.

The pasted list contains two columns: one for the range names and one for the range coordinates associated with each name.

Paste a List of Range Names

1. Open the workbook that contains the range names you want to paste.

2. Select the cell where you want the pasted list to appear.

Note: Excel will overwrite existing data, so select a location where there is no existing cell data or where it is okay to delete the existing cell data.

3. Click the **Formulas** tab.

4. Click **Use in Formula**.

5. Click **Paste Names**.

The Paste Name dialog box appears.

6 Click **Paste List**.

Excel closes the Paste Name dialog box.

A Excel pastes the list of range names to the worksheet.

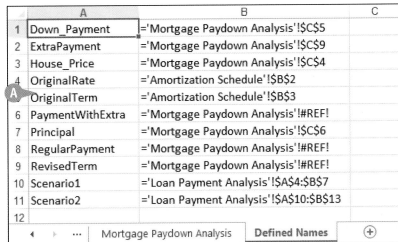

	A	B	C
1	Down_Payment	='Mortgage Paydown Analysis'!$C$5	
2	ExtraPayment	='Mortgage Paydown Analysis'!$C$9	
3	House_Price	='Mortgage Paydown Analysis'!$C$4	
4	OriginalRate	='Amortization Schedule'!$B$2	
5	OriginalTerm	='Amortization Schedule'!$B$3	
6	PaymentWithExtra	='Mortgage Paydown Analysis'!#REF!	
7	Principal	='Mortgage Paydown Analysis'!$C$6	
8	RegularPayment	='Mortgage Paydown Analysis'!#REF!	
9	RevisedTerm	='Mortgage Paydown Analysis'!#REF!	
10	Scenario1	='Loan Payment Analysis'!$A$4:$B$7	
11	Scenario2	='Loan Payment Analysis'!$A$10:$B$13	
12			

Mortgage Paydown Analysis | **Defined Names** | ⊕

TIP

Is there a faster method I can use to paste a list of range names?

Yes, Excel offers a handy keyboard shortcut that you can use. Open the workbook that contains the range names you want to paste, and then select the cell where you want the pasted list to appear. Press F3 to open the Paste Name dialog box, and then click **Paste List**.

CHAPTER 5

Formatting Excel Ranges

Microsoft Excel 2013 offers many commands and options for formatting ranges, including the font, text color, text alignment, background color, number format, column width, row height, and more.

Change the Font and Font Size

Whenen you work in an Excel worksheet, you can add visual appeal to a cell or range by changing the font. In this section and throughout this book, the term *font* is synonymous with *typeface*, and both terms refer to the overall look of each character.

You can also make labels and other text stand out from the rest of the worksheet by changing the font size. The font size is measured in *points*, where there are roughly 72 points in an inch.

Change the Font and Font Size

Change the Font

1 Select the range you want to format.

2 Click the **Home** tab.

3 Click ▼ in the **Font** list.

Ⓐ When you use the mouse pointer (⌣) to point to a typeface, Excel temporarily changes the selected text to that typeface.

4 Click the typeface you want to apply.

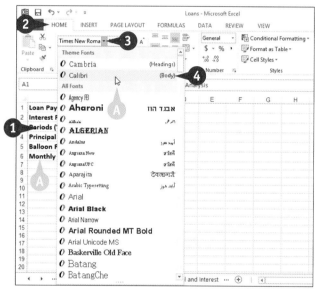

Ⓑ Excel applies the font to the text in the selected range.

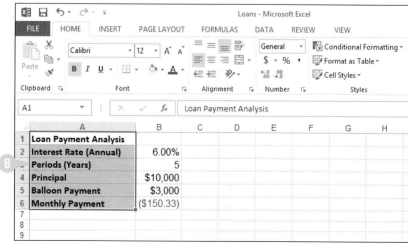

Change the Font Size

1 Select the range you want to format.

2 Click the **Home** tab.

3 Click ▼ in the **Font Size** list.

C When you use the mouse ▷ to point to a font size, Excel temporarily changes the selected text to that size.

4 Click the size you want to apply.

D You can also type the size you want in the Size text box.

E Excel applies the font size to the text in the selected range.

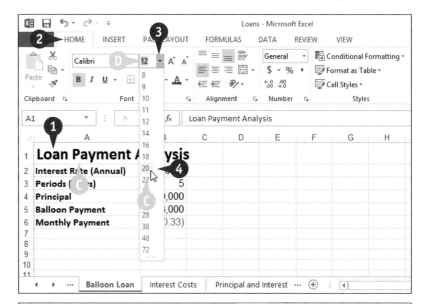

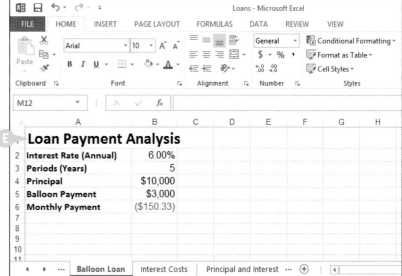

In the Theme Fonts section of the Font list, what do the designations Body and Headings mean?

When you create a workbook, Excel automatically applies a document theme to the workbook, and that theme includes predefined fonts. The theme's default font is referred to as Body, and it is the font used for regular worksheet text. Each theme also defines a Headings font, which Excel uses for cells formatted with a heading or title style.

Can I change the default font and font size?

Yes. Click the **File** tab and then click **Options** to open the Excel Options dialog box. Click the **General** tab, click the **Use this as the default font** ▽, and then click the typeface you want to use as the default. Click the **Font size** ▽ and then click the size you prefer to use as the default. Click **OK**.

Apply Font Effects

You can improve the look and impact of text in an Excel worksheet by applying font effects to a cell or to a range.

Font effects include common formatting such as **bold**, which is often used to make labels stand out from regular text; *italic*, which is often used to add emphasis to text; and underline, which is often used for worksheet titles and headings. You can also apply special effects such as ~~strikethrough~~, superscripts (for example, x^2+y^2), and subscripts (for example, H_2O).

Apply Font Effects

1 Select the range you want to format.

2 Click the **Home** tab.

3 To format the text as bold, click the **Bold** button (**B**).

Ⓐ Excel applies the bold effect to the selected range.

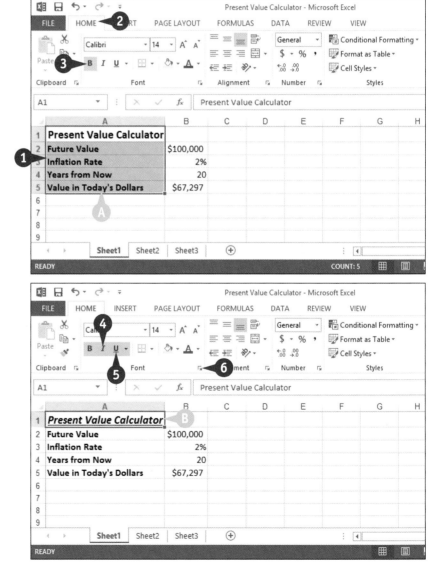

4 To format the text as italic, click the **Italic** button (*I*).

5 To format the text as underline, click the **Underline** button (U).

Ⓑ Excel applies the effects to the selected range.

6 Click the Font dialog box launcher (⌐).

86

The Format Cells dialog box appears with the Font tab displayed.

7 To format the text as strikethrough, click **Strikethrough** (☐ changes to ☑).

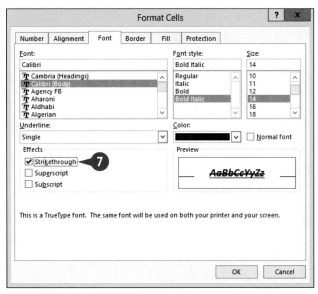

8 To format the text as a superscript, click **Superscript** (☐ changes to ☑).

Ⓒ To format the text as a subscript, click **Subscript** (☐ changes to ☑).

9 Click **OK**.

Excel applies the font effects.

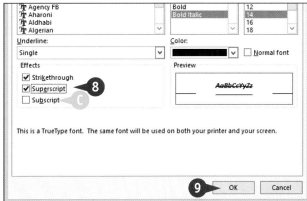

TIP

Are there any font-related keyboard shortcuts I can use?
Yes. Excel supports the following font shortcuts:

Press	To
Ctrl + B	Toggle the selected range as bold
Ctrl + I	Toggle the selected range as italic
Ctrl + U	Toggle the selected range as underline
Ctrl + 5	Toggle the selected range as strikethrough
Ctrl + 1	Display the Format Cells dialog box

Change the Font Color

When you work in an Excel worksheet, you can add visual interest by changing the font color. Most worksheets are meant to convey specific information, but that does not mean the sheet has to be plain. By adding a bit of color to your text, you make your worksheets more appealing. Adding color can also make the worksheet easier to read by, for example, differentiating titles, headings, and labels from regular text.

You can change the font color by applying a color from the workbook's theme, from the Excel palette of standard colors, or from a custom color that you create.

Change the Font Color

Select a Theme or Standard Color

1 Select the range you want to format.

2 Click the **Home** tab.

3 Click ▼ in the **Font Color** list (**A**).

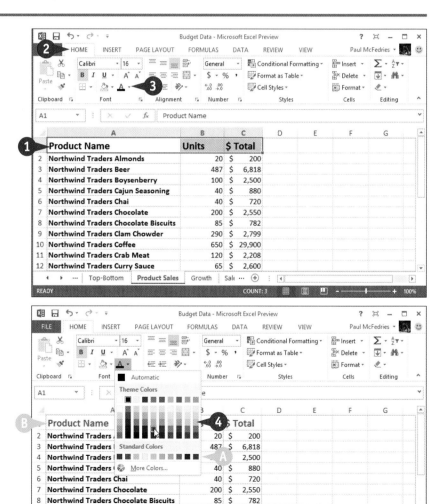

4 Click a theme color.

Ⓐ Alternatively, click one of the Excel standard colors.

Ⓑ Excel applies the color to the selected range.

Select a Custom Color

1 Select the range you want to format.

2 Click the **Home** tab.

3 Click ▼ in the **Font Color** list (⏷).

4 Click **More Colors.**

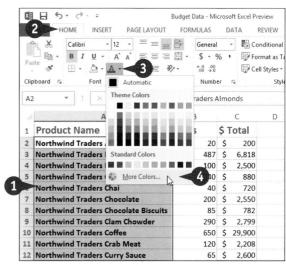

The Colors dialog box appears.

5 Click the color you want to use.

Ⓒ You can also click the **Custom** tab and then either click the color you want or enter the values for the Red, Green, and Blue components of the color.

6 Click **OK.**

Excel applies the color to the selected range.

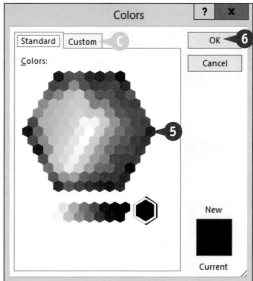

TIP

How can I make the best use of fonts in my documents?

• Do not use many different typefaces in a single document. Stick to one, or at most two, typefaces to avoid the ransom note look.

• Avoid overly decorative typefaces because they are often difficult to read.

• Use bold only for document titles, subtitles, and headings.

• Use italics only to emphasize words and phrases, or for the titles of books and magazines.

• Use larger type sizes only for document titles, subtitles, and, possibly, the headings.

• If you change the text color, be sure to leave enough contrast between the text and the background. In general, dark text on a light background is the easiest to read.

Align Text Within a Cell

You can make your worksheets easier to read by aligning text and numbers within each cell. By default, Excel aligns numbers with the right side of the cell, and it aligns text with the left side of the cell. You can also align numbers or text with the center of each cell.

Excel also allows you to align your data vertically within each cell. By default, Excel aligns all data with the bottom of each cell, but you can also align text with the top or middle.

Align Text Within a Cell

Align Text Horizontally

1 Select the range you want to format.

2 Click the **Home** tab.

3 In the Alignment group, click the horizontal alignment option you want to use:

Click **Align Text Left** (≡) to align data with the left side of each cell.

Click **Center** (≡) to align data with the center of each cell.

Click **Align Text Right** (≡) to align data with the right side of each cell.

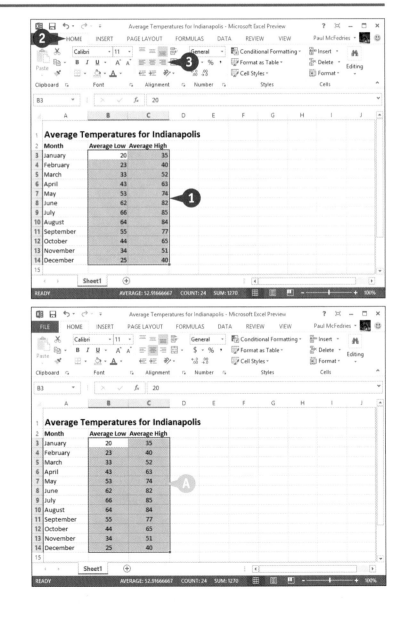

Excel aligns the data horizontally within each selected cell.

Ⓐ In this example, the data in the cells is centered.

Align Text Vertically

1 Select the range you want to format.

2 Click the **Home** tab.

3 In the Alignment group, click the vertical alignment option you want to use:

Click **Top Align** (≡) to align data with the top of each cell.

Click **Middle Align** (≡) to align data with the middle of each cell.

Click **Bottom Align** (≡) to align data with the bottom of each cell.

Excel aligns the data vertically within each selected cell.

Ⓑ In this example, the text is aligned with the middle of the cell.

TIPS

How do I format text so that it aligns with both the left and right sides of the cell?

This is called *justified* text, and it is useful if you have a lot of text in one or more cells. Select the range, click the **Home** tab, and then click the dialog box launcher (⌵) in the Alignment group. The Format Cells dialog box appears with the Alignment tab displayed. In the **Horizontal** list, click ⌄ and then click **Justify**. Click **OK** to justify the cells.

How do I indent cell text?

Select the range you want to indent, click the **Home** tab, and then click the Alignment group's dialog box launcher (⌵). In the Alignment tab, click the **Horizontal** list ⌄ and then click **Left (Indent)**. Use the **Indent** text box to type the indent, in characters, and then click **OK**. You can also click the **Increase Indent** (≡) or **Decrease Indent** (≡) button in the Home tab's Alignment group.

Center Text Across Multiple Columns

You can make a worksheet more visually appealing and easier to read by centering text across multiple columns. This feature is most useful when you have text in a cell that you use as a label or title for a range. Centering the text across the range makes it easier to see that the label or title applies to the entire range.

Center Text Across Multiple Columns

1 Select a range that consists of the text you want to work with and the cells across which you want to center the text.

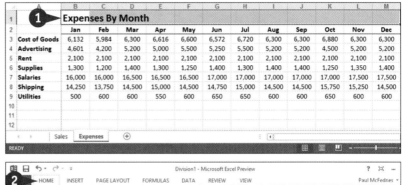

2 Click the **Home** tab.

3 In the Alignment group, click the dialog box launcher (⌐).

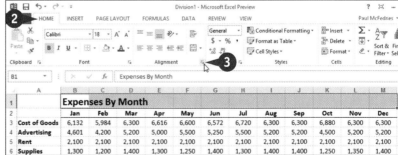

Excel opens the Format Cells dialog box with the Alignment tab displayed.

4 Click the **Horizontal** ⌄ and then click **Center Across Selection**.

5 Click **OK**.

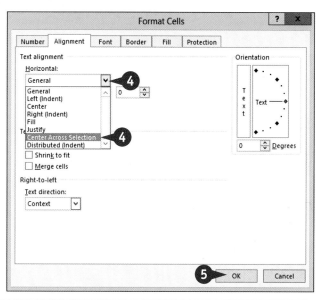

Ⓐ Excel centers the text across the selected cells.

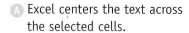

	A	B	C	D	E	F	G	H	I	J	K	L	M
1						Expenses By Month							
2		Jan	Feb	Mar	Apr	May	Jun	Jul	Aug	Sep	Oct	Nov	Dec
3	Cost of Goods	6,132	5,984	6,300	6,616	6,600	6,572	6,720	6,300	6,300	6,880	6,300	6,300
4	Advertising	4,601	4,200	5,200	5,000	5,500	5,250	5,500	5,200	5,200	4,500	5,200	5,200
5	Rent	2,100	2,100	2,100	2,100	2,100	2,100	2,100	2,100	2,100	2,100	2,100	2,100
6	Supplies	1,300	1,200	1,400	1,300	1,250	1,400	1,300	1,400	1,400	1,250	1,350	1,400
7	Salaries	16,000	16,000	16,500	16,500	16,500	17,000	17,000	17,000	17,000	17,000	17,500	17,500
8	Shipping	14,250	13,750	14,500	15,000	14,500	14,750	15,000	14,500	14,500	15,750	15,250	14,500
9	Utilities	500	600	600	550	600	650	650	600	600	650	600	600
10													
11													
12													

Sales   Expenses

READY

TIP

Is there an easier way to center text across multiple columns?
Yes, although this technique also merges the selected cells into a single cell. (See Chapter 3 to learn more about merging cells.) Follow these steps:

1 Repeat Steps **1** and **2**.

2 In the Alignment group, click the **Merge & Center** button (▦).

Excel merges the selected cells into a single cell and centers the text within that cell.

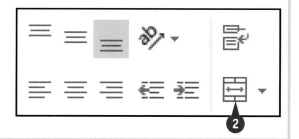

Rotate Text Within a Cell

You can add visual interest to your text by slanting the text upward or downward in the cell. You can also use this technique to make a long column heading take up less horizontal space on the worksheet.

You can choose a predefined rotation, or you can make cell text angle upward or downward by specifying the degrees of rotation.

Rotate Text Within a Cell

1 Select the range containing the text you want to angle.

2 Click the **Home** tab.

3 Click **Orientation** (✏).

A If you want to use a predefined orientation, click one of the menu items and skip the rest of the steps.

4 Click **Format Cell Alignment**.

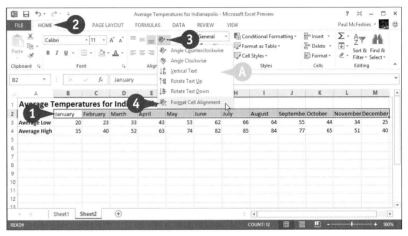

The Format Cells dialog box appears with the Alignment tab displayed.

5 Click an orientation marker.

B You can also use the Degrees spin box to type or click a degree of rotation. (See the Tip at the end of this section.)

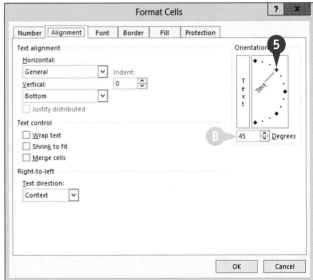

C You can click the vertical text area to display your text vertically instead of horizontally in the cell.

6 Click **OK**.

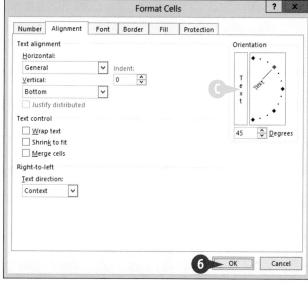

D Excel rotates the cell text.

E The row height automatically increases to contain the slanted text.

F You can reduce the column width to free up space and make your cells more presentable.

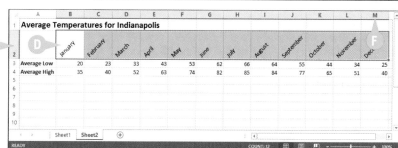

How does the Degrees spin box work?
If you use the Degrees spin box to set the text orientation, you can set the orientation to a positive number, such as 25, and Excel angles the text in an upward direction. If you set the text orientation to a negative number, such as −40, Excel angles the text in a downward direction.

You can specify values in the range from 90 degrees (which is the same as clicking the Rotate Text Up command in the Orientation menu) to −90 degrees (which is the same as clicking the Rotate Text Down command).

Add a Background Color to a Range

You can make a range stand out from the rest of the worksheet by applying a background color to the range. Note, however, that if you want to apply a background color to a range based on the values in that range — for example, red for negative values and green for positive — it is easier to apply a conditional format, as described in "Apply a Conditional Format to a Range," later in this chapter.

You can change the background color by applying a color from the workbook's theme, from the Excel palette of standard colors, or from a custom color that you create.

Add a Background Color to a Range

Select a Theme or Standard Color

1. Select the range you want to format.

2. Click the **Home** tab.

3. Click ▼ in the **Fill Color** list ( ).

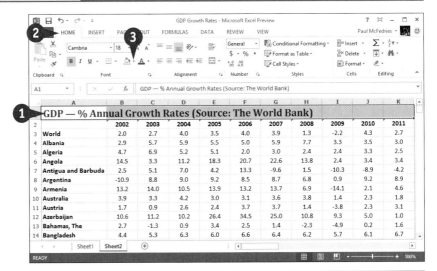

4. Click a theme color.

Ⓐ Alternatively, click one of the standard Excel colors.

Ⓑ Excel applies the color to the selected range.

Ⓒ To remove the background color from the range, click **No Fill**.

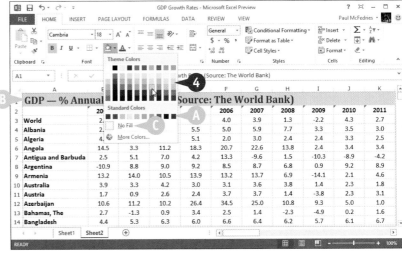

Select a Custom Color

1 Select the range you want to format.

2 Click the **Home** tab.

3 Click ▼ in the **Fill Color** list (🖌).

4 Click **More Colors**.

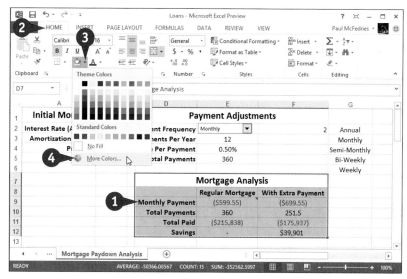

The Colors dialog box appears.

5 Click the color you want to use.

Ⓓ You can also click the **Custom** tab and then either click the color you want or enter the values for the Red, Green, and Blue components of the color.

6 Click **OK**.

Excel applies the color to the selected range.

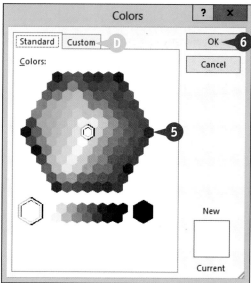

Are there any pitfalls to watch out for when I apply background colors?

Yes. The biggest pitfall is applying a background color that clashes with the range text. For example, the default text color is black, so if you apply any dark background color, the text will be very difficult to read. Always use either a light background color with dark-colored text, or a dark background color with light-colored text.

Can I apply a background that fades from one color to another?

Yes. This is called a *gradient* effect. Select the range, click the **Home** tab, and then click the Font group's dialog box launcher (🖼). Click the **Fill** tab and then click **Fill Effects**. In the Fill Effects dialog box, use the **Color 1** ▼ and the **Color 2** ▼ to choose your colors. Click an option in the **Shading styles** section (○ changes to ◉), and then click **OK**.

Apply a Number Format

You can make your worksheet easier to read by applying a number format to your data. For example, if your worksheet includes monetary data, you can apply the Currency format to display each value with a dollar sign and two decimal places.

Excel offers ten number formats, most of which apply to numeric data. However, you can also apply the Date format to date data, the Time format to time data, and the Text format to text data.

Apply a Number Format

1 Select the range you want to format.

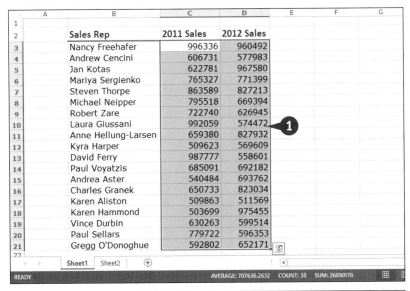

2 Click the **Home** tab.

3 Click the **Number Format** ▼.

4 Click the number format you want to use.

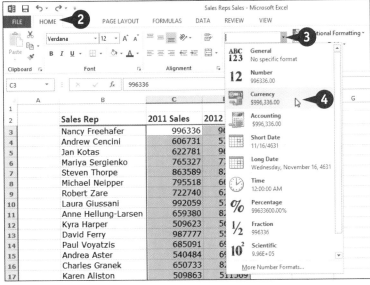

Ⓐ Excel applies the number format to the selected range.

Ⓑ For monetary values, you can also click **Accounting Number Format** ($).

Ⓒ For percentages, you can also click **Percent Style** (%).

Ⓓ For large numbers, you can also click **Comma Style** (⁹).

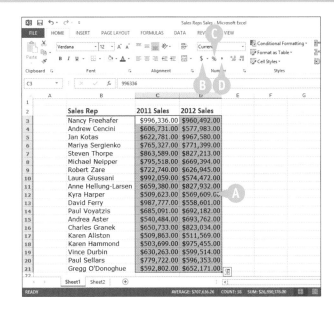

TIP

Is there a way to get more control over the number formats?

Yes. You can use the Format Cells dialog box to control properties such as the display of negative numbers, the currency symbol used, and how dates and times appear. Follow these steps:

❶ Select the range you want to format.

❷ Click the **Home** tab.

❸ Click the Number group's dialog box launcher (⌐).

The Format Cells dialog box appears with the Number tab displayed.

❹ In the Category list, click the type of number format you want to apply.

❺ Use the controls that Excel displays to customize the number format.

The controls you see vary, depending on the number format you chose in Step **4**.

❻ Click **OK**.

Excel applies the number format.

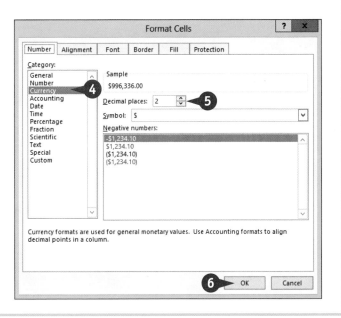

Change the Number of Decimal Places Displayed

You can make your numeric values easier to read and interpret by adjusting the number of decimal places that Excel displays. For example, you might want to ensure that all dollar-and-cent values show two decimal places, while dollar-only values show no decimal places. Similarly, you can adjust the display of percentage values to suit your audience by showing more decimals (greater accuracy but more difficult to read) or fewer decimals (less accuracy but easier to read).

You can either decrease or increase the number of decimal places that Excel displays.

Change the Number of Decimal Places Displayed

Decrease the Number of Decimal Places

1 Select the range you want to format.

2 Click the **Home** tab.

3 Click the **Decrease Decimal** button ( ).

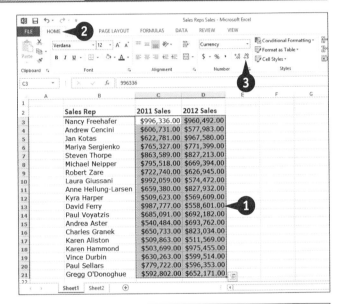

Ⓐ Excel decreases the number of decimal places by one.

4 Repeat Step **3** until you get the number of decimal places you want.

Increase the Number of Decimal Places

1. Select the range you want to format.

2. Click the **Home** tab.

3. Click the **Increase Decimal** button (.00→.0).

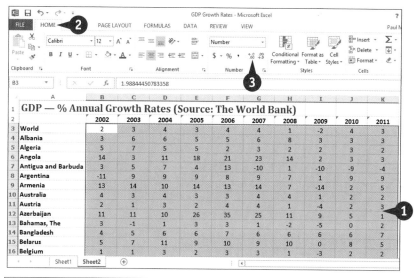

B. Excel increases the number of decimal places by one.

4. Repeat Step **3** until you get the number of decimal places you want.

TIP

My range currently has values that display different numbers of decimal places. What happens when I change the number of decimal places?

In this situation, Excel uses the value that has the most displayed decimal places as the basis for formatting all the values. For example, if the selected range has values that display no, one, two, or four decimal places, Excel uses the value with four decimals as the basis. If you click **Decrease Decimal**, Excel displays every value with three decimal places; if you click **Increase Decimal**, Excel displays every value with five decimal places.

Apply an AutoFormat to a Range

You can save time when formatting your Excel worksheets by using the AutoFormat feature. This feature offers a number of predefined formatting options that you can apply to a range all at once. The formatting options include the number format, font, cell alignment, borders, patterns, row height, and column width.

The AutoFormats are designed for data in a tabular format, particularly where you have headings in the top row and left column, numeric data in the rest of the cells, and a bottom row that shows the totals for each column.

Apply an AutoFormat to a Range

1 Select the range you want to format.

2 Click **AutoFormat** ().

Note: See Chapter 1 to learn how to add a button to the Quick Access Toolbar. In this case, you must add the QuickFormat button.

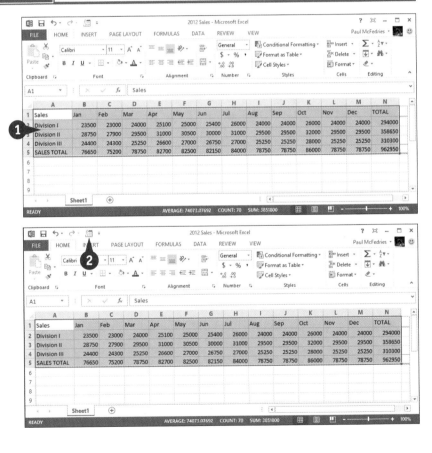

The AutoFormat dialog box appears.

3 Click the AutoFormat you want to use.

4 Click **OK**.

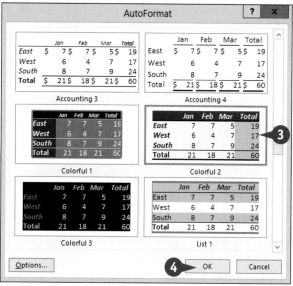

A Excel applies the AutoFormat to the selected range.

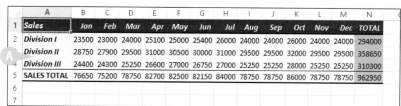

TIPS

Is there a way to apply an AutoFormat without using some of its formatting?

Yes. Excel enables you to control all six formats that are part of each AutoFormat: Number, Font, Alignment, Border, Patterns, and Width/Height. Follow Steps **1** to **3** to choose the AutoFormat you want to apply. Click **Options** to expand the dialog box and display the Formats to apply group. Deselect the option for each format you do not want to apply (☑ changes to ☐), and then click **OK**.

How do I remove an AutoFormat?

If you do not like or no longer need the AutoFormat you applied to the cells, you can revert them to a plain, unformatted state. Select the range and then click ▦ to display the AutoFormat dialog box. At the bottom of the format list, click **None**, and then click **OK**. Excel removes the AutoFormat from the selected range.

Apply a Conditional Format to a Range

You can make a worksheet easier to analyze by applying a conditional format to a range. A *conditional format* is formatting that Excel applies only to cells that meet the condition you specify. For example, you can tell Excel to apply the formatting only if a cell's value is greater than some specified amount.

When you set up your conditional format, you can specify the font, border, and background pattern, which helps to ensure that the cells that meet your criteria stand out from the other cells in the range.

Apply a Conditional Format to a Range

① Select the range you want to work with.

② Click the **Home** tab.

③ Click **Conditional Formatting**.

④ Click **Highlight Cells Rules**.

⑤ Click the operator you want to use for your condition.

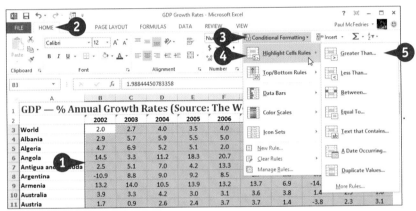

An operator dialog box appears, such as the Greater Than dialog box shown here.

⑥ Type the value you want to use for your condition.

Ⓐ You can also click the **Collapse Dialog** button (⊞) and then click a worksheet cell.

Depending on the operator, you may need to specify two values.

⑦ Click the **with** ☑ and then click the formatting you want to use.

Ⓑ To create your own format, click **Custom Format**.

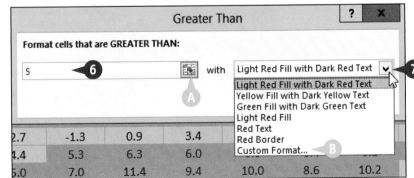

8 Click **OK**.

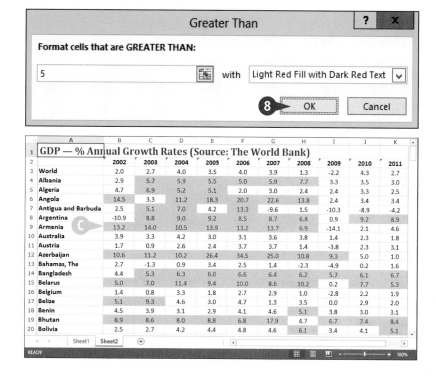

Greater Than ? X

Format cells that are GREATER THAN:

5   with   Light Red Fill with Dark Red Text ▾

8 ➤ OK   Cancel

C Excel applies the formatting to cells that meet your condition.

A	B	C	D	E	F	G	H	I	J	K
1 GDP — % Annual Growth Rates (Source: The World Bank)										
2	2002	2003	2004	2005	2006	2007	2008	2009	2010	2011
3 World	2.0	2.7	4.0	3.5	4.0	3.9	1.3	-2.2	4.3	2.7
4 Albania	2.9	5.7	5.9	5.5	5.0	5.9	7.7	3.3	3.5	3.0
5 Algeria	4.7	6.9	5.2	5.1	2.0	3.0	2.4	2.4	3.3	2.5
6 Angola	14.5	3.3	11.2	18.3	20.7	22.6	13.8	2.4	3.4	3.4
7 Antigua and Barbuda	2.5	5.1	7.0	4.2	13.3	-9.6	1.5	-10.3	-8.9	-4.2
8 Argentina	-10.9	8.8	9.0	9.2	8.5	8.7	6.8	0.9	9.2	8.9
9 Armenia	13.2	14.0	10.5	13.9	13.2	13.7	6.9	-14.1	2.1	4.6
10 Australia	3.9	3.3	4.2	3.0	3.1	3.6	3.8	1.4	2.3	1.8
11 Austria	1.7	0.9	2.6	2.4	3.7	3.7	1.4	-3.8	2.3	3.1
12 Azerbaijan	10.6	11.2	10.2	26.4	34.5	25.0	10.8	9.3	5.0	1.0
13 Bahamas, The	2.7	-1.3	0.9	3.4	2.5	1.4	-2.3	-4.9	0.2	1.6
14 Bangladesh	4.4	5.3	6.3	6.0	6.6	6.4	6.2	5.7	6.1	6.7
15 Belarus	5.0	7.0	11.4	9.4	10.0	8.6	10.2	0.2	7.7	5.3
16 Belgium	1.4	0.8	3.3	1.8	2.7	2.9	1.0	-2.8	2.2	1.9
17 Belize	5.1	9.3	4.6	3.0	4.7	1.3	3.5	0.0	2.9	2.0
18 Benin	4.5	3.9	3.1	2.9	4.1	4.6	5.1	3.8	3.0	3.1
19 Bhutan	8.9	8.6	8.0	8.8	6.8	17.9	4.7	6.7	7.4	8.4
20 Bolivia	2.5	2.7	4.2	4.4	4.8	4.6	6.1	3.4	4.1	5.1

Sheet1 Sheet2 ⊕

READY   100%

TIPS

Can I set up more than one condition for a single range?

Yes. Excel enables you to specify multiple conditional formats. For example, you could set up one condition for cells that are greater than some value, and a separate condition for cells that are less than some other value. You can apply unique formats to each condition. Follow Steps **1** to **8** to configure the new condition.

How do I remove a conditional format from a range?

If you no longer require a conditional format, you can delete it. Follow Steps **1** to **3** to select the range and display the Conditional Formatting menu, and then click **Manage Rules**. Excel displays the Conditional Formatting Rules Manager dialog box. Click the **Show formatting rules for** ▾ and then click **This Worksheet**. Click the conditional format you want to remove and then click **Delete Rule**. Click **OK** to return to the worksheet.

Apply a Style to a Range

You can reduce the time it takes to format your worksheets by applying the predefined Excel styles to your ranges. Excel comes with more than 20 predefined styles for different worksheet elements such as headings, numbers, calculations, and special range types such as explanatory text, worksheet notes, and warnings. Excel also offers two dozen styles associated with the current document theme.

Each style includes the number format, cell alignment, font typeface and size, border, and fill color.

Apply a Style to a Range

1 Select the range you want to format.

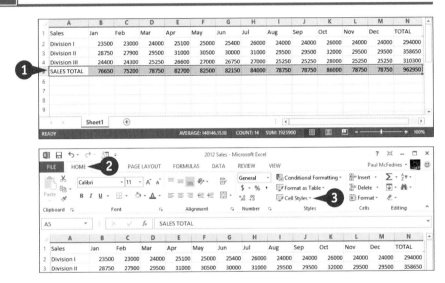

2 Click the **Home** tab.

3 Click **Cell Styles**.

Excel displays the Cell Styles gallery.

④ Click the style you want to apply.

Note: If the style is not exactly the way you want, you can right-click the style, click **Modify**, and then click **Format** to customize the style.

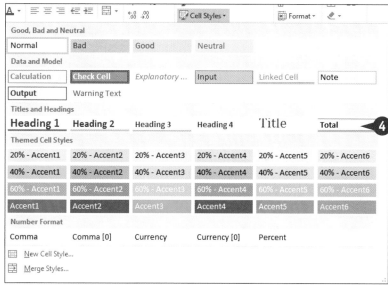

Ⓐ Excel applies the style to the range.

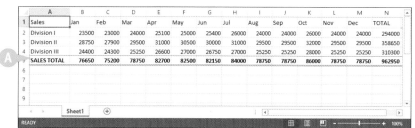

Are there styles I can use to format tabular data?
Yes. Excel comes with a gallery of table styles that offer formatting options that highlight the first row, apply different formats to alternating rows, and so on. Select the range that includes your data, click the **Home** tab, and then click **Format as Table**. In the gallery that appears, click the table format you want to apply.

Can I create my own style?
Yes. This is useful if you find yourself applying the same set of formatting options over and over. By saving those options as a custom style, you can apply it by following Steps **1** to **4**. Apply your formatting to a cell or range, and then select that cell or range. Click **Home**, click **Cell Styles**, and then click **New Cell Style**. In the Style dialog box, type a name for your style, and then click **OK**.

Change the Column Width

You can make your worksheets neater and more readable by adjusting the column widths to suit the data contained in each column.

For example, if you have a large number or a long line of text in a cell, Excel may display only part of the cell value. To avoid this, you can increase the width of the column. Similarly, if a column only contains a few characters in each cell, you can decrease the width to fit more columns on the screen.

Change the Column Width

1 Click in any cell in the column you want to resize.

2 Click the **Home** tab.

3 Click **Format**.

4 Click **Column Width**.

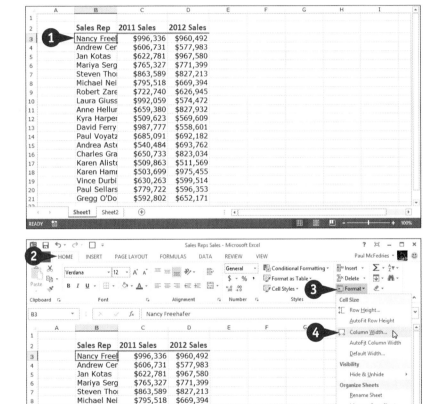

The Column Width dialog box appears.

5 In the Column width text box, type the width you want to use.

6 Click **OK**.

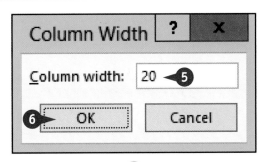

Ⓐ Excel adjusts the column width.

Ⓑ You can also move ✛ over the right edge of the column heading (✛ changes to ✚) and then click and drag the edge to set the width.

	A	B		D	E
1					
2		Sales Rep	2011 Sales	2012 Sales	
3		Nancy Freenafer	$996,336	$960,492	
4		Andrew Cencini	$606,731	$577,983	
5		Jan Kotas	$622,781	$967,580	
6		Mariya Sergienko	$765,327	$771,399	
7		Steven Thorpe	$863,589	$827,213	
8		Michael Neipper	$795,518	$669,394	
9		Robert Zare	$722,740	$626,945	
10		Laura Giussani	$992,059	$574,472	
11		Anne Hellung-Larsen	$659,380	$827,932	
12		Kyra Harper	$509,623	$569,609	
13		David Ferry	$987,777	$558,601	
14		Paul Voyatzis	$685,091	$692,182	
15		Andrea Aster	$540,484	$693,762	
16		Charles Granek	$650,733	$823,034	
17		Karen Aliston	$509,863	$511,569	
18		Karen Hammond	$503,699	$975,455	
19		Vince Durbin	$630,263	$599,514	
20		Paul Sellars	$779,722	$596,353	
21		Gregg O'Donoghue	$592,802	$652,171	

Sheet1 Sheet2 ⊕

TIPS

Is there an easier way to adjust the column width to fit the contents of a column?

Yes. You can use the Excel AutoFit feature, which automatically adjusts the column width to fit the widest item in a column. Click any cell in the column, click **Home**, click **Format**, and then click **AutoFit Column Width**. Alternatively, move ✛ over the right edge of the column heading (✛ changes to ✚) and then double-click.

Is there a way to change all the column widths at once?

Yes. Click ◢ to select the entire worksheet, and then follow the steps in this section to set the width you prefer. If you have already adjusted some column widths and you want to change all the other widths, click **Home**, click **Format**, and then click **Default Width** to open the Standard Width dialog box. Type the new standard column width, and then click **OK**.

Change the Row Height

You can make your worksheet more visually appealing by increasing the row heights to create more space. This is particularly useful in worksheets that are crowded with text. Changing the row height is also useful if the current height is too small and your cell text is cut off at the bottom.

If you want to change the row height to display multiline text within a cell, you must also turn on text wrapping within the cell. See the following section, "Wrap Text Within a Cell."

Change the Row Height

1 Select a range that includes at least one cell in every row you want to resize.

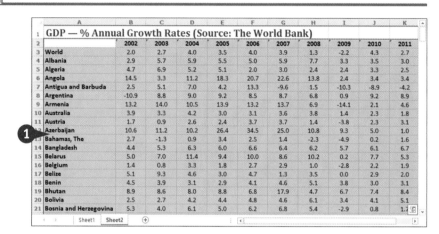

2 Click the **Home** tab.

3 Click **Format**.

4 Click **Row Height**.

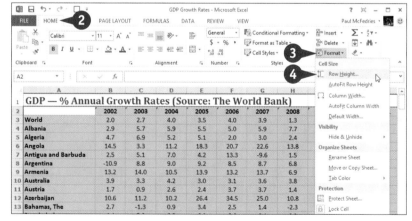

The Row Height dialog box appears.

5 In the Row height text box, type the height you want to use.

6 Click **OK**.

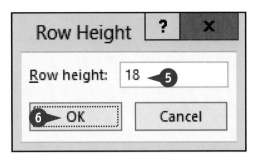

A Excel adjusts the row heights.

B You can also move ⊕ over the bottom edge of a row heading (⊕ changes to ✛) and then click and drag the bottom edge to set the height.

	A	B	C	D	E	F	G	H	I	J	K
1	GDP — % Annual Growth Rates (Source: The World Bank)										
2		2002	2003	2004	2005	2006	2007	2008	2009	2010	2011
3	World	2.0	2.7	4.0	3.5	4.0	3.9	1.3	-2.2	4.3	2.7
4	Albania	2.9	5.7	5.9	5.5	5.0	5.9	7.7	3.3	3.5	3.0
5	Algeria	4.7	6.9	5.2	5.1	2.0	3.0	2.4	2.4	3.3	2.5
6	Angola	14.5	3.3	11.2	18.3	20.7	22.6	13.8	2.4	3.4	3.4
7	Antigua and Barbuda	2.5	5.1	7.0	4.2	13.3	-9.6	1.5	-10.3	-8.9	-4.2
8	Argentina	-10.9	8.8	9.0	9.2	8.5	8.7	6.8	0.9	9.2	8.9
9	Armenia	13.2	14.0	10.5	13.9	13.2	13.7	6.9	-14.1	2.1	4.6
10	Australia	3.9	3.3	4.2	3.0	3.1	3.6	3.8	1.4	2.3	1.8
11	Austria	1.7	0.9	2.6	2.4	3.7	3.7	1.4	-3.8	2.3	3.1
12	Azerbaijan	10.6	11.2	10.2	26.4	34.5	25.0	10.8	9.3	5.0	1.0
13	Bahamas, The	2.7	-1.3	0.9	3.4	2.5	1.4	-2.3	-4.9	0.2	1.6
14	Bangladesh	4.4	5.3	6.3	6.0	6.6	6.4	6.2	5.7	6.1	6.7
15	Belarus	5.0	7.0	11.4	9.4	10.0	8.6	10.2	0.2	7.7	5.3
16	Belgium	1.4	0.8	3.3	1.8	2.7	2.9	1.0	-2.8	2.2	1.9
17	Belize	5.1	9.3	4.6	3.0	4.7	1.3	3.5	0.0	2.9	2.0
18	Benin	4.5	3.9	3.1	2.9	4.1	4.6	5.1	3.8	3.0	3.1

Sheet1 Sheet2 ⊕

TIPS

Is there an easier way to adjust the row height to fit the contents of a row?

Yes. You can use the Excel AutoFit feature, which automatically adjusts the row height to fit the tallest item in a row. Click in any cell in the row, click **Home**, click **Format**, and then click **AutoFit Row Height**. Alternatively, move ⊕ over the bottom edge of the row heading (⊕ changes to ✛) and then double-click.

Is there a way to change all the row heights at once?

Yes. Click ◢ to select the entire worksheet. You can then either follow the steps in this section to set the height manually, or move ⊕ over the bottom edge of any row heading (⊕ changes to ✛) and then click and drag the edge to set the height of all the rows.

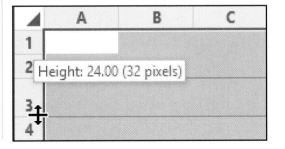

Wrap Text Within a Cell

You can make a long text entry in a cell more readable by formatting the cell to wrap the text. *Wrapping* cell text means that the text is displayed on multiple lines within the cell instead of just a single line.

If you type more text in a cell than can fit horizontally, Excel either displays the text over the next cell if it is empty or displays only part of the text if the next cell contains data. To prevent Excel from showing only truncated cell data, you can format the cell to wrap text within the cell.

Wrap Text Within a Cell

1 Select the cell that you want to format.

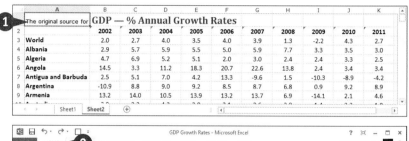

2 Click the **Home** tab.

3 Click **Wrap Text** (▤).

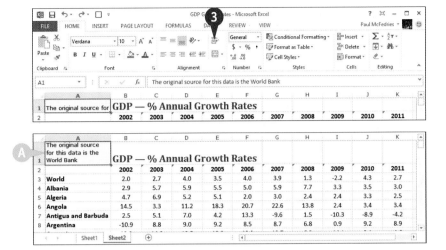

Excel turns on text wrapping for the selected cell.

A If the cell has more text than can fit horizontally, Excel wraps the text onto multiple lines and increases the row height to compensate.

My text is only slightly bigger than the cell. Is there a way to view all of the text without turning on text wrapping?

Yes. There are several things you can try. For example, you can widen the column until you see all your text; see "Change the Column Width," earlier in this chapter.

Alternatively, you can try reducing the cell font size. One way to do this is to choose a smaller value in the **Font Size** list of the Home tab's Font group. However, an easier way is to click the Alignment group's dialog box launcher (▣) to open the Format Cells dialog box with the Alignment tab displayed. Click the **Shrink to fit** check box (☐ changes to ☑) and then click **OK**.

Add Borders to a Range

You can make a range stand out from the rest of your worksheet data by adding a border around the range. For example, if you have a range of cells that are used as the input values for one or more formulas, you could add a border around the input cells to make it clear that the cells in that range are related to each other.

You can also use borders to make a range easier to read. For example, if your range has totals on the bottom row, you can add a double border above the totals.

Add Borders to a Range

1 Select the range that you want to format.

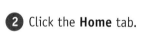

2 Click the **Home** tab.

3 Click the **Borders** ▼.

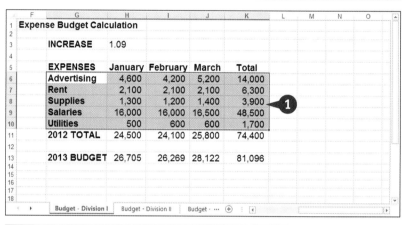

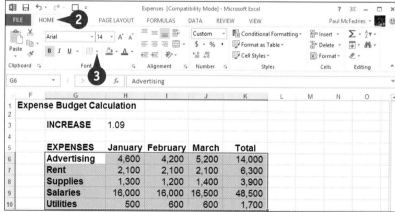

4 Click the type of border you
want to use.

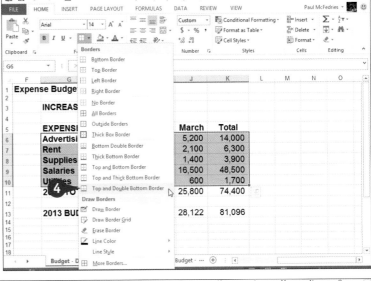

A Excel applies the border to
the range.

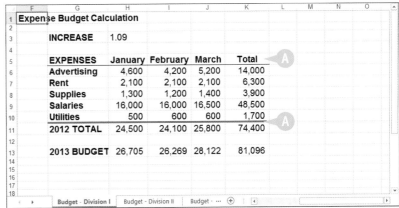

**How do I get my borders to stand out from the
worksheet gridlines?**

One way to make your borders stand out is to click
the **Borders** ▾ , click **Line Style**, and then click a
thicker border style. You can also click **Line Color**
and then click a color that is not a shade of gray.
However, perhaps the most effective method is to
turn off the worksheet gridlines. Click the **View** tab,
and then in the Show group, click the **Gridlines**
check box (☑ changes to ☐).

**None of the border types is quite right for my
worksheet. Can I create a custom border?**

Yes. You can draw the border manually. Click the
Borders ▾ and then click **Draw Border**. Use the
Line Style and **Line Color** lists to configure your
border. Click a cell edge to add a border to that
edge; click and drag a range to add a border around
that range. If you prefer to create a grid where the
border surrounds every cell, click the **Draw Border
Grid** command instead.

Copy Formatting from One Cell to Another

You can save yourself a great deal of time by copying existing formatting to other areas of a worksheet. As you have seen in this chapter, although formatting cells is not difficult, it can be time-consuming to apply the font, color, alignment, number format, and other options. After you spend time formatting text or data, rather than spending time repeating the steps for other data, you can use the Format Painter tool to copy the formatting with a couple of mouse clicks.

Copy Formatting from One Cell to Another

1 Select the cell that has the formatting you want to copy.

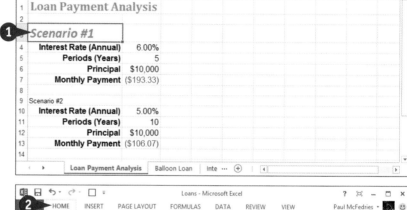

2 Click the **Home** tab.

3 Click **Format Painter** (✸).

✛ changes to ✛✑.

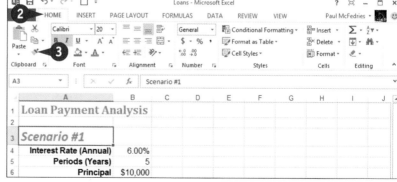

4 Click the cell to which you want to copy the formatting.

Note: If you want to apply the formatting to multiple cells, click and drag 🖐 over the cells.

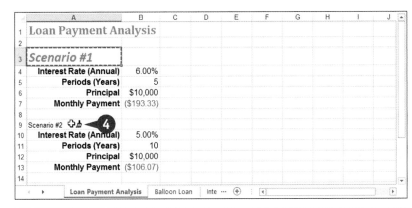

Ⓐ Excel copies the formatting to the cell.

Is there an easy way to copy formatting to multiple cells or ranges?

Yes. If the cells are together, you can click and drag over the cells to apply the copied formatting. If the cells or ranges are not together, Excel offers a shortcut that means you do not have to select the Format Painter multiple times to copy formatting to multiple ranges.

Click the cell that contains the formatting you want to copy, click the **Home** tab, and then double-click 🖌. Click each cell to which you want to copy the formatting, or click and drag over each range that you want to format. When you are done, click 🖌 to cancel the Format Painter command.

CHAPTER 6

Building Formulas

Are you ready to start creating powerful and useful worksheets by building your own formulas? This chapter explains formulas, shows you how to build them, and shows you how to incorporate the versatile worksheet functions in Excel into your formulas.

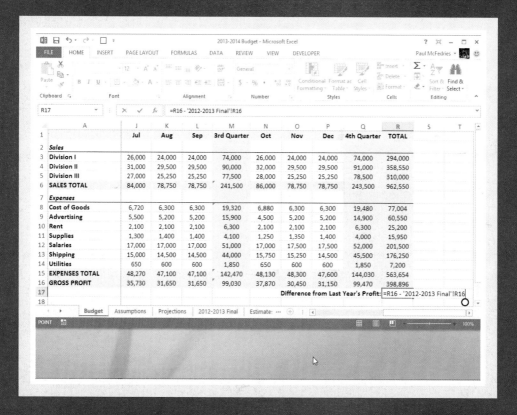

Understanding Excel Formulas

Although you can use Excel to create simple databases to store text, numbers, dates, and other data, the spreadsheets you create are also designed to analyze data and make calculations. Therefore, to get the most out of Excel, you need to understand formulas so that you can use them to analyze and perform calculations on your worksheet data.

To build accurate and useful formulas, you need to know the components of a formula, including operators and operands. You also need to understand arithmetic and comparison formulas and you need to understand the importance of precedence when building a formula.

Formulas

A *formula* is a set of symbols and values that perform some kind of calculation and produce a result. All Excel formulas have the same general structure: an equal sign (=) followed by one or more operands and operators. The equal sign tells Excel to interpret everything that follows in the cell as a formula. For example, if you type **=5+8** into a cell, Excel interprets the 5+8 text as a formula, and displays the result (13) in the cell.

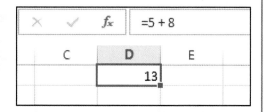

Operands

Every Excel formula includes one or more *operands*, which are the data that Excel uses in the calculation. The simplest type of operand is a constant value, which is usually a number. However, most Excel formulas include references to worksheet data, which can be a cell address (such as A1), a range address (such as B1:B5), or a range name. Finally, you can also use any of the built-in Excel functions as an operand.

Operators

In an Excel formula that contains two or more operands, each operand is separated by an *operator*, which is a symbol that combines the operands in some way, usually mathematically. Example operators include the plus sign (+) and the multiplication sign (*). For example, the formula =B1+B2 adds the values in cells B1 and B2.

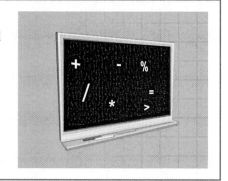

Arithmetic Formulas

An arithmetic formula combines numeric operands — numeric constants, functions that return numeric results, and fields or items that contain numeric values — with mathematical operators to perform a calculation. Because Excel worksheets primarily deal with numeric data, arithmetic formulas are by far the most common formulas used in worksheet calculations.

The table lists the seven arithmetic operators that you can use to construct arithmetic formulas.

Operator	Name	Example	Result
+	Addition	=10 + 5	15
–	Subtraction	=10 – 5	5
–	Negation	=–10	–10
*	Multiplication	=10 * 5	50
/	Division	=10 / 5	2
%	Percentage	=10%	0.1
^	Exponentiation	=10 ^ 5	100000

Comparison Formulas

A comparison formula combines numeric operands — numeric constants, functions that return numeric results, and fields or items that contain numeric values — with special operators to compare one operand with another. A comparison formula always returns a logical result. This means that if the comparison is true, then the formula returns the value 1, which is equivalent to the logical value TRUE; if the comparison is false, then the formula returns the value 0, which is equivalent to the logical value FALSE.

The table lists the six operators that you can use to construct comparison formulas.

Operator	Name	Example	Result
=	Equal to	=10 = 5	0
<	Less than	=10 < 5	0
< =	Less than or equal to	=10 < = 5	0
>	Greater than	=10 > 5	1
> =	Greater than or equal to	=10 > = 5	1
< >	Not equal to	=10 < > 5	1

Operator Precedence

Most of your formulas include multiple operands and operators. In many cases, the order in which Excel performs the calculations is crucial. For example, consider the formula =3 + 5 ^ 2. If you calculate from left to right, the answer you get is 64 (3 + 5 equals 8, and 8 ^ 2 equals 64). However, if you perform the exponentiation first and then the addition, the result is 28 (5 ^ 2 equals 25, and 3 + 25 equals 28). Therefore, a single formula can produce multiple answers, depending on the order in which you perform the calculations.

To solve this problem, Excel evaluates a formula according to a predefined order of precedence, which is determined by the formula operators, as shown in the table.

Operator	Operation	Precedence
( )	Parentheses	1st
–	Negation	2nd
%	Percentage	3rd
^	Exponentiation	4th
* and /	Multiplication and division	5th
+ and –	Addition and subtraction	6th
= < < = > > < >	Comparison	7th

Build a Formula

You can add a formula to a worksheet cell using a technique similar to adding data to a cell. To ensure that Excel treats the text as a formula, be sure to begin with an equal sign (=) and then type your operands and operators.

When you add a formula to a cell, Excel displays the formula result in the cell, not the actual formula. For example, if you add the formula =C3+C4 to a cell, that cell displays the sum of the values in cells C3 and C4. To see the formula, click the cell and examine the formula bar.

Build a Formula

1 Click in the cell in which you want to build the formula.

2 Type =.

Ⓐ Your typing also appears in the formula bar.

Note: You can also type the formula into the formula bar.

3 Type or click an operand. For example, to reference a cell in your formula, click in the cell.

Ⓑ Excel inserts the address of the clicked cell into the formula.

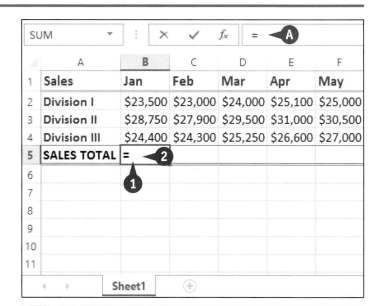

④ Type an operator.

⑤ Repeat Steps **3** and **4** to add other operands and operators to your formula.

⑥ Click ✓ or press Enter.

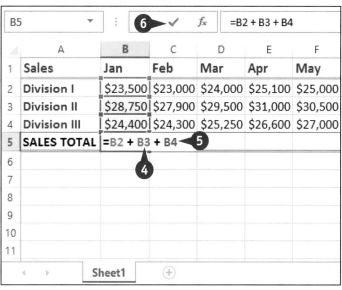

Ⓒ Excel displays the formula result in the cell.

If Excel displays only the result of the formula, how do I make changes to the formula?

Excel displays the formula result in the cell, but it still keeps track of the original formula. To display the formula again, you have two choices: Click the cell and then edit the formula using the formula bar, or double-click the cell to display the original formula in the cell and then edit the formula. In both cases, click ✓ or press Enter when you finish editing the formula.

If I have many formulas, is there an easy way to view them?

Yes. You can configure the worksheet to show the formulas instead of their results. Click **File** and then click **Options** to open the Excel Options dialog box. Click the **Advanced** tab, scroll to the **Display options for this worksheet** section, click the **Show formulas in cells instead of their calculated results** check box (☐ changes to ☑), and then click **OK**. You can also toggle between formulas and results by pressing Ctrl+`.

Understanding Excel Functions

To build powerful and useful formulas, you often need to include one or more Excel functions as operands. To get the most out of functions and to help you build formulas quickly and easily, you need to understand a few things about functions. For example, you need to understand the advantages of using functions and you need to know the basic structure of every function. To get a sense of what is available and how you might use functions, you need to review the Excel function types.

Functions

A *function* is a predefined formula that performs a specific task. For example, the SUM function calculates the total of a list of numbers, and the PMT (payment) function calculates a loan or mortgage payment.

You can use functions on their own, preceded by =, or as part of a larger formula.

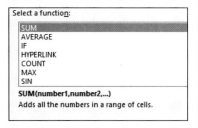

Function Advantages

Functions are designed to take you beyond the basic arithmetic and comparison formulas by offering two main advantages. First, functions make simple but cumbersome formulas easier to use. For example, calculating a loan payment requires a complex formula, but the Excel PMT function makes this easy. Second, functions enable you to include complex mathematical expressions in your worksheets that otherwise would be difficult or impossible to construct using simple arithmetic operators.

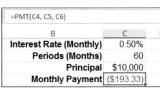

Function Structure

Every worksheet function has the same basic structure: NAME(Argument1, Argument2, ...). The NAME part identifies the function. In worksheet formulas and custom PivotTable formulas, the function name always appears in uppercase letters: PMT, SUM, AVERAGE, and so on. The items that appear within the parentheses are the functions' *arguments*. The arguments are the inputs that functions use to perform calculations. For example, the function SUM(B2, B3, B4) adds the values in cells B2, B3, and B4.

	B	C	D	E	F
=SUM(B2, B3, B4)					
	Jan	Feb	Mar	Apr	May
	$23,500	$23,000	$24,000	$25,100	$25,000
	$28,750	$27,900	$29,500	$31,000	$30,500
	$24,400	$24,300	$25,250	$26,600	$27,000
	$76,650				

Mathematical Functions

The following table lists some common mathematical functions:

Function	Description
MOD(number,divisor)	Returns the remainder of a number after dividing by the divisor
PI( )	Returns the value Pi
PRODUCT(number1, number2,...)	Multiplies the specified numbers
RAND( )	Returns a random number between 0 and 1
RANDBETWEEN (number1,number2)	Returns a random number between the two numbers
ROUND(number,digits)	Rounds the number to a specified number of digits
SQRT(number)	Returns the positive square root of the number
SUM(number1, number2,...)	Adds the arguments

Statistical Functions

The following table lists some common statistical functions:

Function	Description
AVERAGE(number1,number2,...)	Returns the average of the arguments
COUNT(number1,number2,...)	Counts the numbers in the argument list
MAX(number1,number2,...)	Returns the maximum value of the arguments
MEDIAN(number1,number2,...)	Returns the median value of the arguments
MIN(number1,number2,...)	Returns the minimum value of the arguments
MODE(number1,number2,...)	Returns the most common value of the arguments
STDEV(number1,number2,...)	Returns the standard deviation based on a sample
STDEVP(number1,number2,...)	Returns the standard deviation based on an entire population

Financial Functions

Most of the Excel financial functions use the following arguments:

Argument	Description
rate	The fixed rate of interest over the term of the loan or investment
nper	The number of payments or deposit periods over the term of the loan or investment
pmt	The periodic payment or deposit
pv	The present value of the loan (the principal) or the initial deposit in an investment
fv	The future value of the loan or investment
type	The type of payment or deposit: 0 (the default) for end-of-period payments or deposits; 1 for beginning-of-period payments or deposits

The following table lists some common financial functions:

Function	Description
FV(rate,nper,pmt,pv,type)	Returns the future value of an investment or loan
IPMT(rate,per,nper,pv,fv,type)	Returns the interest payment for a specified period of a loan
NPER(rate,pmt,pv,fv,type)	Returns the number of periods for an investment or loan
PMT(rate,nper,pv,fv,type)	Returns the periodic payment for a loan or investment
PPMT(rate,per,nper,pv,fv,type)	Returns the principal payment for a specified period of a loan
PV(rate,nper,pmt,fv,type)	Returns the present value of an investment
RATE(nper,pmt,pv,fv,type,guess)	Returns the periodic interest rate for a loan or investment

Add a Function to a Formula

To get the benefit of an Excel function, you need to use it within a formula. You can use a function as the only operand in the formula, or you can include the function as part of a larger formula. To make it easy to choose the function you need and to add the appropriate arguments, Excel offers the Insert Function feature. This is a dialog box that enables you to display functions by category and then choose the function you want from a list. You then see the Function Arguments dialog box that enables you to easily see and fill in the arguments used by the function.

Add a Function to a Formula

1 Click in the cell in which you want to build the formula.

2 Type **=**.

3 Type any operands and operators you need before adding the function.

4 Click the **Insert Function** button (*fx*).

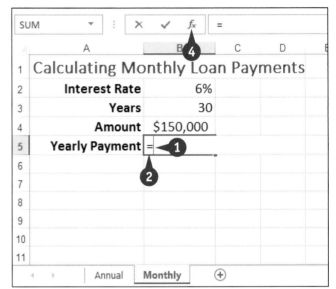

The Insert Function dialog box appears.

5 Click ⌄ and then click the category that contains the function you want to use.

6 Click the function.

7 Click **OK**.

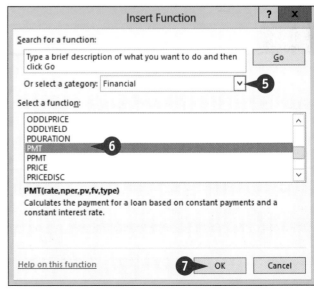

The Function Arguments dialog box appears.

8 Click inside an argument box.

9 Click the cell that contains the argument value.

You can also type the argument value.

10 Repeat Steps **8** and **9** to fill as many arguments as you need.

A The function result appears here.

11 Click **OK**.

B Excel adds the function to the formula.

C Excel displays the formula result.

Note: In this example, the result appears in the parentheses to indicate a negative value. In loan calculations, money that you pay out is always a negative amount.

Note: If your formula requires any other operands and operators, press **F2** and then type what you need to complete your formula.

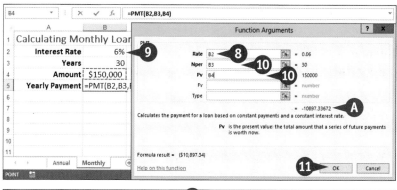

TIPS

Do I have to specify a value for every function argument?

Not necessarily. Some function arguments are required to obtain a result, but others are optional. In the PMT function, for example, the rate, nper, and pv arguments are required, but the fv and type arguments are optional. When the Function Arguments dialog box displays a result for the function, you know you have entered all of the required arguments.

How do I calculate a monthly financial result if I only have yearly values?

This is a common problem. For example, if your loan payment worksheet contains an annual interest rate and a loan term in years, how do you calculate the monthly payment using the PMT function? You need to convert the rate and term to monthly values. That is, you divide the annual interest rate by 12, and you multiply the term by 12. For example, if the annual rate is in cell B2, the term in years is in B3, and the loan amount is in B4, then the function PMT(B2/12, B3*12, B4) calculates the monthly payment.

Add a Row or Column of Numbers

You can quickly add worksheet numbers by building a formula that uses the Excel SUM function. When you use the SUM function in a formula, you can specify as the function's arguments a series of individual cells. For example, SUM(A1, B2, C3) calculates the total of the values in cells A1, B2, and C3.

However, you can also use the SUM function to specify just a single argument, which is a range reference to either a row or a column of numbers. For example, SUM(C3:C21) calculates the total of the values in all the cells in the range C3 to C21.

Add a Row or Column of Numbers

1 Click in the cell where you want the sum to appear.

2 Type **=sum(**.

A When you begin a function, Excel displays a banner that shows you the function's arguments.

Note: In the function banner, bold arguments are required, and arguments that appear in square brackets are optional.

3 Use the Excel mouse pointer (⊕) to click and drag the row or column of numbers that you want to add.

B Excel adds a reference for the range to the formula.

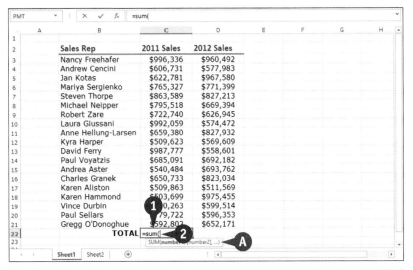

128

4 Type).

5 Click ✓ or press Enter.

C Excel displays the formula.

D Excel displays the sum in the cell.

TIPS

Can I use the SUM function to total rows and columns at the same time?

Yes, the SUM function works not only with simple row and column ranges, but with any rectangular range. After you type **=sum(**, use the mouse ✥ to click and drag the entire range that you want to sum.

Can I use the SUM function to total only certain values in a row or column?

Yes. The SUM function can accept multiple arguments, so you can enter as many cells or ranges as you need. After you type **=sum(**, hold down Ctrl and either click each cell that you want to include in the total, or use the mouse ✥ to click and drag each range that you want to sum.

Build an AutoSum Formula

You can reduce the time it takes to build a worksheet as well as reduce the possibility of errors by using the Excel AutoSum feature. This tool adds a SUM function formula to a cell and automatically adds the function arguments based on the structure of the worksheet data. For example, if there is a column of numbers above the cell where you want the SUM function to appear, AutoSum automatically includes that column of numbers as the SUM function argument.

Build an AutoSum Formula

1 Click in the cell where you want the sum to appear.

Note: For AutoSum to work, the cell you select should be below or to the right of the range you want to sum.

2 Click the **Home** tab.

3 Click the **Sum** button (Σ).

A If you want to use a function other than SUM, click the **Sum** ▼ and then click the operation you want to use: Average, Count Numbers, Max, or Min.

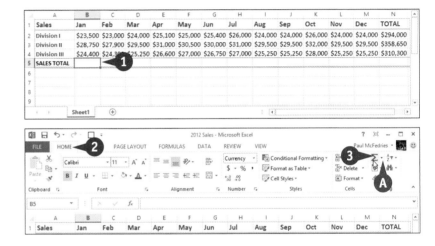

B Excel adds a SUM function formula to the cell.

Note: You can also press `Alt`+`=` instead of clicking Σ.

C Excel guesses that the range above (or to the left of) the cell is the one you want to add.

If Excel guessed wrong, you can select the correct range manually.

4 Click ✓ or press `Enter`.

D Excel displays the formula.

E Excel displays the sum in the cell.

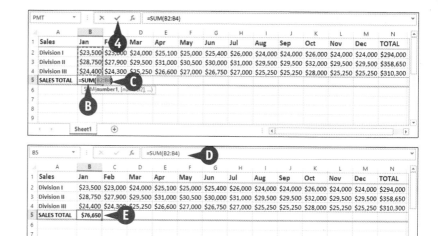

TIPS

Is there a way to see the sum of a range without adding an AutoSum formula?

Yes. You can use the Excel status bar to do this. When you select any range, Excel adds the range's numeric values and displays the result in the middle of the status bar — for example, SUM: 76,650. By default, Excel also displays the Average and Count. If you want to see a different calculation, right-click the result in the status bar and then click the operation you want to use: Numerical Count, Maximum, or Minimum.

Is there a faster way to add an AutoSum formula?

Yes. If you know the range you want to sum, and that range is either a vertical column with a blank cell below it or a horizontal row with a blank cell to its right, select the range (including the blank cell) and then click Σ or press `Alt`+`=`. Excel populates the blank cell with a SUM formula that totals the selected range.

Add a Range Name to a Formula

You can make your formulas easier to build, more accurate, and easier to read by using range names as operands instead of cell and range addresses. For example, the formula =SUM(B2:B10) is difficult to decipher on its own, particularly if you cannot see the range B2:B10 to examine its values. However, if you use the formula =SUM(Expenses), instead, it becomes immediately obvious what the formula is meant to do.

See Chapter 4 to learn how to define names for ranges in Excel.

Add a Range Name to a Formula

1 Click in the cell in which you want to build the formula, type =, and then type any operands and operators you need before adding the range name.

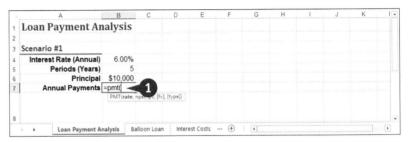

2 Click the **Formulas** tab.

3 Click **Use in Formula**.

A Excel displays a list of the range names in the current workbook.

4 Click the range name you want to use.

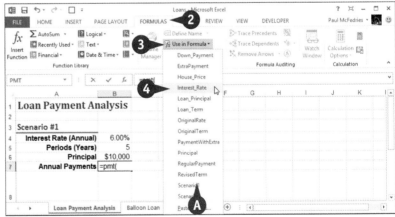

B Excel inserts the range name into the formula.

5 Type any operands and operators you need to complete your formula.

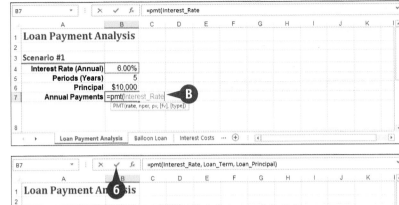

C If you need to insert other range names into your formula, repeat Steps **2** to **5** for each name.

6 Click ✓ or press **Enter**.

Excel calculates the formula result.

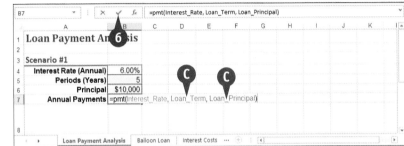

TIPS

If I create a range name after I build my formula, is there an easy way to convert the range reference to the range name?

Yes. Excel offers an Apply Names feature that replaces range references with their associated range names throughout a worksheet. Click the **Formulas** tab, click the **Define Name** ▼ , and then click **Apply Names** to open the Apply Names dialog box. In the Apply names list, click the range name you want to use, and then click **OK**. Excel replaces the associated range references with the range name in each formula in the current worksheet.

Do I have to use the list of range names to insert range names into my formula?

No. As you build your formula, you can type the range name manually, if you know it. Alternatively, as you build your formula, click the cell or select the range that has the defined name, and Excel adds the name to your formula instead of the range address. If you want to work from a list of defined range names, click an empty area of the worksheet, click **Formulas**, click **Use in Formula**, click **Paste Names**, and then click **Paste List**.

Reference Another Worksheet Range in a Formula

You can add flexibility to your formulas by adding references to ranges that reside in other worksheets. This enables you to take advantage of work you have done in other worksheets, so you do not have to waste time repeating your work in the current worksheet.

Referencing a range in another worksheet also gives you the advantage of having automatically updated information. For example, if the data in the other worksheet range changes, Excel automatically updates your formula to include the changed data.

Reference Another Worksheet Range in a Formula

1 Click in the cell in which you want to build the formula, type =, and then type any operands and operators you need before adding the range reference.

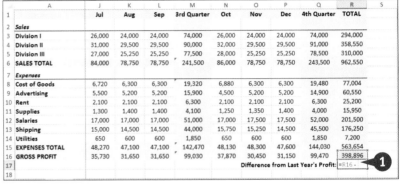

2 Press **Ctrl** + **Page down** until the worksheet you want to use appears.

134

3 Select the range you want to use.

4 Press `Ctrl` + `Page up` until you return to the original worksheet.

	J	K	L	M	N	O	P	Q	R	S
1	Jul	Aug	Sep	3rd Quarter	Oct	Nov	Dec	4th Quarter	TOTAL	
2										
3	23,920	22,080	22,080	68,080	23,920	22,080	22,080	68,080	270,480	
4	28,520	27,140	27,140	82,800	29,440	27,140	27,140	83,720	329,866	
5	24,840	23,230	23,230	71,300	25,760	23,230	23,230	72,220	285,200	
6	77,280	72,450	72,450	222,180	79,120	72,450	72,450	224,020	885,546	
7										
8	6,492	6,086	6,086	18,663	6,646	6,086	6,086	18,818	74,386	
9	5,775	5,460	5,460	16,695	4,725	5,460	5,460	15,645	63,578	
10	2,205	2,205	2,205	6,615	2,205	2,205	2,205	6,615	26,460	
11	1,365	1,470	1,470	4,305	1,313	1,418	1,470	4,200	16,748	
12	17,850	17,850	17,850	53,550	17,850	18,375	18,375	54,600	211,575	
13	15,750	15,225	15,225	46,200	16,538	16,013	15,225	47,775	185,063	
14	683	630	630	1,943	683	630	630	1,943	7,560	
15	50,119	48,926	48,926	147,971	49,959	50,186	49,451	149,595	585,368	
16	27,161	23,524	23,524	74,209	29,161	22,264	22,999	74,425	300,178	
17										
18										

Budget — ons   Projections   2012-2013 Final

A A reference to the range on the other worksheet appears in your formula.

5 Type any operands and operators you need to complete your formula.

6 Click ✓ or press `Enter`.

Excel calculates the formula result.

=R16 - '2012-2013 Final'!R16

	K	L	M	N	O	P	Q	R	S	T
	Aug	Sep	3rd Quarter	Oct	Nov	Dec	4th Quarter	TOTAL		
	26,000	24,000	24,000	74,000	26,000	24,000	24,000	74,000	294,000	
	31,000	29,500	29,500	90,000	32,000	29,500	29,500	91,000	358,550	
	27,000	25,250	25,250	77,500	28,000	25,250	25,250	78,500	310,000	
AL	84,000	78,750	78,750	241,500	86,000	78,750	78,750	243,500	962,550	
ods	6,720	6,300	6,300	19,320	6,880	6,300	6,300	19,480	77,004	
g	5,500	5,200	5,200	15,900	4,500	5,200	5,200	14,900	60,550	
	2,100	2,100	2,100	6,300	2,100	2,100	2,100	6,300	25,200	
	1,300	1,400	1,400	4,100	1,250	1,350	1,400	4,000	15,950	
	17,000	17,000	17,000	51,000	17,000	17,500	17,500	52,000	201,500	
	15,000	14,500	14,500	44,000	15,750	15,250	14,500	45,500	176,250	
	650	600	600	1,850	650	600	600	1,850	7,200	
TOTAL	48,270	47,100	47,100	142,470	48,130	48,300	47,600	144,030	563,654	
OFIT	35,730	31,650	31,650	99,030	37,870	30,450	31,150	99,470	398,896	

Difference from Last Year's Profit: =R16 - '2012-2013 Final'!R16

Budget   Assumptions   Projections   2012-2013 Final   Estimate:

TIPS

Can I manually reference a range in another worksheet?

Yes. Rather than selecting the other worksheet range with your mouse, you can type the range reference directly into your formula. Type the worksheet name, surrounded by single quotation marks (' ') if the name contains a space; type an exclamation mark (!); then type the cell or range address. Here is an example: **'Expenses 2013'!B2:B10**.

Can I reference a range in another workbook in my formula?

Yes. First make sure the workbook you want to reference is open. When you reach the point in your formula where you want to add the reference, click the Excel icon (🗗) in the Windows taskbar, and then click the other workbook to switch to it. Click the worksheet that has the range you want to reference, and then select the range. Click 🗗 and then click the original workbook to switch back to it. Excel adds the other workbook range reference to your formula.

Move or Copy a Formula

You can restructure or reorganize a worksheet by moving an existing formula to a different part of the worksheet. When you move a formula, Excel preserves the formula's range references.

Excel also enables you to make a copy of a formula, which is a useful technique if you require a duplicate of the formula elsewhere or if you require a formula that is similar to an existing formula. When you copy a formula, Excel adjusts the range references to the new location.

Move or Copy a Formula

Move a Formula

1. Click the cell that contains the formula you want to move.
2. Position ✥ over any outside border of the cell (✥ changes to ✥).
3. Click and drag the cell to the new location (✥ changes to ↖).

A. Excel displays an outline of the cell.

B. Excel displays the address of the new location.

4. Release the mouse button.

C. Excel moves the formula to the new location.

D. Excel does not change the formula's range references.

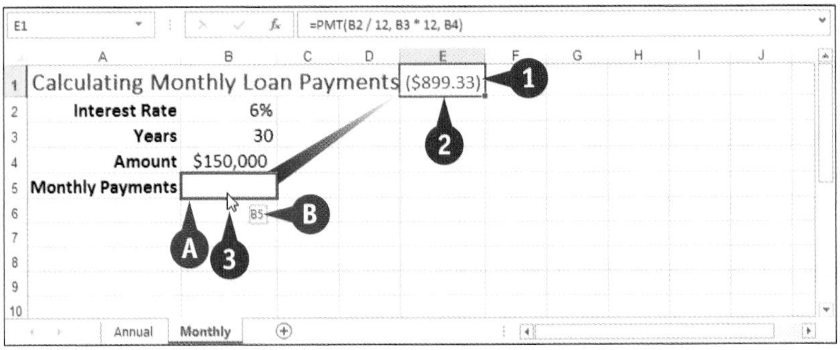

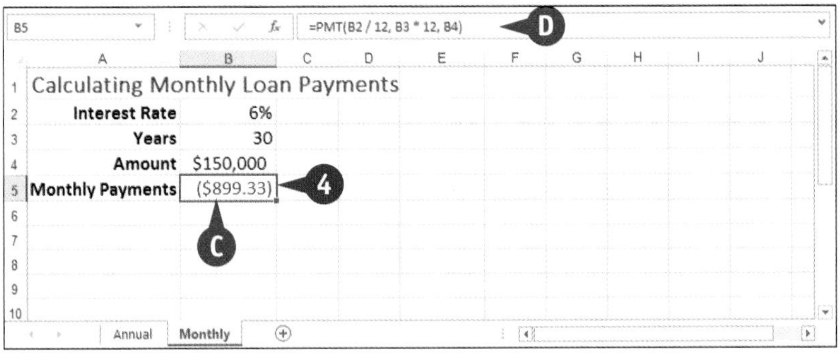

Copy a Formula

1 Click the cell that contains the formula you want to copy.

2 Press and hold **Ctrl**.

3 Position ✛ over any outside border of the cell (✛ changes to ↖).

4 Click and drag the cell to the location where you want the copy to appear.

E Excel displays an outline of the cell.

F Excel displays the address of the new location.

5 Release the mouse button.

6 Release **Ctrl**.

G Excel creates a copy of the formula in the new location.

H Excel adjusts the range references.

Note: You can make multiple copies by dragging the bottom-right corner of the cell. Excel fills the adjacent cells with copies of the formula. See the following section, "Switch to Absolute Cell References," for an example.

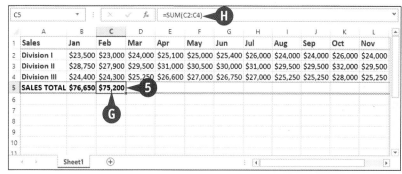

TIP

Why does Excel adjust the range references when I copy a formula?

When you make a copy of a formula, Excel assumes that you want that copy to reference different ranges than in the original formula. In particular, Excel assumes that the ranges you want to use in the new formula are positioned relative to the ranges used in the original formula, and that the relative difference is equal to the number of rows and columns you dragged the cell to create the copy.

For example, suppose your original formula references cell A1, and you make a copy of the formula in the cell one column to the right. In that case, Excel also adjusts the cell reference one column to the right, so it becomes B1 in the new formula. To learn how to control this behavior, see the following section, "Switch to Absolute Cell References."

Switch to Absolute Cell References

You can make some formulas easier to copy by switching to absolute cell references. When you use a regular cell address — called a *relative cell reference* — such as A1 in a formula, Excel adjusts that reference when you copy the formula to another location. To prevent that reference from changing, you must change it to the *absolute cell reference* format: $A$1.

See the first tip at the end of this section to learn more about the difference between relative and absolute cell references.

Switch to Absolute Cell References

1 Double-click the cell that contains the formula you want to edit.

2 Select the cell reference you want to change.

3 Press F4.

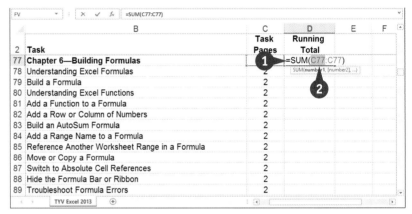

A Excel switches the address to an absolute cell reference.

4 Repeat Steps **2** and **3** to switch any other cell addresses that you require in the absolute reference format.

5 Click ✓ or press Enter.

B Excel adjusts the formula.

6 Copy the formula.

Note: See the previous section, "Move or Copy a Formula," to learn how to copy a formula.

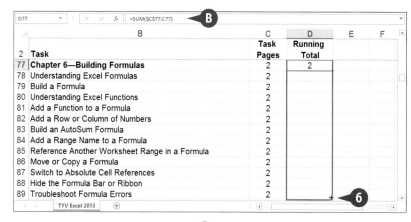

C Excel preserves the absolute cell references in the copied formulas.

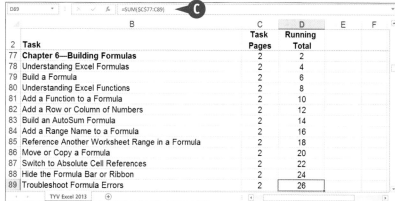

TIPS

What is the difference between absolute cell references and relative cell references?

When you use a cell reference in a formula, Excel treats that reference as being relative to the formula's cell. For example, if the formula is in cell B5 and it references cell A1, Excel effectively treats A1 as the cell four rows up and one column to the left. If you copy the formula to cell D10, then the cell four rows up and one column to the left now refers to cell C6, so in the copied formula Excel changes A1 to C6. If the original formula instead refers to $A$1, then the copied formula in cell D10 also refers to $A$1.

How do I restore a cell address back to a relative cell reference?

You can use the F4 keyboard technique, which actually runs the address through four different reference formats. Press F4 once to switch to the absolute cell reference format, such as $A$1. Press F4 again to switch to a mixed reference format that uses a relative column and absolute row (A$1). Press F4 a third time to switch to a mixed reference format that uses an absolute column and relative row ($A1). Finally, press F4 a fourth time to return to the relative cell reference (A1).

Hide the Formula Bar or Ribbon

You can give yourself a bit more room in the Excel window by hiding the formula bar or Ribbon. Hiding the formula bar is a good idea if you never use the formula bar to enter or edit cell data and you never use formula bar features such as the Name box, the Enter button, and the Insert Function button. After hiding the formula bar, if you find that you need it, you can quickly restore it to the Excel window.

You can also gain more worksheet room by hiding the Ribbon. When you hide the Ribbon, Excel keeps the tabs visible, so you can still access the commands.

Hide the Formula Bar or Ribbon

Hide the Formula Bar

1 Click the **View** tab.

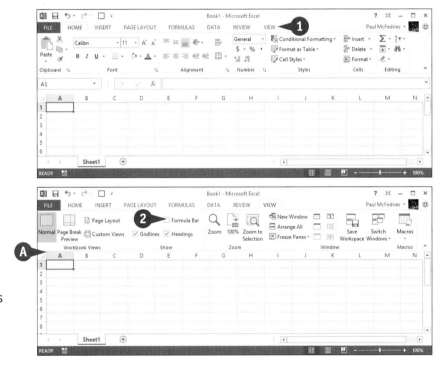

2 Click **Formula Bar** (☑ changes to ☐).

A Excel removes the formula bar from the window.

Note: To restore the formula bar, repeat Steps **1** and **2** (☐ changes to ☑).

Hide the Ribbon

1 Click **Unpin the Ribbon** (⌃).

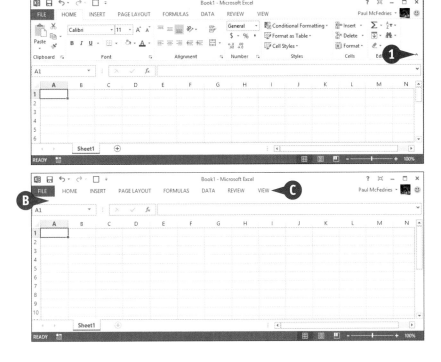

B Excel hides the Ribbon.

C Excel keeps the Ribbon tabs visible.

Note: To restore the Ribbon, click any tab and then click **Pin the Ribbon** (⇥).

Note: You can also hide and display the Ribbon by pressing Ctrl + F1.

TIP

If I have a long entry in a cell, I only see part of the entry in the formula bar. Can I fix that?

Yes, you can use the Expand Formula Bar feature in Excel to expand the formula to show multiple lines of data instead of just a single line. On the right side of the formula bar, click the **Expand Formula Bar** button (⌄) or press Ctrl + Shift + U to increase the size of the formula bar as shown here. If you still cannot see the entire cell entry, either click and drag the bottom edge of the formula bar to expand it even further, or click ▪ and ▪ to scroll through the entry.

When you are done, click the **Collapse Formula Bar** button (⌃) or press Ctrl + Shift + U to return the formula bar to its normal state.

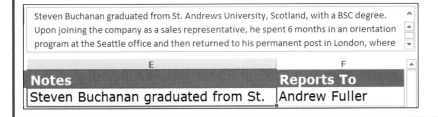

Troubleshoot Formula Errors

Despite your best efforts, a formula may return an inaccurate or erroneous result. To help you fix such problem formulas, there are a few troubleshooting techniques you can use, such as checking for incorrect range references or function arguments, confirming your data, and checking for punctuation errors such as missing colons or parentheses.

If Excel displays an error such as #DIV/0 instead of a result, then you also need to understand these error messages so that you can troubleshoot and correct the problem.

Confirm Range References

If your formula is returning an unexpected or inaccurate result, the first thing to check is your range and cell references. For example, if your data is in the range A1:A10, but your formula uses A1:A9, then the result will be inaccurate. The easiest way to check the range and cell references is to double-click the cell containing the formula. Excel highlights the range referenced by the formula, so you can see at a glance which range your formula is using.

	A	B	C
7	*Expenses*		
8	**Cost of Goods**	5,924	5,781
9	**Advertising**	4,830	4,410
10	Rent	2,205	2,205
11	**Supplies**	1,365	1,260
12	**Salaries**	16,800	16,800
13	**Shipping**	14,963	14,438
14	Utilities	525	630
15	TOTA	=SUM(B8:B11)	

Confirm Range Data

If your formula is correct but it is still producing unexpected results, the problem might lie with the data instead of the formula. Double-check your range data to make sure that it is accurate and up to date.

C5 f_x =SUM(C2:C4)

	A	B	C	D
1	*Sales*	Jan	Feb	Mar
2	**Division I**	21,620	1	22,080
3	**Division II**	26,450	1	27,140
4	**Division III**	22,448	1	23,230
5	**SALES TOTAL**	70,518	3	72,450

Confirm Punctuation

Many formulas produce inaccurate or erroneous results because of incorrect punctuation. Look for missing colons in range references; missing or misplaced quotation marks in string data or links to other worksheets or workbooks; and missing commas in function arguments. Also check parentheses to make sure you have one closing parenthesis for each opening parenthesis, and that your parentheses are in the correct locations within the formula.

	A	B	C
1	Loan Payment Analysis		
2	Interest Rate (Annual)	6.00%	
3	Periods (Years)	5	
4	Principal	$10,000	
5	Monthly Payment	=PMT(B2 / 12 B3 * 12 B4)	
6		PMT(rate, nper, pv, [fv], [type])	

Confirm Operator Precedence

The order in which Excel calculates numeric formulas can make a big difference to the final result, particularly if you are mixing addition and subtraction with multiplication and division. Confirm the correct order of precedence that your formula requires; compare this with the

	A	B	C	D	E
1					
2	Calculating the Pre-Tax Cost of an Item				
3					
4	Variables:		Pre-Tax Cost Calculation:		
5	Total Cost	$10.65		Result	Formula in D
6	Tax Rate	7%	Without controlling precedence →	$10.72	=B5 / 1 + B6
7			Controlling precedence →	$9.95	=B5 / (1 + B6)
8					

natural order of operator precedence in Excel, as described in "Understanding Excel Formulas," earlier in this chapter; and then use parentheses to force the correct order if necessary.

Understand the Excel Error Values

Excel may display an error value instead of a formula result. Here are descriptions of the six main error types:

Error	Description
#DIV/0	Your formula is dividing by zero. Check the divisor input cells for values that are either zero or blank.
#N/A	Your formula cannot return a legitimate result. Check that your function arguments are appropriate for each function.
#NAME?	Your formula uses a name that Excel does not recognize. Check your range names and function names.
#NUM!	Your formula uses a number inappropriately. Check the arguments for your mathematical functions to make sure they use the correct types of numbers.
#REF#	Your formula contains an invalid cell reference. This usually occurs when you delete a cell referenced by a formula. Adjust the formula to use a different cell.
#VALUE!	Your formula uses an inappropriate value in a function argument. Check your function arguments to make sure they use the correct data type.

CHAPTER 7

Manipulating Worksheets

An Excel worksheet is where you enter your headings and data and build your formulas. You will spend most of your time in Excel operating within a worksheet, so you need to know how to navigate and perform worksheet tasks such as renaming, moving, copying, and deleting.

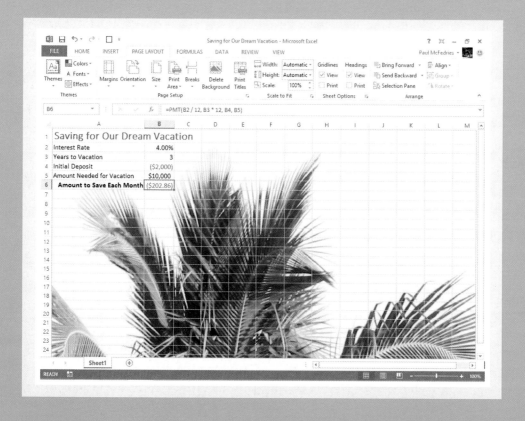

Navigate a Worksheet

You can use a few keyboard techniques that make it easier to navigate data after you have entered it in a worksheet.

It is usually easiest to use your mouse to click in the next cell you want to work with. If you are using Excel on a tablet or PC that has a touchscreen, then you can tap the next cell you want to use. However, if you are entering data, then using the keyboard to navigate to the next cell is often faster because your hands do not have to leave the keyboard.

Keyboard Techniques for Navigating a Worksheet	
Press	**To move**
←	Left one cell
→	Right one cell
↑	Up one cell
↓	Down one cell
Home	To the beginning of the current row
Page down	Down one screen
Page up	Up one screen
Alt + Page down	One screen to the right
Alt + Page up	One screen to the left
Ctrl + Home	To the beginning of the worksheet
Ctrl + End	To the bottom-right corner of the used portion of the worksheet
Ctrl +arrow keys	In the direction of the arrow to the next non-blank cell if the current cell is blank, or to the last non-blank cell if the current cell is not blank

Rename a Worksheet

You can make your Excel workbooks easier to understand and navigate by providing each worksheet with a name that reflects the contents of the sheet.

Excel provides worksheets with generic names such as Sheet1 and Sheet2, but you can change these to more descriptive names such as Sales 2013, Amortization, or Budget Data. Note, however, that although worksheet names can include any combination of letters, numbers, symbols, and spaces, they cannot be longer than 31 characters.

Rename a Worksheet

1 Display the worksheet you want to rename.

2 Click the **Home** tab.

3 Click **Format**.

4 Click **Rename Sheet**.

Ⓐ You can also double-click the worksheet's tab.

Ⓑ Excel opens the worksheet name for editing and selects the text.

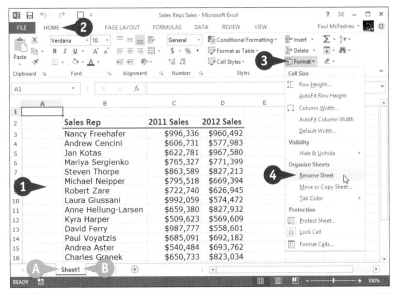

5 If you want to edit the existing name, press either ⬅ or ➡ to deselect the text.

6 Type the new worksheet name.

7 Press Enter.

Excel assigns the new name to the worksheet.

Create a New Worksheet

When you create a new workbook, Excel includes a single worksheet that you can use to build a spreadsheet model or store data. If you want to build a new model or store a different set of data, and this new information is related to the existing data in the workbook, you can create a new worksheet to hold the new information. Excel supports multiple worksheets in a single workbook, so you can add as many worksheets as you need for your project or model.

In most cases, you will add a blank worksheet, but Excel also comes with several predefined worksheet templates that you can use.

Create a New Worksheet

Insert a Blank Worksheet

1 Open the workbook to which you want to add the worksheet.

2 Click the **Home** tab.

3 Click the **Insert** ▼.

4 Click **Insert Sheet**.

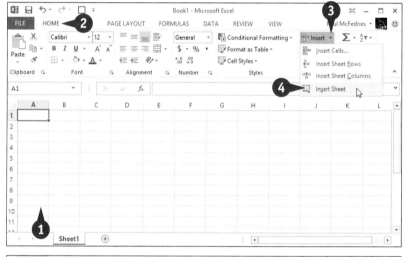

A Excel inserts the worksheet.

Note: You can also insert a blank worksheet by pressing **Shift**+**F11**.

B Another way to add a blank worksheet is to click the **Insert Worksheet** button (⊕).

Insert a Worksheet from a Template

1 Open the workbook to which you want to add the worksheet.

2 Right-click a worksheet tab.

3 Click **Insert**.

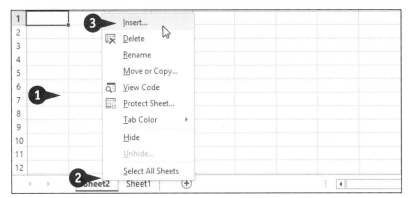

The Insert dialog box appears.

4 Click the **Spreadsheet Solutions** tab.

5 Click the type of worksheet you want to add.

C You can also click **Templates on Office.com** to download worksheet templates from the web.

6 Click **OK**.

D Excel inserts the worksheet.

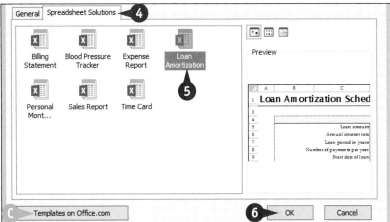

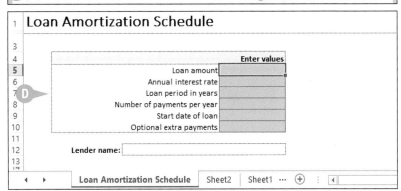

How do I navigate from one worksheet to another?

The easiest way is to click the tab of the worksheet you want to use. You can also click the following controls:

◀	Move to the previous worksheet.	Ctrl + ◀	Move to the first worksheet.
▶	Move to the next worksheet.	Ctrl + ▶	Move to the last worksheet.

Move a Worksheet

You can organize an Excel workbook and make it easier to navigate by moving your worksheets to different positions within the workbook. You can also move a worksheet to another workbook.

When you add a new worksheet to a workbook, Excel adds the sheet to the left of the existing sheets. However, it is unlikely that you will add each new worksheet in the order you want them to appear in the workbook. For example, in a budget-related workbook, you might prefer to have all the sales-related worksheets together, all the expense-related worksheets together, and so on.

Move a Worksheet

1 If you want to move the worksheet to another workbook, open that workbook and then return to the current workbook.

2 Click the tab of the worksheet you want to move.

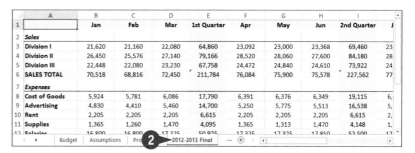

3 Click the **Home** tab.

4 Click **Format**.

5 Click **Move or Copy Sheet**.

Ⓐ You can also right-click the tab and then click **Move or Copy Sheet**.

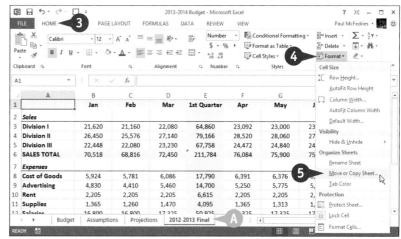

The Move or Copy dialog box appears.

6 If you want to move the sheet to another workbook, click the **To book** ☑ and then click the workbook.

7 Use the **Before sheet** list to click a destination worksheet.

When Excel moves the worksheet, it will appear to the left of the sheet you selected in Step **7**.

8 Click **OK**.

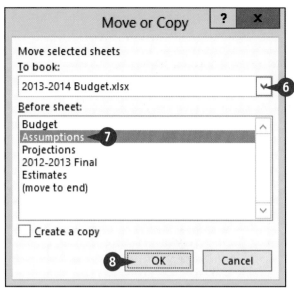

Ⓑ Excel moves the worksheet.

	A	B	C	D	E	F	G	H	I	J
1		Jan	Feb	Mar	1st Quarter	Apr	May	Jun	2nd Quarter	
2	*Sales*									
3	**Division I**	21,620	21,160	22,080	64,860	23,092	23,000	23,368	69,460	23
4	**Division II**	26,450	25,576	27,140	79,166	28,520	28,060	27,600	84,180	28
5	**Division III**	22,448	22,080	23,230	67,758	24,472	24,840	24,610	73,922	24
6	**SALES TOTAL**	70,518	68,816	72,450	211,784	76,084	75,900	75,578	227,562	77
7	*Expenses*									
8	**Cost of Goods**	5,924	5,781	6,086	17,790	6,391	6,376	6,349	19,115	6,
9	**Advertising**	4,830	4,410	5,460	14,700	5,250	5,775	5,513	16,538	5,
10	Rent	2,205	2,205	2,205	6,615	2,205	2,205	2,205	6,615	2,
11	**Supplies**	1,365	1,260	1,470	4,095	1,365	1,313	1,470	4,148	1,
12	Salaries	16,800	16,800	17,325	50,925	17,325	17,325	17,850	52,500	17

2012-2013 Final | Assumptions | Projections

Ⓑ

TIP

Is there an easier way to move a worksheet within the same workbook?

Yes. It is usually much easier to use your mouse to move a worksheet within the same workbook:

1 Move the mouse pointer (⇖) over the tab of the workbook you want to move.

2 Click and drag the worksheet tab left or right to the new position within the workbook (⇖ changes to ⇘).

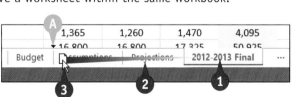

Ⓐ As you drag, an arrow shows the position of the worksheet.

3 When you have the worksheet positioned where you want it, drop the worksheet tab.

Excel moves the worksheet.

Copy a Worksheet

Excel enables you to make a copy of a worksheet, which is a useful technique if you require a new worksheet that is similar to an existing worksheet. You can copy the sheet to the same workbook or to another workbook.

One of the secrets of productivity in Excel is to not repeat work that you have already done. For example, if you have already created a worksheet and you find that you need a second sheet that is very similar, then you should not create the new worksheet from scratch. Instead, you should copy the existing worksheet and then edit the new sheet as needed.

Copy a Worksheet

1 If you want to copy the worksheet to another workbook, open that workbook and then return to the current workbook.

2 Click the tab of the worksheet you want to copy.

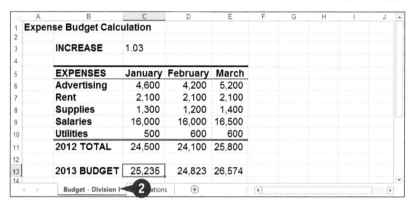

3 Click the **Home** tab.

4 Click **Format**.

5 Click **Move or Copy Sheet**.

Ⓐ You can also right-click the tab and then click **Move or Copy Sheet**.

The Move or Copy dialog box appears.

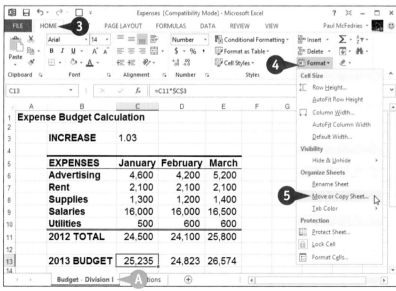

6 If you want to copy the sheet to another workbook, click the **To book** ⌄ and then click the workbook.

7 Use the **Before sheet** list to click a destination worksheet.

When Excel copies the worksheet, the copy will appear to the left of the sheet you selected in Step **7**.

8 Click the **Create a copy** check box (☐ changes to ☑).

9 Click **OK**.

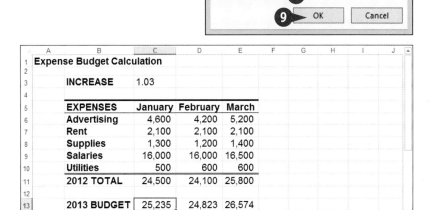

Move or Copy   ?   X

Move selected sheets
To book:

Expenses.xls   **6** ⌄

Before sheet:

Budget - Division I
Calculations   **7**
(move to end)

☑ Create a copy   **8**

9   OK   Cancel

B Excel copies the worksheet.

C Excel gives the new worksheet the same name as the original, but with (2) appended.

Note: See "Rename a Worksheet," earlier in this chapter, to learn how to edit the name of the copied worksheet.

	A	B	C	D	E	F	G	H	I	J
1	**Expense Budget Calculation**									
2										
3	**INCREASE**		1.03							
4										
5	**EXPENSES**	**January**	**February**	**March**						
6	**Advertising**	4,600	4,200	5,200						
7	**Rent**	2,100	2,100	2,100						
8	**Supplies**	1,300	1,200	1,400						
9	**Salaries**	16,000	16,000	16,500						
10	**Utilities**	500	600	600						
11	**2012 TOTAL**	24,500	24,100	25,800						
12										
13	**2013 BUDGET**	25,235	24,823	26,574						
14										

Budget - Div **B** Budget - Division I (2) **C** ⊕

TIP

Is there an easier way to copy a worksheet within the same workbook?

Yes. It is usually much easier to use your mouse to copy a worksheet within the same workbook:

1 Move the mouse ⌖ over the tab of the workbook you want to copy.

2 Hold down **Ctrl**.

3 Click and drag the worksheet tab left or right (⌖ changes to ⌖).

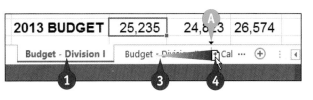

2013 BUDGET | 25,235 | 24,823 | 26,574

A

Budget - Division I   Budget - Divi... Cal ··· ⊕

1   **3**   **4**

A As you drag, an arrow shows the position of the worksheet.

4 When you have the worksheet positioned where you want it, drop the worksheet tab.

Excel copies the worksheet.

Delete a Worksheet

If you have a worksheet that you no longer need, you can delete it from the workbook. This reduces the size of the workbook and makes the workbook easier to navigate.

You cannot undo a worksheet deletion, so check the worksheet contents carefully before proceeding with the deletion. To be extra safe, save the workbook before performing the worksheet deletion. If you delete the wrong sheet accidentally, close the workbook without saving your changes.

Delete a Worksheet

1 Click the tab of the worksheet you want to delete.

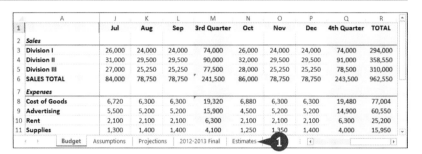

2 Click the **Home** tab.

3 Click the **Delete** ▼.

4 Click **Delete Sheet**.

Ⓐ You can also right-click the tab and then click **Delete Sheet**.

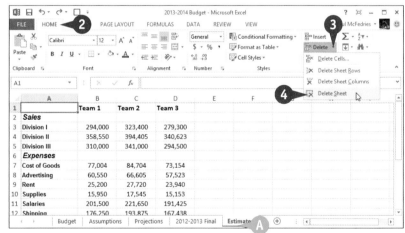

If the worksheet contains data, Excel asks you to confirm that you want to delete the worksheet.

5 Click **Delete**.

Ⓑ Excel removes the worksheet.

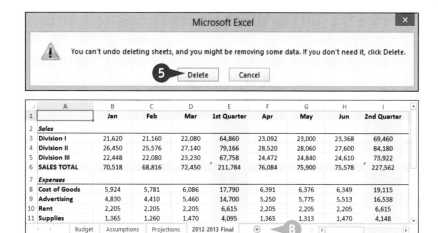

TIP

I have several worksheets that I need to delete. Do I have to delete them individually?

No. You can select all the sheets you want to remove and then run the deletion. To select multiple worksheets, click the tab of one of the worksheets, hold down **Ctrl**, and then click the tabs of the other worksheets.

If your workbook has many worksheets and you want to delete most of them, an easy way to select the sheets is to right-click any worksheet tab and then click **Select All Sheets**. Hold down **Ctrl**, and then click the tabs of the worksheets that you do not want to delete.

After you have selected your worksheets, follow Steps **3** to **5** to delete all the selected worksheets at once.

Change the Gridline Color

You can add some visual interest to your worksheet by changing the color that Excel uses to display the gridlines. The default color is black, but Excel offers a palette of 56 colors that you can choose from.

Changing the gridline color also has practical value because it enables you to differentiate between the gridlines and the borders that you add to a range or a table. See Chapter 5 to learn how to add borders to your worksheet ranges.

Change the Gridline Color

1 Click the tab of the worksheet you want to customize.

2 Click the **File** tab.

3 Click **Options**.

The Excel Options dialog box appears.

4 Click **Advanced**.

5 Scroll down to the **Display options for this worksheet** section.

6 Click the **Gridline color** ⌄.

7 Click the color you want to use.

8 Click **OK**.

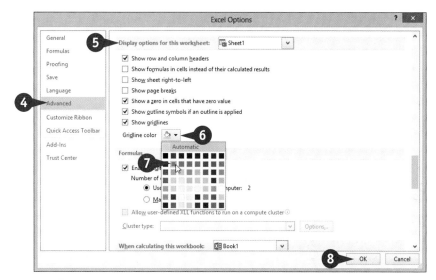

A Excel displays the gridlines using the color you selected.

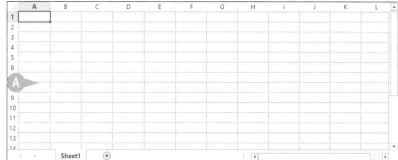

TIP

Can I change the gridline color for all the sheets in my workbook?
Yes. One method would be to follow the steps in this section for each worksheet in your workbook. However, an easier method is to first select all the sheets in the workbook. To do this, right-click any worksheet tab and then click **Select All Sheets**.

You can now follow Steps **2** to **8** to apply the new gridline color to all your worksheets. Once you have done that, right-click any worksheet tab and then click **Ungroup Sheets** to collapse the grouping.

Toggle Worksheet Gridlines On and Off

You can make your worksheet look cleaner and make the worksheet text easier to read by turning off the sheet gridlines. When you do this, Excel displays the worksheet with a plain white background, which often makes the worksheet easier to read. This is particularly true on a worksheet where you have added numerous borders to your ranges, as described in Chapter 5.

If you find you have trouble selecting ranges with the gridlines turned off, you can easily turn them back on again.

Toggle Worksheet Gridlines On and Off

Turn Gridlines Off

1 Click the tab of the worksheet you want to work with.

2 Click the **View** tab.

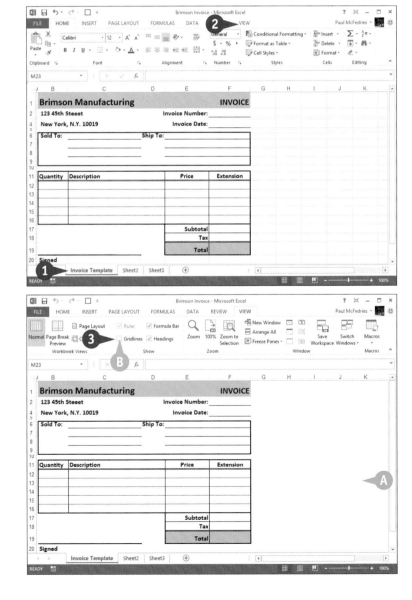

3 Click **Gridlines** (☑ changes to ☐).

Ⓐ Excel turns off the gridline display.

Turn Gridlines On

Ⓑ To turn the gridlines back on, click **Gridlines** (☐ changes to ☑).

158

Toggle Worksheet Headings On and Off

You can give yourself a bit more room to work by turning off the worksheet's row headings — the numbers 1, 2, and so on to the left of the worksheet — and column headings — the letters A, B, and so on above the worksheet.

If you find you have trouble reading your worksheet or building formulas with the headings turned off, you can easily turn them back on again.

Toggle Worksheet Headings On and Off

Turn Headings Off

1 Click the tab of the worksheet you want to work with.

2 Click the **View** tab.

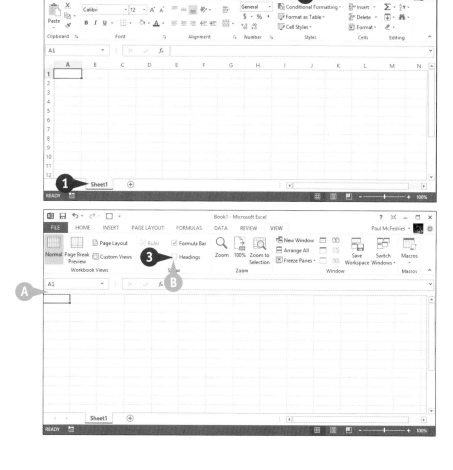

3 Click **Headings** (☑ changes to ☐).

A Excel turns off the headings.

Turn Headings On

B To turn the headings back on, click **Headings** (☐ changes to ☑).

Set the Worksheet Tab Color

You can make a workbook easier to navigate by color-coding the worksheet tabs. For example, if you have a workbook with sheets associated with several projects, you could apply a different tab color for each project. Similarly, you could format the tabs of incomplete worksheets with one color, and completed worksheets with another color.

Excel offers 10 standard colors as well as 60 colors associated with the current workbook theme. You can also apply a custom color if none of the standard or theme colors suits your needs.

Set the Worksheet Tab Color

1 Click the tab of the worksheet you want to format.

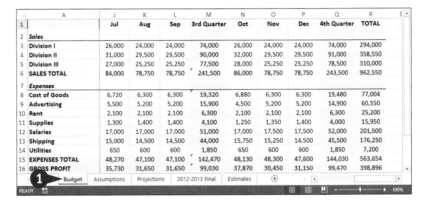

2 Click the **Home** tab.

3 Click **Format**.

4 Click **Tab Color**.

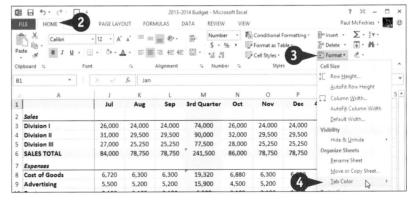

Excel displays the Tab Color palette.

5 Click the color you want to use for the current tab.

A To apply a custom color, click **More Colors** and then use the Colors dialog box to choose the color you want.

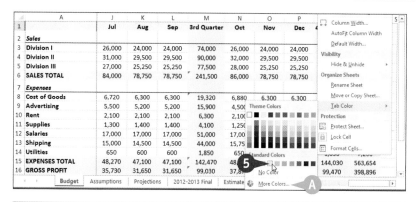

B Excel applies the color to the tab.

Note: You can also right-click the tab, click **Tab Color**, and then click the color you want to apply.

Note: The tab color appears very faintly when the tab is selected, but the color appears quite strongly when any other tab is selected.

If I want to apply the same color to several worksheets, do I have to format them individually?

No. You can select all the sheets you want to format and then apply the tab color. To select multiple worksheets, click the tab of one of the worksheets, hold down Ctrl, and then click the tabs of the other worksheets. After you have selected your worksheets, follow Steps **2** to **5** to apply the tab color to all the selected worksheets at once.

How do I remove a tab color?

If you no longer require a worksheet to have a colored tab, you can remove the color. Follow Steps **1** to **4** to select the worksheet and display the Tab Color palette, and then click **No Color**. Excel removes the color from the worksheet's tab.

Set the Worksheet Background

Y ou can add visual interest to a worksheet by replacing the standard white sheet background with a photo, drawing, or other image. For example, a worksheet that tracks the amount needed for a future vacation could show a photo from the proposed destination as the background.

When choosing the image you want to use as the background, be sure to select a picture that will not make the worksheet text difficult to read. For example, if your sheet text is a dark color, choose a light-colored image as the background.

Set the Worksheet Background

1 Click the tab of the worksheet you want to customize.

2 Click the **Page Layout** tab.

3 Click **Background** (🖼).

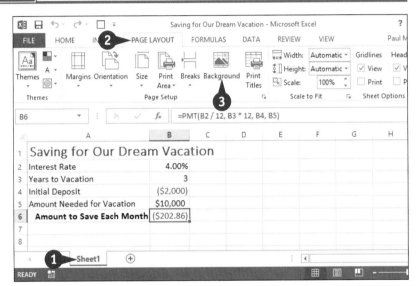

The Insert Pictures dialog box appears.

4 Click **From a file**.

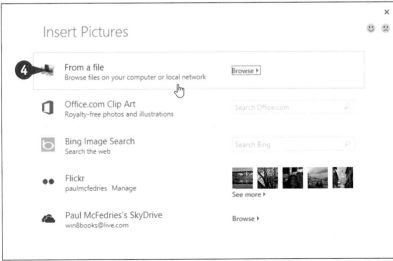

The Sheet Background dialog box appears.

5 Select the location of the image you want to use.

6 Click the image.

7 Click **Insert**.

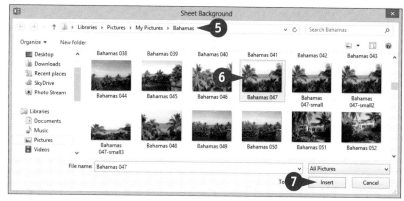

A Excel formats the worksheet background with the image you selected.

TIPS

How do I apply a background color instead of a background image?

Excel does not have a command that changes the background color of the entire worksheet. Instead, you must first select all the cells in the worksheet by clicking **Select All** (◢). Click the **Home** tab, click the **Fill Color** ▼ , and then click the color you want to use. Excel applies the color to the background of every cell.

How do I remove the background image from the worksheet?

If you find that having the background image makes it difficult to read the worksheet text, then you should remove the background. Click the tab of the worksheet, click **Page Layout**, and then click **Delete Background** (▩). Excel removes the background image from the worksheet.

Zoom In on or Out of a Worksheet

You can get a closer look at a portion of a worksheet by zooming in on that range. When you zoom in on a range, Excel increases the magnification of the range, which makes it easier to see the range data, particularly when the worksheet font is quite small.

On the other hand, if you want to get a sense of the overall structure of a worksheet, you can also zoom out. When you zoom out, Excel decreases the magnification, so you see more of the worksheet.

Zoom In on or Out of a Worksheet

1 Click the tab of the worksheet you want to zoom.

2 Click the **View** tab.

3 Click **Zoom** (🔍).

Ⓐ You can also run the Zoom command by clicking the zoom level in the status bar.

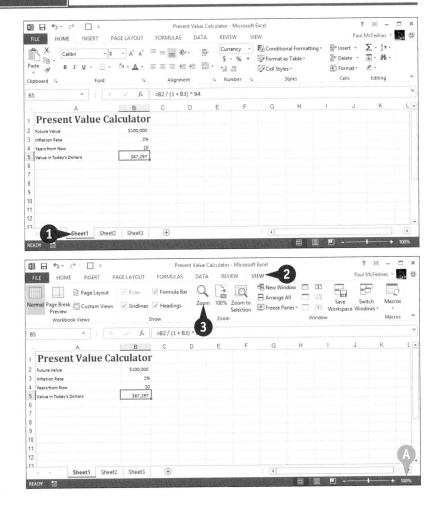

164

The Zoom dialog box appears.

4 Click the magnification level you want to use (○ changes to ●).

B You can also click **Custom** (○ changes to ●) and then type a magnification level in the text box.

Note: Select a magnification level above 100% to zoom in on the worksheet; select a level under 100% to zoom out of the worksheet.

5 Click **OK**.

Excel changes the magnification level and redisplays the worksheet.

C You can click **100%** () to return to the normal zoom level.

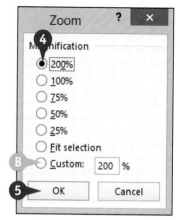

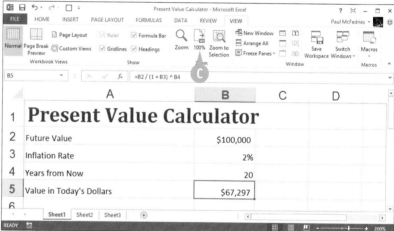

TIPS

How can I zoom in on a particular range?

Excel offers the Zoom to Selection feature that enables you to quickly and easily zoom in on a range. First, select the range that you want to magnify. Click the **View** tab and then click **Zoom to Selection** (). Excel magnifies the selected range to fill the entire Excel window.

Is there an easier way to zoom in and out of a worksheet?

Yes, you can use the Zoom slider, which appears on the far-right side of the Excel status bar. Drag the slider to the right to zoom in on the worksheet, or drag to the left to zoom out. You can also click the **Zoom In** () or **Zoom Out** () button to change the magnification.

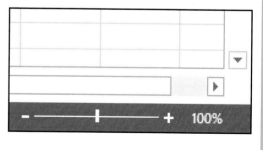

Split a Worksheet into Two Panes

You can make it easier to examine your worksheet data by splitting the worksheet into two scrollable panes that each show different parts of the worksheet. This is useful if you have cell headings at the top of the worksheet that you want to keep in view as you scroll down the worksheet.

Splitting a worksheet into two panes is also useful if you want to keep some data or a formula result in view while you scroll to another part of the worksheet.

Split a Worksheet into Two Panes

1 Click the tab of the worksheet you want to split.

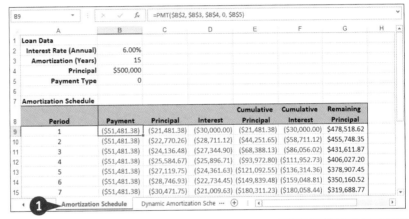

2 Select a cell in column A that is below the point where you want the split to occur.

For example, if you want to place the first five rows in the top pane, select cell A6.

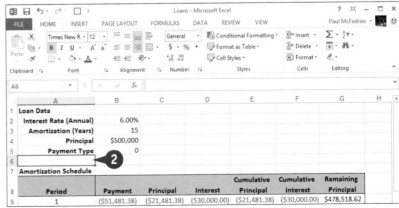

3 Click the **View** tab.

4 Click **Split** (▭).

A Excel splits the worksheet into two horizontal panes at the selected cell.

B You can adjust the size of the panes by clicking and dragging the split bar up or down.

To remove the split, either click ▭ again, or double-click the split bar.

Can I split a worksheet into two vertical panes?
Yes. To do this, you must first select a cell in the top row of the worksheet. Specifically, select the top cell in the column to the right of where you want the split to occur. For example, if you want to show only column A in the left pane, select cell B1. When you click ▭, Excel splits the worksheet into two vertical panes.

Can I split a worksheet into four panes?
Yes. This is useful if you have three or four worksheet areas that you want to examine separately. To perform a four-way split, first select the cell where you want the split to occur. Note that this cell must not be in either row 1 or column A. When you click ▭, Excel splits the worksheet into four panes. The cell you selected becomes the upper-left cell in the bottom-right pane.

Hide and Unhide a Worksheet

You can hide a worksheet so that it no longer appears in the workbook. This is useful if you need to show the workbook to other people, but the workbook contains a worksheet with sensitive or private data that you do not want others to see. You might also want to hide a worksheet if it contains unfinished work that is not ready for others to view.

To learn how to protect a workbook so that other people cannot unhide a worksheet, see Chapter 15.

Hide and Unhide a Worksheet

Hide a Worksheet

1 Click the tab of the worksheet you want to hide.

2 Click the **Home** tab.

3 Click **Format**.

4 Click **Hide & Unhide**.

5 Click **Hide Sheet**.

Ⓐ You can also right-click the worksheet tab and then click **Hide Sheet**.

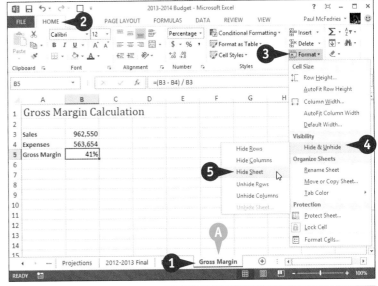

Ⓑ Excel temporarily removes the worksheet from the workbook.

168

Unhide a Worksheet

1 Click the **Home** tab.

2 Click **Format**.

3 Click **Hide & Unhide**.

4 Click **Unhide Sheet**.

Ⓒ You can also right-click any worksheet tab and then click **Unhide Sheet**.

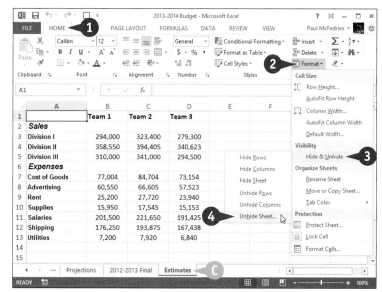

The Unhide dialog box appears.

5 Click the worksheet you want to restore.

6 Click **OK**.

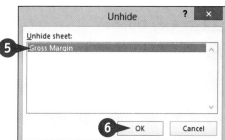

Ⓓ Excel returns the worksheet to the workbook.

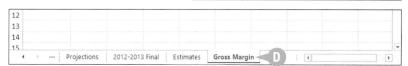

TIP

I have several worksheets that I need to hide. Do I have to hide them individually?

No. You can select all the sheets you want to work with and then hide them. To select multiple worksheets, click the tab of one of the worksheets, hold down **Ctrl**, and then click the tabs of the other worksheets.

If your workbook has many worksheets and you want to hide most of them, an easy way to select the sheets is to right-click any worksheet tab and then click **Select All Sheets**. Hold down **Ctrl**, and then click the tabs of the worksheets that you do not want to hide.

After you have selected your worksheets, follow Steps **3** to **5** to hide all the selected worksheets at once.

CHAPTER 8

Dealing with Workbooks

Everything you do in Excel takes place within a *workbook*, which is the standard Excel file. This chapter shows you how to get more out of workbooks by creating new files; saving, opening, and closing files; checking spelling; and more.

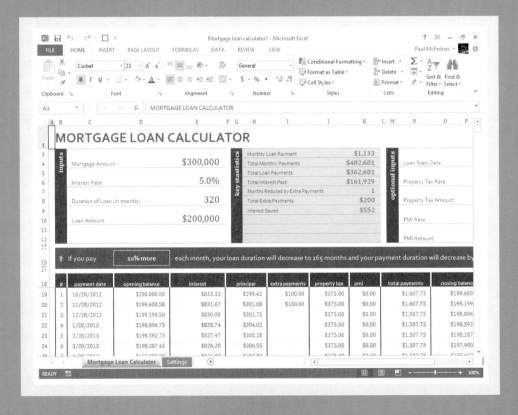

Create a New Blank Workbook

To perform new work in Excel, you need to first create a new, blank Excel workbook. When you launch Excel, it prompts you to create a new workbook and you can click Blank Workbook to start with a blank file that contains a single empty worksheet. However, for subsequent files you must use the File tab to create a new blank workbook.

If you prefer to create a workbook based on one of the Excel templates, see the following section, "Create a New Workbook from a Template."

Create a New Blank Workbook

1 Click the **File** tab.

2 Click **New**.

3 Click **Blank Workbook**.

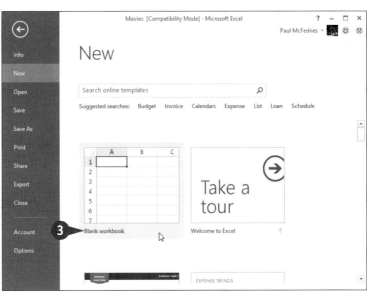

A Excel creates the blank workbook and displays it in the Excel window.

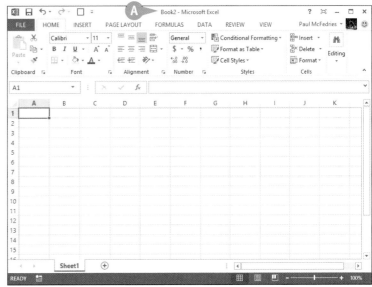

TIPS

Is there a faster method I can use to create a new workbook?

Yes. Excel offers a keyboard shortcut for faster workbook creation. From the keyboard, press `Ctrl`+`N`.

When I start Excel and then open an existing workbook, Excel often removes the new, blank workbook that it opened automatically. How can I prevent this?

Excel assumes that you want to use a fresh workbook when you start the program, so it prompts you to create a new workbook. However, if you do not make any changes to the blank workbook and then open an existing file, Excel assumes you do not want to use the new workbook, so it closes it. To prevent this from happening, make a change to the blank workbook before opening another file.

Create a New Workbook from a Template

You can save time and effort by creating a new workbook based on one of the Excel template files. Each template includes a working spreadsheet model that contains predefined headings, labels, and formulas, as well as preformatted colors, fonts, styles, borders, and more. In many cases, you can use the new workbook as is and just fill in your own data.

Excel 2013 offers more than two dozen templates, and many more are available through Microsoft Office Online.

Create a New Workbook from a Template

1 Click the **File** tab.

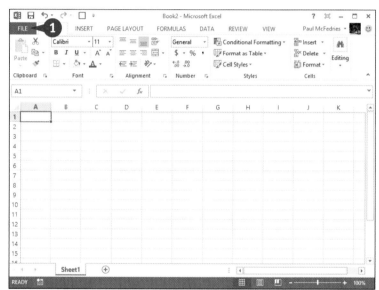

2 Click **New**.

Ⓐ To use an Office Online template, use the Search Online Templates text box to type a word or two that defines the type of template you want to use.

3 Click the template you want to use.

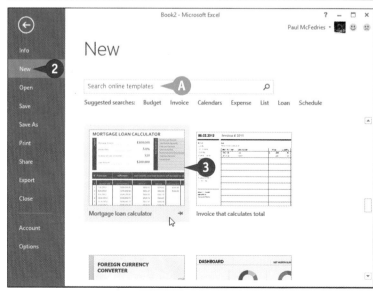

B A preview of the template appears.

4 Click **Create**.

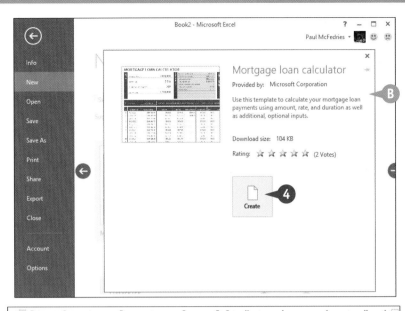

C Excel creates the new workbook and displays it in the Excel window.

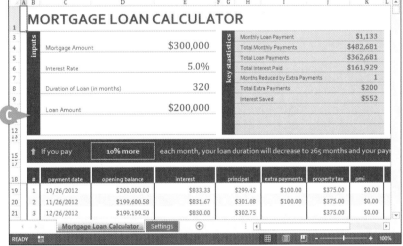

Can I create my own template?
Yes. If you have a specific workbook structure that you use frequently, you should save it as a template so that you do not have to re-create the same structure from scratch each time. Open the workbook, click **File**, and then click **Save as**. In the Save As dialog box, click **Computer**, and then click **Browse**. Click the **Save as type** ☑ and then click **Excel Template**. Type a name in the **File name** text box and then click **Save**. To use the template, click **File** and click **Open**; then, in the Open dialog box, click **Computer**, click **Browse**, and then click your template file.

Save a Workbook

After you create a workbook in Excel and make changes to it, you can save the document to preserve your work. When you edit a workbook, Excel stores the changes in your computer's memory, which is erased each time you shut down your computer. Saving the document preserves your changes on your computer's hard drive. To ensure that you do not lose any work if your computer crashes or Excel freezes up, you should save your work every few minutes.

Save a Workbook

1 Click **Save** (🖫).

You can also press **Ctrl**+**S**.

If you have saved the document previously, your changes are now preserved, and you do not need to follow the rest of the steps in this section.

The Save As tab appears.

2 Click **Computer**.

3 Click **Browse**.

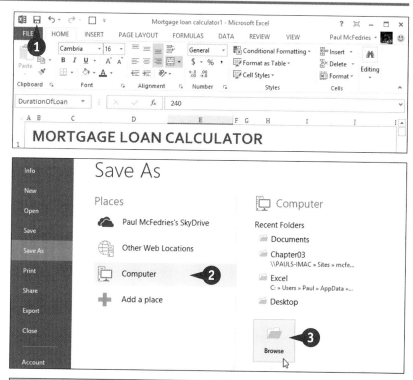

The Save As dialog box appears.

4 Select a folder in which to store the file.

5 Click in the **File name** text box and type the name that you want to use for the document.

6 Click **Save**.

Excel saves the file.

Note: To learn how to save a workbook in an older Excel format, see Chapter 15.

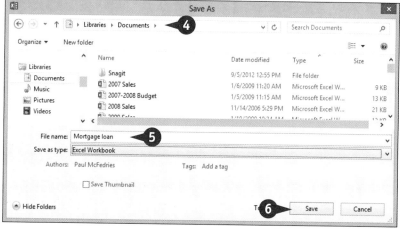

The Arrange Windows dialog box appears.

4 Click a view mode (○ changes to ◉).

Tiled arranges the workbooks evenly on the Windows desktop.

Horizontal stacks the workbooks one above the other.

Vertical displays the workbooks side by side.

Cascade arranges the workbooks in an overlapping cascade pattern.

5 Click **OK**.

A Excel arranges the workbook windows.

This example shows two workbooks arranged with the Vertical view mode.

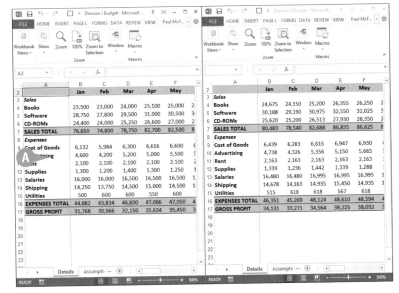

TIPS

How do I return to viewing one workbook at a time?

Click the workbook you want to use, and then click the workbook window's **Maximize** button (▭). This maximizes the workbook on the Windows desktop, so you only see that workbook. To switch to another open workbook, click the Excel icon (▥) in the taskbar to display thumbnail versions of the open workbooks, and then click the one you want to view.

Is it possible to view two different sections of a single workbook at the same time?

Yes. Excel enables you to create a second window for a workbook and you can then arrange the two windows as described in this section. Switch to the workbook you want to view, click the **View** tab, and then click **New Window** (▤). Follow Steps **1** to **3** to open the Arrange Windows dialog box and select a view option. Click the **Windows of active workbook** check box (☐ changes to ☑), and then click **OK**.

Find Text in a Workbook

Most spreadsheet models require at most a screen or two in a single worksheet, so locating the text you want is usually not difficult. However, you might be working with a large spreadsheet model that takes up either multiple screens in a single worksheet or multiple worksheets. In such large workbooks, locating specific text can be difficult and time-consuming. You can make this task easier and faster using the Excel Find feature, which searches the entire workbook in the blink of an eye.

Find Text in a Workbook

1 Click the **Home** tab.

2 Click **Find & Select**.

3 Click **Find**.

Note: You can also run the Find command by pressing <kbd>Ctrl</kbd>+<kbd>F</kbd>.

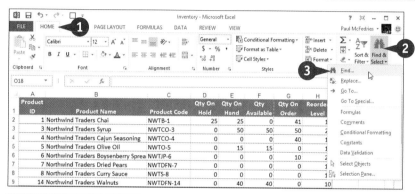

The Find and Replace dialog box appears.

4 Click in the **Find what** text box and type the text you want to find.

5 Click **Find Next**.

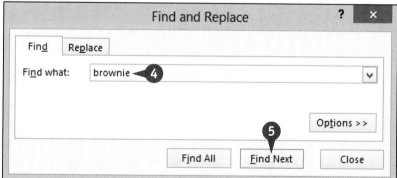

Ⓐ Excel selects the next cell that contains an instance of the search text.

Note: If the search text does not exist in the document, Excel displays a dialog box to let you know.

❻ If the selected instance is not the one you want, click **Find Next** until Excel finds the correct instance.

❼ Click **Close** to close the Find and Replace dialog box.

Ⓑ Excel leaves the cell selected.

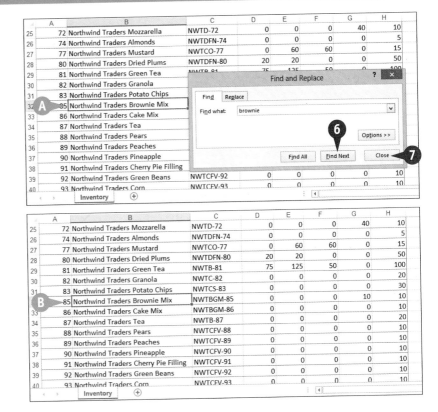

TIPS

When I search for a particular term, Excel only looks in the current worksheet. How can I get Excel to search the entire workbook?
In the Find and Replace dialog box, click **Options** to expand the dialog box. Click the **Within** ☑ and then click **Workbook**. This option tells Excel to examine the entire workbook for your search text.

When I search for a name such as *Bill*, Excel also matches the non-name *bill*. Is there a way to fix this?
Yes. In the Find and Replace dialog box, click **Options** to expand the dialog box. Select the **Match case** check box (☐ changes to ☑). This option tells Excel to match the search text only if it has the same mix of uppercase and lowercase letters that you specify in the **Find what** text box. If you type **Bill**, for example, the program matches only *Bill* and not *bill*.

Replace Text in a Workbook

Do you need to replace a word or part of a word with some other text? If you only need to replace one or two instances of the text, you can usually perform the replacement quickly and easily. However, if you have many instances of the text to replace, the replacement can take a long time and the more instances there are, the more likely it is that you will make a mistake. You can save time and do a more accurate job if you let the Excel Replace feature replace the text for you.

Replace Text in a Workbook

1 Click the **Home** tab.

2 Click **Find & Replace**.

3 Click **Replace**.

Note: You can also run the Replace command by pressing Ctrl + H.

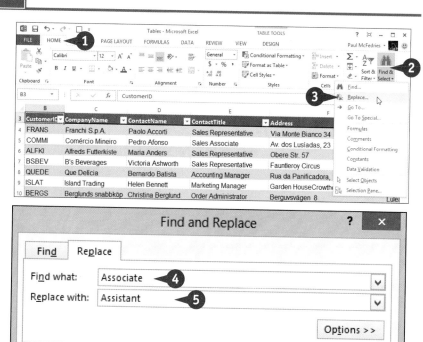

The Find and Replace dialog box appears.

4 In the **Find what** text box, type the text you want to find.

5 Click in the **Replace with** text box and type the text you want to use as the replacement.

6 Click **Find Next**.

Ⓐ Excel selects the cell that contains the next instance of the search text.

Note: If the search text does not exist in the document, Excel displays a dialog box to let you know.

⑦ If the selected instance is not the one you want, click **Find Next** until Excel finds the correct instance.

⑧ Click **Replace**.

Ⓑ Excel replaces the selected text with the replacement text.

Ⓒ Excel selects the next instance of the search text.

⑨ Repeat Steps **7** and **8** until you have replaced all of the instances you want to replace.

⑩ Click **Close** to close the Find and Replace dialog box.

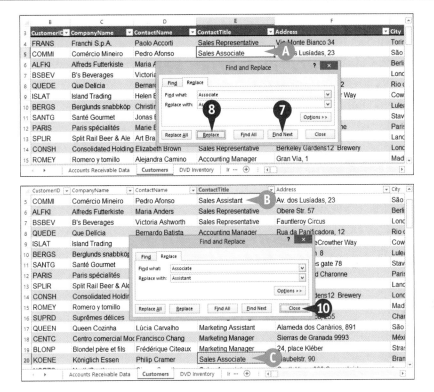

Is there a faster way to replace every instance of the search text with the replacement text?
Yes. In the Find and Replace dialog box, click **Replace All**. This tells Excel to replace every instance of the search text with the replacement text. However, you should exercise some caution with this feature because it may make some replacements that you did not intend. Click **Find Next** a few times to make sure the matches are correct. Also, consider clicking **Options** and then selecting the **Match case** check box (☐ changes to ☑), as described in the previous section, "Find Text in a Workbook."

Check Spelling and Grammar

Although Excel workbooks are mostly concerned with numbers, formulas, and data, a workbook that contains misspelled words might not be taken as seriously as one that is free of jarring typos. You can eliminate any text errors in your Excel workbooks by taking advantage of the spell-checker, which identifies potentially misspelled words and offers suggested corrections.

When the spell-checker flags a word as misspelled, you can correct the word, tell the spell-checker to ignore it, or add it to the spell-checker's dictionary.

Check Spelling and Grammar

1 Click the **Review** tab.

2 Click **Spelling** ( ).

Note: You can also press F7.

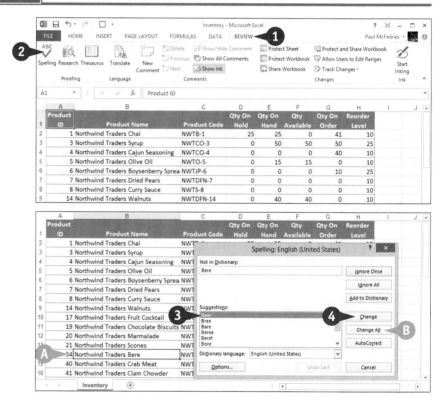

A The Spelling dialog box appears and selects the cell that contains the first error.

3 Click the correction you want to use.

4 Click **Change**.

B Click **Change All** to correct every instance of the error.

C The spell-checker displays the next error.

5 If you want to correct the word, repeat Step **4**.

D If you do not want to correct the word, click one of the following buttons:

Click **Ignore Once** to skip this instance of the error.

Click **Ignore All** to skip all instances of the error.

Click **Add to Dictionary** to include the word in the spell-checker's dictionary.

6 When the check is complete, click **OK**.

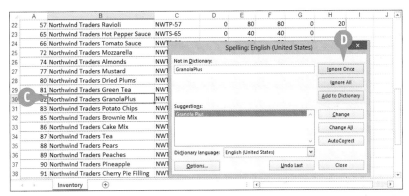

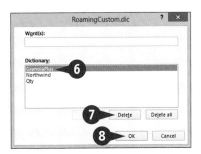

Microsoft Excel

Spell check complete. You're good to go!

6 OK

TIP

Can I remove a word that I added to the spell-checker's dictionary?
Yes. Follow these steps:

1 Click **File**.

2 Click **Options** to open the Excel Options dialog box.

3 Click **Proofing**.

4 Click **Custom Dictionaries** to open the Custom Dictionaries dialog box.

5 Click **Edit Word List**.

6 Click the term you want to remove.

7 Click **Delete**.

8 Click **OK** to return to the Custom Dictionaries dialog box.

9 Click **OK** to return to the Excel Options dialog box.

10 Click **OK**.

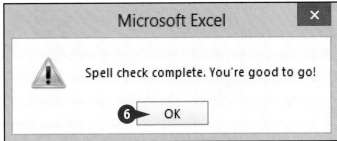

Close a Workbook

When you finish adding and editing text in an Excel workbook, you should close the workbook to reduce desktop clutter. If the workbook is very large or contains many images, closing the file also frees up memory and other system resources.

When you close a workbook, Excel automatically checks to see if you have made changes to the workbook since the last time you saved it. If Excel determines that the workbook contains unsaved changes, it prompts you to save the file. To avoid losing your work, be sure to save the workbook.

Close a Workbook

1 Display the workbook you want to close.

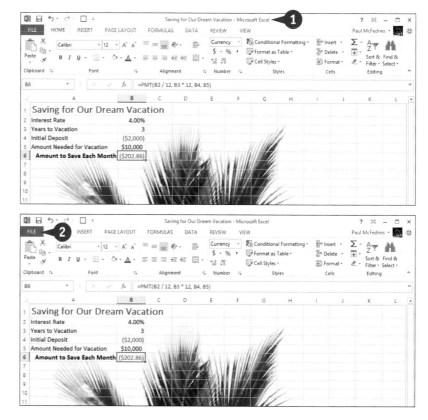

2 Click the **File** tab.

3 Click **Close**.

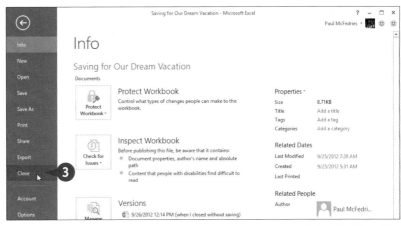

If you have unsaved changes in the workbook, Excel asks if you want to save your work.

4 Click **Save**.

Ⓐ If you do not want to preserve your changes, click **Don't Save**.

Ⓑ If you decide to keep the document open, click **Cancel**.

The program saves your work and then closes the document.

TIP

Are there faster methods I can use to close a document?
Yes. You can also close a document using a keyboard shortcut or a mouse click. From your keyboard, press Ctrl + W to close the current document; then, with your mouse, click the **Close** button (✕) in the upper-left corner of the document window.

CHAPTER 9

Formatting Workbooks

Excel offers several settings that enable you to control the look of a workbook, including the workbook colors, fonts, and special effects. You can also apply a workbook theme and add a header and footer to a workbook.

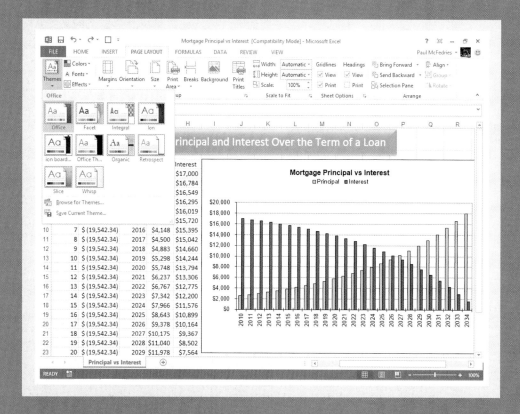

Modify the Workbook Colors

You can give your workbook a new look by selecting a different color scheme. Each color scheme affects a dozen workbook elements, including the workbook's text colors, background colors, border colors, chart colors, and more. Excel offers more than 20 color schemes. However, if none of these predefined schemes suits your needs, you can also create your own custom color scheme.

To get the most out of the Excel color schemes, you must apply styles to your ranges, as described in Chapter 5.

Modify the Workbook Colors

1 Open or switch to the workbook you want to format.

2 Click the **Page Layout** tab.

3 Click **Colors** (▦).

④ Click the color scheme you want to apply.

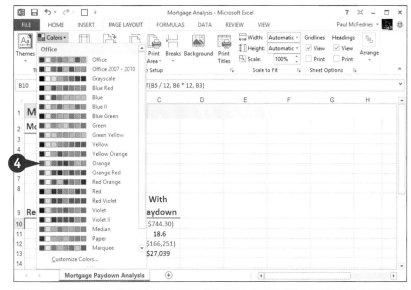

Ⓐ Excel applies the color scheme to the workbook.

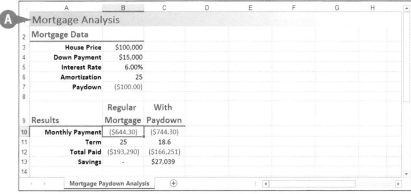

TIP

Can I create my own color scheme?

Yes, by following these steps:

❶ Click the **Page Layout** tab.

❷ Click 🎨.

❸ Click **Customize Colors**.

The Create New Theme Colors dialog box appears.

❹ For each theme color, click ▾ and then click the color you want to use.

Ⓐ The Sample area shows what your theme colors look like.

❺ Type a name for the custom color scheme.

❻ Click **Save**.

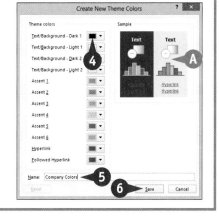

Set the Workbook Fonts

You can add visual appeal to your workbook by selecting a different font scheme. Each font scheme has two defined fonts: a *heading font* for the titles and headings, and a *body font* for the regular worksheet text. Excel offers more than 20 font schemes. However, if none of the predefined schemes is suitable, you can create a custom font scheme.

To get the most out of the Excel font schemes, particularly the heading fonts, you must apply styles to your ranges, as described in Chapter 5.

Set the Workbook Fonts

1 Open or switch to the workbook you want to format.

2 Click the **Page Layout** tab.

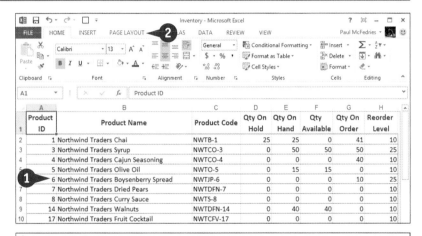

3 Click **Fonts** (A).

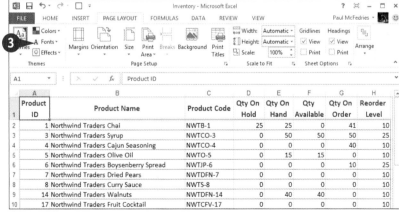

4 Click the font scheme you want to apply.

A Excel applies the heading font to the workbook's headings.

B Excel applies the body font to the workbook's regular text.

A	B	C	D	E	F	G	H
Product ID	Product Name	Product Code	Qty On Hold	Qty On Hand	Qty Available	Qty On Order	Reorder Level
1 Northwind Traders Chai		NWTB-1	25	25	0	41	10
3 Northwind Traders Syrup		NWTCO-3	0	50	50	50	25
4 Northwind Traders Cajun Seasoning		NWTCO-4	0	0	0	40	10
5 Northwind Traders Olive Oil		NWTO-5	0	15	15	0	10
6 Northwind Traders Boysenberry Spread		NWTJP-6	0	0	0	10	25
7 Northwind Traders Dried Pears		NWTDFN-7	0	0	0	0	10
8 Northwind Traders Curry Sauce		NWTS-8	0	0	0	0	10
14 Northwind Traders Walnuts		NWTDFN-14	0	40	40	0	10
17 Northwind Traders Fruit Cocktail		NWTCFV-17	0	0	0	0	10
19 Northwind Traders Chocolate Biscuits Mix		NWTBGM-19	0	0	0	20	5
20 Northwind Traders Marmalade		NWTJP-6	0	0	0	40	10
21 Northwind Traders Scones		NWTBGM-21	0	0	0	0	5
34 Northwind Traders Beer		NWTB-34	23	23	0	0	15
40 Northwind Traders Crab Meat		NWTCM-40	0	0	0	120	30

TIP

Can I create my own font scheme?

Yes, by following these steps:

1 Click the **Page Layout** tab.

2 Click **A** .

3 Click **Customize Fonts**.

The Create New Theme Fonts dialog box appears.

4 Click the **Heading font** and then click the font you want to use for titles and headings.

5 Click the **Body font** and then click the font you want to use for regular sheet text.

A The Sample area shows what your theme fonts look like.

6 Type a name for the custom font scheme.

7 Click **Save**.

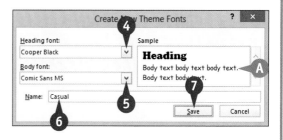

Choose Workbook Effects

You can enhance the look of your workbook by selecting a different effect scheme. The effect scheme applies to charts and graphic objects, and each scheme defines a border style, fill style, and added effect such as a drop shadow or glow. Excel offers more than 20 effect schemes.

To get the most out of the Excel effect schemes, you must apply a style to your chart, as described in Chapter 13, or to your graphic object, as described in Chapter 14.

Choose Workbook Effects

1 Open or switch to the workbook you want to format.

2 Click the **Page Layout** tab.

3 Click **Effects** (⊙).

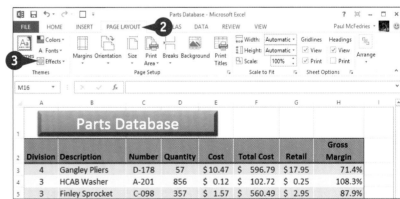

4 Click the effect scheme you want to apply.

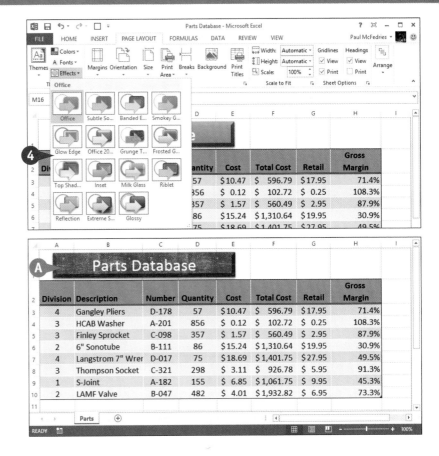

A Excel applies the effect scheme to the workbook's charts and graphics.

Can I create a custom effect scheme?

No. Unlike with the color schemes and font schemes described earlier in this chapter, Excel does not have a feature that enables you to create your own effect scheme.

Why are all the effect schemes the same color?

The color you see in the effect schemes depends on the color scheme you have applied to your workbook. If you apply a different color scheme, as described in "Modify the Workbook Colors," earlier in this chapter, you will see a different color in the effect schemes. If you want to use a custom effect color, create a custom color scheme and change the Accent 1 color to the color you want.

Apply a Workbook Theme

You can give your workbook a completely new look by selecting a different workbook theme. Each theme consists of the workbook's colors, fonts, and effects. Excel offers ten predefined workbook themes.

To get the most out of the Excel workbook themes, you must apply styles to your ranges, as described in Chapter 5; to your charts, as described in Chapter 13; and to your graphic objects, as described in Chapter 14.

Apply a Workbook Theme

1 Open or switch to the workbook you want to format.

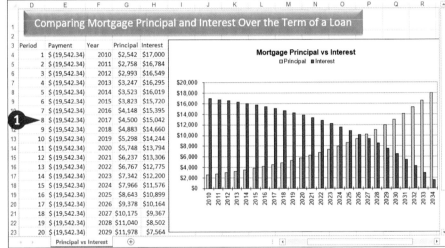

2 Click the **Page Layout** tab.

3 Click **Themes** (⬛).

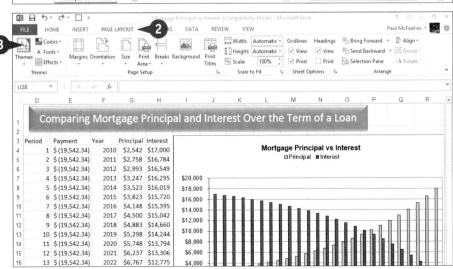

4 Click the workbook theme you want to apply.

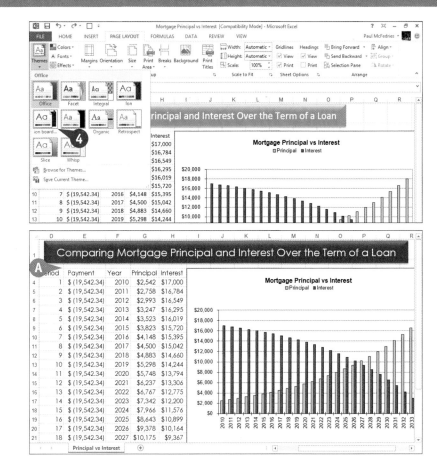

A Excel applies the theme to the workbook.

Note: After you apply the theme, the new font size might require you to adjust the column widths to see your data properly.

Can I create my own workbook theme?

Yes, by following these steps:

1 Format the workbook with a color scheme, font scheme, and effect scheme, as described in the previous three sections.

2 Click the **Page Layout** tab.

3 Click 🔲.

4 Click **Save Current Theme**.

The Save Current Theme dialog box appears.

5 Type a name for the custom theme.

6 Click **Save**.

Add a Workbook Header

If you will be printing a workbook, you can enhance the printout by building a custom header that includes information such as the page number, date, filename, or even a picture.

The *header* is an area on the printed page between the top of the page text and the top margin. Excel offers a number of predefined header items that enable you to quickly add data to the workbook header. If none of the predefined header items suits your needs, Excel also offers tools that make it easy to build a custom header.

Add a Workbook Header

1 Click the **View** tab.

2 Click **Page Layout** ( ).

Excel switches to Page Layout view.

A You can also click the **Page Layout** button ( ).

3 Click the **Click to add header** text.

B Excel opens the header area for editing.

C Excel adds the Header & Footer Tools tab.

4 Click the **Design** tab.

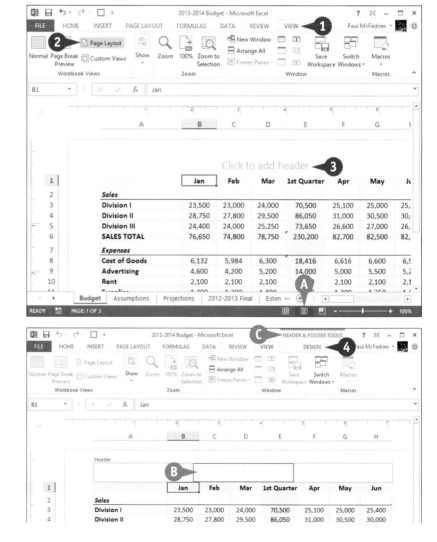

5 Type your text in the header.

6 If you want to include a predefined header item, click **Header** and then click the item.

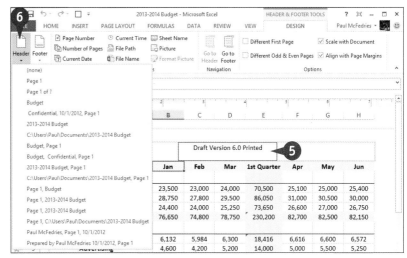

7 Click a button in the Header & Footer Elements group to add that element to the header.

D Excel inserts a code into the header, such as &[Date] for the Current Date element, as shown here.

8 Repeat Steps **5** to **7** to build the header.

9 Click outside the header area.

Excel applies the header. When you are in Page Layout view, you see the current values for elements such as the date.

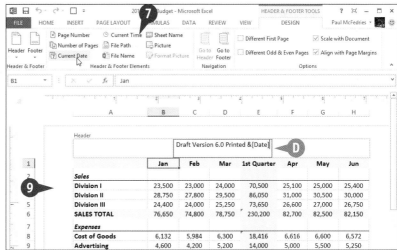

TIP

Can I have multiple headers in a workbook?

Yes. You can have a different header and footer on the first page, which is useful if you want to add a title or explanatory text to the first page. In the Design tab, click the **Different First Page** check box (☐ changes to ☑).

You can also have different headers and footers on the even and odd pages of the printout, such as showing the filename on the even pages and the page numbers on the odd pages. In the Design tab, click the **Different Odd & Even Pages** check box (☐ changes to ☑).

Add a Workbook Footer

If you will be printing a workbook, you can enhance the printout by building a custom footer that includes information such as the current page number, the total number of pages, the worksheet name, and more.

The *footer* is an area on the printed page between the bottom of the page text and the bottom margin. Excel offers a number of predefined footer items that enable you to quickly add data to the workbook footer. If none of the predefined footer items suits your needs, Excel also offers tools that make it easy to build a custom footer.

Add a Workbook Footer

1 Click the **View** tab.

2 Click **Page Layout** (📄).

Excel switches to Page Layout view.

Ⓐ You can also click the **Page Layout** button (📄).

3 Click the **Click to add header** text.

Note: You can also scroll down to the bottom of the page and click the **Click to add footer** text. If you do this, you can skip Step **6**.

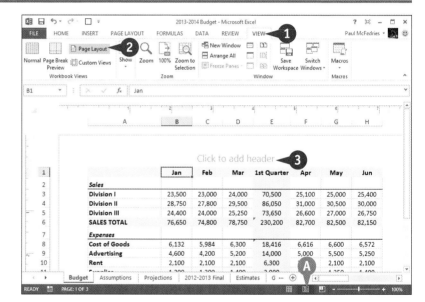

Ⓑ Excel adds the Header & Footer Tools tab.

4 Click the **Design** tab.

5 Click **Go to Footer** (📄).

Ⓒ Excel opens the footer area for editing.

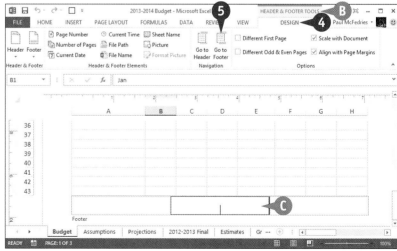

6 Type your text in the footer.

7 If you want to include a predefined footer item, click **Footer** and then click the item.

8 Click a button in the Header & Footer Elements group to add that element to the footer.

Ⓓ Excel inserts a code into the footer, such as &[Pages] for the Number of Pages element, as shown here.

9 Repeat Steps **6** to **8** to build the footer.

10 Click outside the footer area.

Excel applies the footer. When you are in Page Layout view, you see the current values for elements such as the page number.

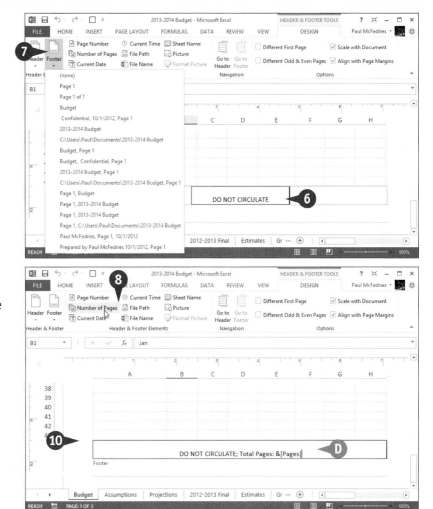

TIP

Can I view my headers and footers before I print the workbook?
Yes. Follow these steps:

1 Click the **File** tab.

2 Click **Print**.

Ⓐ The right side of the Print tab shows you a preview of the workbook printout.

Ⓑ The header appears here.

Ⓒ The footer appears here.

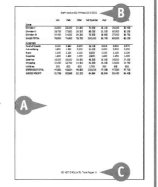

CHAPTER 10

Printing Workbooks

If you want to distribute hard copies of one or more worksheets or an entire workbook, you can use the Excel Print feature. Before you print, you can adjust print-related options such as the margins, page orientation, and paper size.

Adjust the Workbook Margins

You can get more space on the printed page to display your worksheet data by using smaller page margins. The *margins* are the blank areas that surround the printed data. For example, if you find that Excel is printing extra pages because your data is a bit too wide or a bit too long to fit on a single page, you can reduce either the left and right margins or the top and bottom margins.

If you or another person will be writing notes on the printouts, consider using wider margins to allow more room for the notes.

Adjust the Workbook Margins

Using the Ribbon

1 Open the workbook you want to print.

2 Click the **Page Layout** tab.

3 Click **Margins** (⬚).

Ⓐ If you see a margin setting you want to use, click the setting and skip the rest of these steps.

4 Click **Custom Margins**.

The Page Setup dialog box appears with the Margins tab selected.

5 Use the spin boxes to specify the margin sizes in inches.

Note: Do not make the margins too small or your document may not print properly. Most printers cannot handle margins smaller than about 0.25 inch, although you should consult your printer manual to confirm this. In particular, see if your printer offers a "borderless" printing option.

6 Click **OK**.

Excel adjusts the margin sizes.

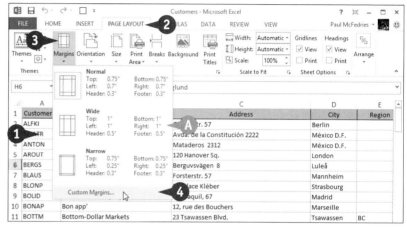

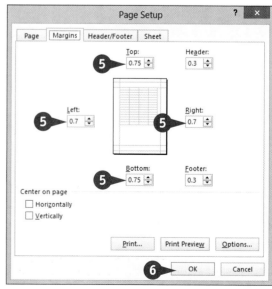

Using the Ruler

1 Open the workbook you want to print.

2 Click **Page Layout** (⬚).

3 Move the ⬚ over the right edge of the ruler's left margin area (⬚ changes to ↔).

4 Click and drag the edge of the margin to set the left margin width.

5 Click and drag the left edge of the right margin area to set the margin width.

6 Move the ⬚ over the bottom edge of the ruler's top margin area (⬚ changes to ↕).

7 Click and drag the edge of the margin to set the top margin width.

8 Click and drag the top edge of the bottom margin area (not shown) to set the bottom margin width.

Note: You need to scroll down to the bottom of the page to see the bottom margin.

Excel adjusts the margin sizes.

TIPS

I increased my margin sizes to get more room around the text. Is there a way to center the text on the page?
Yes. This is a good idea if you want to ensure that you have the same amount of whitespace above and below the text, and to the left and right of the text. Follow Steps **1** to **4** in the "Using the Ribbon" subsection to open the Page Setup dialog box with the Margins tab selected. Click **Horizontally** (☐ changes to ☑), click **Vertically** (☐ changes to ☑), and then click **OK**.

What are the header and footer margins?
The header margin is the space between the workbook header and the top of the page, and the footer margin is the space between the workbook footer and the bottom of the page. (See Chapter 9 to learn how to add a header and footer to your workbook.) In the Margins tab of the Page Setup dialog box, use the **Header** and **Footer** spin boxes to set these margins.

Change the Page Orientation

You can improve the look of your printout by changing the page orientation to suit your data. The page orientation determines whether Excel prints more rows or columns on a page. Portrait orientation is taller, so it prints more rows; landscape orientation is wider, so it prints more columns.

Choose the orientation based on your worksheet data. If your worksheet has many rows and only a few columns, choose portrait; if your worksheet has many columns but just a few rows, choose landscape.

Change the Page Orientation

1 Open the workbook you want to print.

2 Click the **Page Layout** tab.

3 Click **Orientation** ( ).

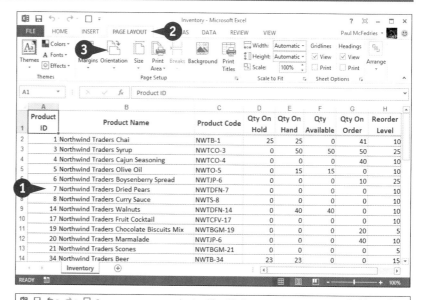

4 Click the orientation you want to use.

A Excel adjusts the orientation.

B Click to see the orientation.

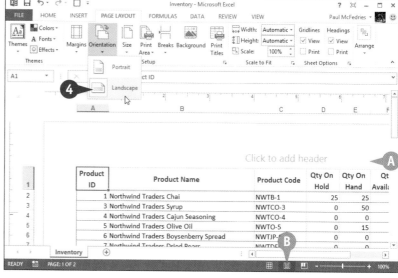

Insert a Page Break

You can control what data appears on each printed page by inserting a page break in your worksheet. A *page break* is a location within a worksheet where Excel begins a new printed page. Excel normally inserts its own page breaks based on the number and height of rows in the sheet, the number and width of the sheet columns, the margin widths, and the page orientation.

A vertical page break starts a new page at a particular column; a horizontal page break starts a new page at a particular row.

Insert a Page Break

1 Open the workbook you want to print.

2 Select the cell to the right of and below where you want the vertical and horizontal page breaks to appear.

Note: Select a cell in row 1 to create just a vertical page break; select a cell in column A to create just a horizontal page break.

3 Click the **Page Layout** tab.

4 Click **Breaks** (⊟).

5 Click **Insert Page Break**.

C Excel inserts the page breaks and indicates the breaks with thicker horizontal and vertical lines.

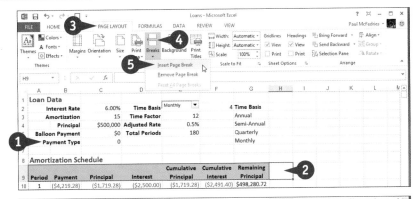

Choose a Paper Size

You can customize your print job by choosing a paper size that is appropriate for your printout. For example, if your worksheet has many rows, you might prefer to print it on a longer sheet of paper, such as a legal-size page (8½ inches wide by 14 inches long). Similarly, if your worksheet has many columns, you might also want to use a longer sheet of paper, but switch to landscape mode, as described in "Change the Page Orientation," earlier in this chapter.

Check your printer manual to make sure your printer can handle the paper size you select.

Choose a Paper Size

1 Open the workbook you want to print.

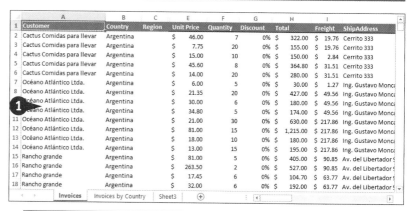

2 Click the **Page Layout** tab.

3 Click **Size** (□).

Ⓐ If you see a page size you want to use, click the size and skip the rest of these steps.

4 Click **More Paper Sizes**.

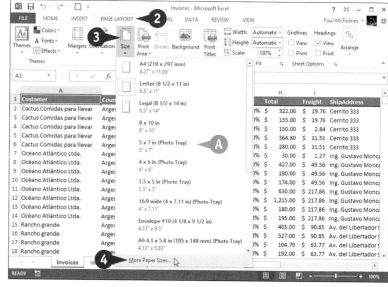

The Page Setup dialog box appears with the Page tab selected.

5 Click the **Paper size** ⌄ and then click the size you want to use.

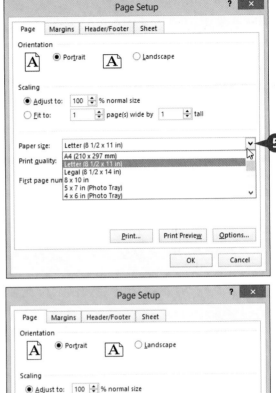

6 Click **OK**.

Excel uses the new paper size option when you print the workbook.

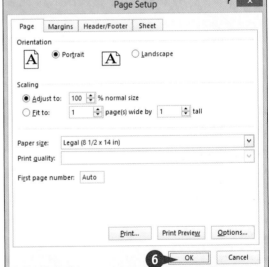

Is there a way to ensure that all my worksheet columns fit onto a single page?
Yes. First, try selecting a wider page size as described in this section. You can also try reducing the left and right margins, as described in "Adjust the Workbook Margins," earlier in this chapter. Alternatively, switch to the landscape orientation, as described in "Change the Page Orientation," earlier in this chapter.

You can also follow Steps **1** to **4** to display the Page Setup dialog box with the Page tab selected. Click **Fit to** (○ changes to ◉), and set the **page(s) wide by** spin box to 1. Set the **tall** spin box to a number large enough that all of your printed rows will fit on a single page. (If you are not sure about the correct number, you can click **Print Preview** to check.) Click **OK**.

Set the Print Area

You can control the cells that Excel includes in the printout by setting the print area for the worksheet. The print area is a range of cells that you select. When Excel prints the workbook, it only prints the cells within the print area.

You normally define a single range of cells as the print area, but it is possible to set up two or more ranges as the print area. See the first Tip at the end of this section for more information.

Set the Print Area

1 Open the workbook you want to print.

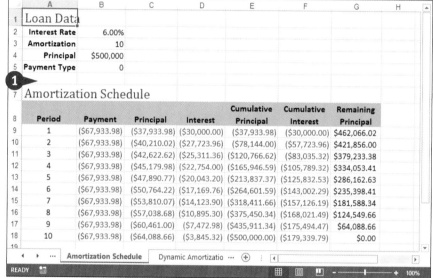

2 Select the range that you want to print.

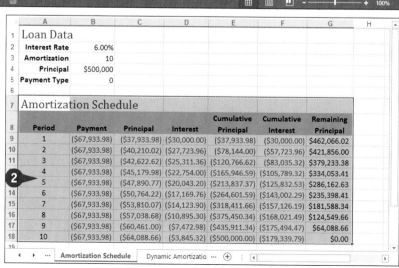

3 Click the **Page Layout** tab.

4 Click **Print Area** (📇).

5 Click **Set Print Area**.

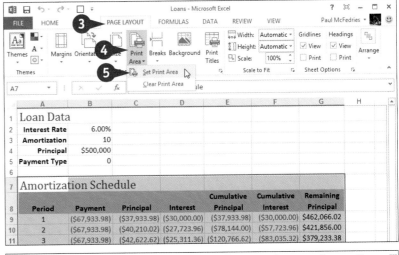

A Excel displays a border around the print area.

When you print the worksheet, Excel prints only the cells within the print area.

Can I define two different ranges as the print area?

Yes. The easiest way to do this is to follow the steps in this section to set the first range as the print area. Next, select the second range, click the **Page Layout** tab, click 📇, and then click **Add to Print Area**. You can repeat this procedure to add as many ranges as you require to the print area.

How do I remove an existing print area?

First, note that if you just want to set a new print area, you do not need to remove the existing print area first. Instead, select the range you want to use and then follow Steps **3** to **5**. Excel replaces the original print area with the new one. If you no longer want a print area defined, click the **Page Layout** tab, click 📇, and then click **Clear Print Area**.

Configure Titles to Print on Each Page

You can make your printout easier to read by configuring the worksheet to print the range titles on each page of the printout. For example, if your data has a row of headings at the top, you can configure the worksheet to display those headings at the top of each printout page.

Similarly, if your data has a column of headings at the left, you can configure the worksheet to display those headings on the left side of each printout page.

Configure Titles to Print on Each Page

1 Open the workbook you want to print.

2 Click the tab of the worksheet you want to configure.

3 Click the **Page Layout** tab.

4 Click **Print Titles** ( ).

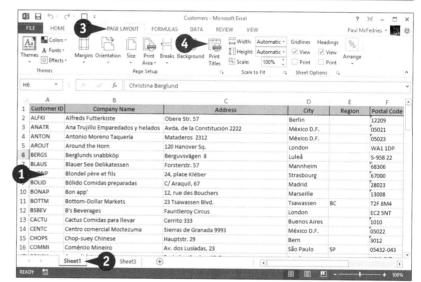

Excel opens the Page Setup dialog box with the Sheet tab displayed.

5 Click inside the **Rows to repeat at top** range box.

6 Click **Collapse Dialog** ( ).

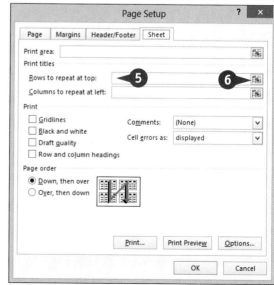

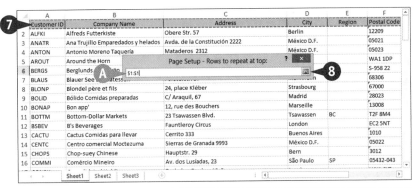

A Excel collapses the Page Setup dialog box.

The mouse pointer changes from ⬚ to ➡.

7 Use the Excel mouse pointer row select (➡) to click the row that you want to appear at the top of each printed page.

If you want more than one row to repeat at the top of each page, use the mouse ➡ to click the last row that you want to repeat.

8 Click **Restore Dialog** (▦).

B The address of the row appears in the **Rows to repeat at top** box.

9 Click **OK**.

When you print this worksheet, Excel displays the selected row at the top of each page.

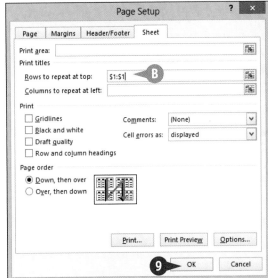

TIP

How do I configure my worksheet to print a column of headings on each page?

If your headings appear in a column rather than a row, you can still configure the sheet to print them on each page. Follow these steps:

1 Follow Steps **1** to **4** to open the Page Setup dialog box with the Sheet tab displayed.

2 Click inside the **Columns to repeat at left** range box.

3 Click ▦.

4 Use the Excel mouse pointer column select (⬇) to click the column that you want to appear on the left of each printed page.

5 Click ▦.

6 Click **OK**.

Preview the Printout

You can save time and paper by using the Print Preview feature to examine your printout on-screen before you send it to the printer. You can use Print Preview to make sure settings such as margins, page orientation, page breaks, print areas, and sheet titles all result in the printout you want.

If you see a problem in the preview, you can use the Print Preview screen to make adjustments to some printout options.

Preview the Printout

1 Open the workbook you want to print.

2 Click the tab of the worksheet you want to preview.

3 Click the **File** tab.

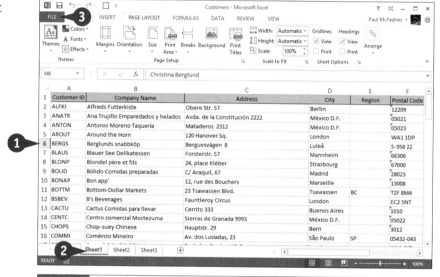

4 Click **Print**.

The Print window appears.

Ⓐ Excel displays a preview of the printout.

Note: If you do not see the preview, click **Show Print Preview**.

5 Click **Print Preview Next Page** (▶) to scroll through the printout pages.

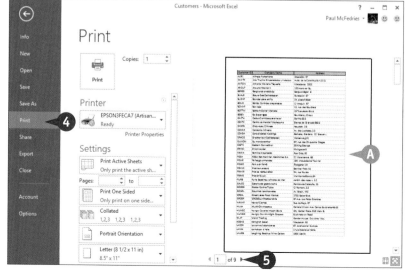

6 Click **Print Preview Previous Page** (◀) to return to a printout page.

B You can click the **Page Orientation** ▼ to change the page orientation.

C You can click the **Page Size** ▼ to change the page size.

D You can click the **Margins** ▼ to change the margins.

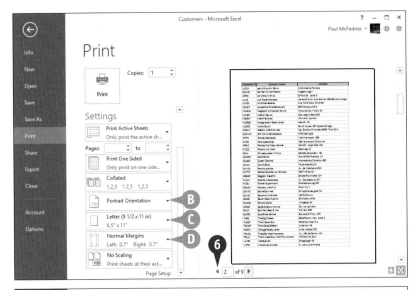

7 When you are done, click **Back** (⊙) to return to the workbook.

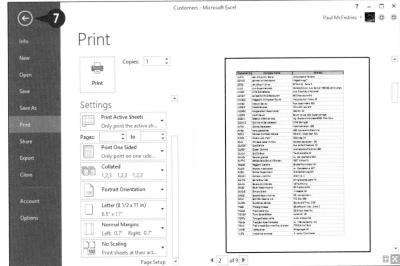

TIP

Can I fine-tune the margins in Print Preview?

Yes. The **Margins** list only offers a few predefined margin sets. To define custom margins in Print Preview, follow these steps:

1 Click **Show Margins** (▢).

A Print Preview augments the preview with lines that indicate the margins.

2 Click and drag a line to adjust that margin.

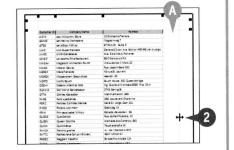

Print a Workbook

When you need a hard copy of your document, either for your files or to distribute to someone else, you can send the document to your printer.

This section assumes that you have a printer connected to your computer and that the printer is turned on. Also, before printing you should check that your printer has enough paper to complete the print job.

Print a Workbook

1 Open the workbook you want to print.

2 If you only want to print a single worksheet, click the tab of that worksheet.

Note: To print multiple worksheets, hold down **Ctrl** and click the top of each sheet you want to print.

3 Click the **File** tab.

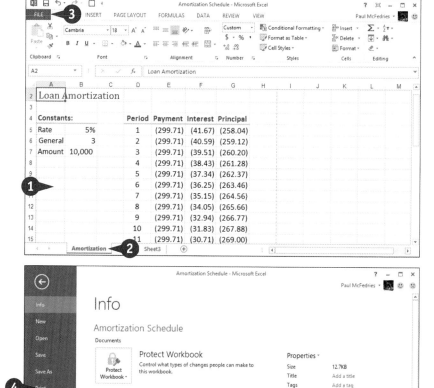

4 Click **Print**.

Note: You can also press **Ctrl** + **P** .

The Print window appears.

5 Select the number of copies you want to print using the spin box.

Ⓐ If you have more than one printer, click the **Printer** ▼ and then click the printer that you want to use.

Ⓑ By default, Print Active Sheets appears in the Settings list, which tells Excel to print only the selected sheets. If you want to print all the sheets in the workbook, click the **Print What** ▼ and then click **Print Entire Workbook**.

6 Click **Print**.

Excel prints the document.

Ⓒ The printer icon (🖨) appears in the taskbar's notification area while the document prints.

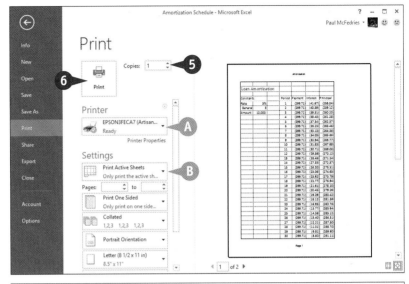

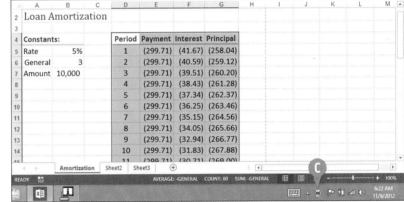

TIPS

Is there a faster way to print?

Yes. If you only want to print a single copy of the selected worksheet, you can use the Excel Quick Print command to send the worksheet directly to your default printer. Click ▾ in the Quick Access Toolbar, and then click **Quick Print** to add this command to the toolbar. You can then click **Quick Print** (🖨) to print the current worksheet without having to go through the Print window.

Can I print just part of a worksheet?

Yes, you can tell Excel to print just a range. Begin by selecting the range or ranges you want to print. (See Chapter 3 to learn how to select a range.) Follow Steps **3** and **4** to open the Print window and choose the number of copies. Click the **Print What** ▼ and then click **Print Selection**. Click **Print**.

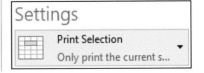

CHAPTER 11

Working with Tables

The forte of Excel is spreadsheet work, of course, but its row-and-column layout also makes it a natural flat-file database manager. That is, instead of entering data and then using the Excel tools to build formulas and analyze that data, you can also use Excel simply to store data in a special structure called a table.

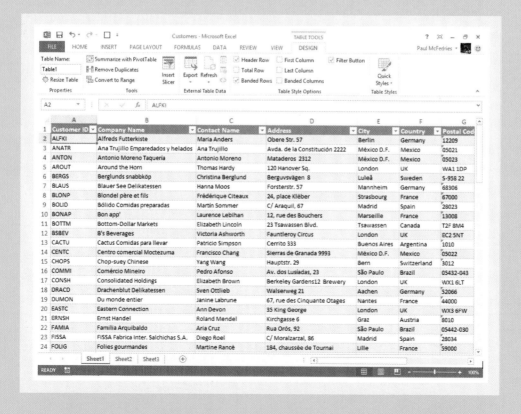

Understanding Tables

In Excel, a *table* is a rectangular range of cells used to store data. The table is a collection of related information with an organizational structure that makes it easy to find or extract data from its contents.

To get the most out of Excel tables, you need to understand a few basic concepts, such as how a table is like a database, the advantages of tables, and how tables help with data analysis.

A Table Is a Database

A table is a type of database where the data is organized into rows and columns: Each column represents a database field, which is a single type of information, such as a name, address, or phone number; each row represents a database record, which is a collection of associated field values, such as the information for a specific contact.

Advantages of a Table

A table differs from a regular Excel range in that Excel offers a set of tools that makes it easier for you to work with the data within a table. As you see in this chapter, these tools make it easy to convert existing worksheet data into a table, add new records and fields to a table, delete existing records and fields, insert rows to show totals, and apply styles.

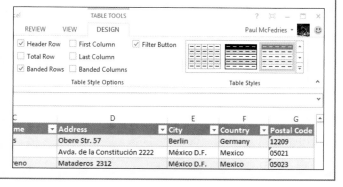

Data Analysis

Tables are also useful tools for analyzing your data. For example, as you see in "Create a PivotTable," later in this chapter, you can easily use a table as the basis of a PivotTable, which is a special object for summarizing and analyzing data. In Chapter 12 you also learn how to sort table records and how to filter table data to show only specific records.

Get to Know Table Features

Although a table looks much like a regular Excel range, it offers a number of features that differentiate it from a range. To understand these differences and make it as easy as possible to learn how to build and use tables, you need to know the various features in a typical table, such as the table rows and columns, the table headers, and the filter buttons.

Ⓐ Table Column

A single type of information, such as names, addresses, or phone numbers. In an Excel table, each column is the equivalent of a database field.

Ⓑ Column Headers

The unique names you assign to every table column that serve to label the type of data in each column. These names are always found in the first row of the table.

Ⓒ Table Cell

An item in a table column that represents a single instance of that column's data, such as a name, address, or phone number. In an Excel table, each cell is equivalent to a database field value.

Ⓓ Table Row

A collection of associated table cells, such as the data for a single contact. In Excel tables, each row is the equivalent of a database record.

Ⓔ Column Filter Button

A feature that gives you access to a set of commands that perform various actions on a column, such as sorting or filtering the column data.

	C	D	E	F	G	H	I
1	Contact N	Address	City	Country	Postal Code	Contact Title	Phone
2	Maria Anders	Obere Str. 57	Berlin	Germany	12209	Sales Representative	030-0074321
3	Ana Trujillo	Avda. de la Constitución 2222	México D.F.	Mexico	05021	Owner	(5) 555-4729
4	Antonio Moreno	Mataderos 2312	México D.F.	Mexico	05023	Owner	(5) 555-3932
5	Thomas Hardy	120 Hanover Sq.	London	UK	WA1 1DP	Sales Representative	(171) 555-7788
6	Christina Berglund	Berguvsvägen 8	Luleå	Sweden	S-958 22	Order Administrator	0921-12 34 65
7	Hanna Moos	Forsterstr. 57	Mannheim	Germany	68306	Sales Representative	0621-08460
8	Frédérique Citeaux	24, place Kléber	Strasbourg	France	67000	Marketing Manager	88.60.15.31
9	Martín Sommer	C/ Araquil, 67	Madrid	Spain	28023	Owner	(91) 555 22 82
10	Laurence Lebihan	12, rue des Bouchers	Marseille	France	13008	Owner	91.24.45.40
11	Elizabeth Lincoln	23 Tsawassen Blvd.	ssen	Canada	T2F 8M4	Accounting Manager	(604) 555-4729
12	Victoria Ashworth	Fauntleroy Circus	London	UK	EC2 5NT	Sales Representative	(171) 555-1212
13	Patricio Simpson	Cerrito 333	Buenos Aires	Argentina	1010	Sales Agent	(1) 135-5555
14	Francisco Chang	Sierras de Granada 9993	México D.F.	Mexico	05022	Marketing Manager	(5) 555-3392
15	Yang Wang	Hauptstr. 29	Bern	Switzerland	3012	Owner	0452-076545
16	Pedro Afonso	Av. dos Lusíadas, 23	São Paulo	Brazil	05432-043	Sales Associate	(11) 555-7647
17	Elizabeth Brown	Berkeley Gardens12 Brewery	London	UK	WX1 6LT	Sales Representative	(171) 555-2282
18	Sven Ottlieb	Walserweg 21	Aachen	Germany	52066	Order Administrator	0241-039123

Sheet1 Sheet2 Sheet3 ⊕

Convert a Range to a Table

In Excel 2013, you cannot create a table from scratch and then fill that table with data. Instead, you must first create a range that includes at least some of the data you want in your table and then convert that range to a table.

Note that you do not need to enter all of your data before converting the range to a table. Once you have the table, you can add new rows and columns as needed, as described later in this chapter. However, it is best to decide up front whether you want your table to have column headers.

Convert a Range to a Table

1 Click a cell within the range that you want to convert to a table.

2 Click the **Insert** tab.

3 Click **Table** ( ).

Note: You can also choose the Table command by pressing Ctrl + T .

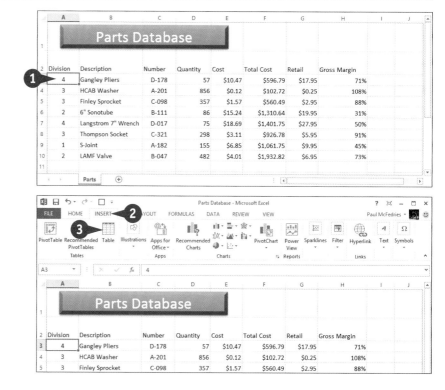

The Create Table dialog box appears.

Ⓐ Excel selects the range that it will convert to a table.

Ⓑ If you want to change the range, click 🔣, drag the Excel mouse pointer (✛) over the new range, and then click 🔣.

④ If your range has labels that you want to use as column headers, click **My table has headers** (☐ changes to ☑).

⑤ Click **OK**.

Excel converts the range to a table.

Ⓒ Excel applies a table format to the range.

Ⓓ The Table Tools contextual tab appears.

Ⓔ Filter buttons appear in each column heading.

⑥ Click the **Design** tab to see the Excel table design tools.

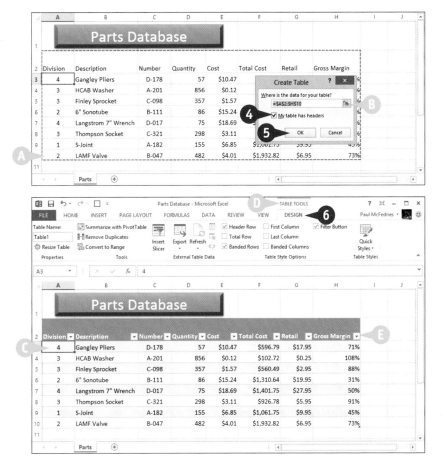

TIPS

Do I need to add labels to the top of each column before converting my range to a table?

No, you do not need to add labels before performing the conversion. In this case, follow Steps **1** to **3** to display the Create Table dialog box, then click **My table has headers** (☑ changes to ☐). After you click **OK**, Excel converts the range to a table and automatically adds headers to each column. These headers use the generic names Column1, Column2, and so on.

If I selected the wrong range for my table, is there a way to tell Excel the correct range?

Yes, although you cannot change the location of the headers. To redefine the range used in the table, first select any cell in the table. Under the Table Tools contextual tab, click the **Design** tab and then click **Resize Table** (⊕) to open the Resize Table dialog box. Drag the mouse ✛ over the new range and then click **OK**.

Select Table Data

If you want to work with part of a table, you first need to select that part of the table. For example, if you want to apply a format to an entire column or copy an entire row, you first need to select that column or row.

The normal range-selection techniques in Excel often do not work well with a table. For example, selecting an entire worksheet column or row does not work because no table uses up an entire worksheet column or row. Instead, Excel provides several tools for selecting a table column (just the data or the data and the header), a table row, or the entire table.

Select Table Data

Select a Table Column

1. Click any cell in the column you want to select.

2. Right-click the selected cell.

3. Click **Select**.

4. Click **Table Column Data**.

   Excel selects all the column's data cells.

Select a Table Column and Header

1. Click any cell in the column you want to select.

2. Right-click the selected cell.

3. Click **Select**.

4. Click **Entire Table Column**.

   Excel selects the column's data and header.

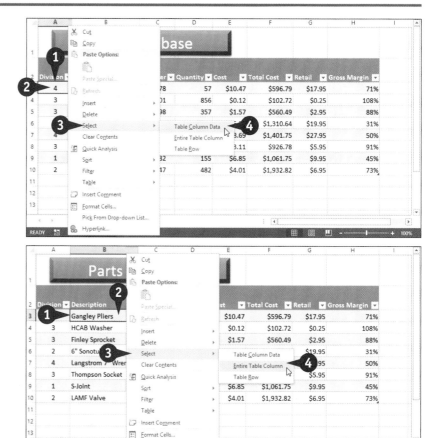

Select a Table Row

1 Click any cell in the row you want to select.

2 Right-click the selected cell.

3 Click **Select**.

4 Click **Table Row**.

Excel selects all the data within the row.

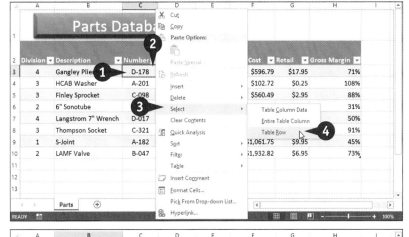

Select the Entire Table

1 Click any cell within the table.

2 Press Ctrl + A.

Excel selects the entire table.

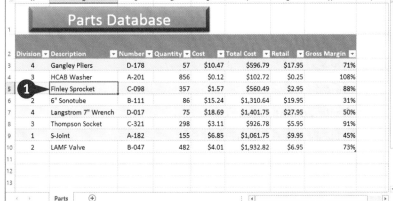

TIP

Can I select multiple columns or rows in a table?

Yes. To select two or more table columns, first select one cell in each of the columns that you want to include in your selection. If the columns are not side-by-side, click the first cell and then hold down Ctrl as you click each of the other cells. Right-click any selected cell, click **Select**, and then click **Table Column Data** (or **Entire Table Column** if you also want to include the column headers in the selection).

To select two or more table rows, first select one cell in each of the rows that you want to include in your selection. Again, if the rows are not adjacent, click the first cell and then hold down Ctrl as you click each of the other cells. Right-click any selected cell, click **Select**, and then click **Table Row**.

Insert a Table Row

You can add a new record to your Excel table by inserting a new row. You can insert a row either within the table or at the end of the table.

Once you have entered the initial set of data into your table, you will likely add most new records within the table by inserting a new row above a current row. However, when you are in the initial data entry phase, you will most likely prefer to add new records by adding a row to the end of the table.

Insert a Table Row

1 Select a cell in the row below which you want to insert the new row.

2 Click the **Home** tab.

3 Click **Insert** (插入图标).

4 Click **Insert Table Rows Above**.

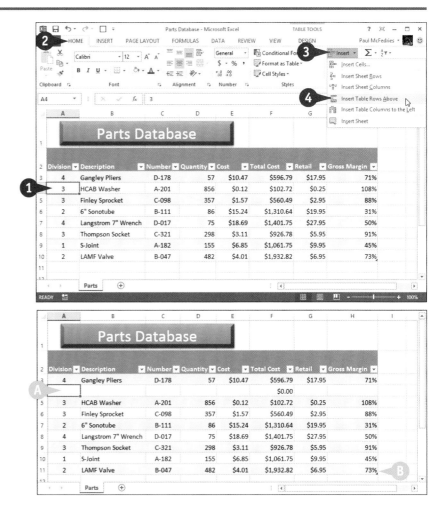

A Excel inserts the new row.

B To insert a new row at the end of the table, select the lower-right table cell and then press Tab.

Insert a Table Column

You can add a new field to your Excel table by inserting a new column. You can insert a column either within the table or at the end of the table.

To make data entry easier and more efficient, you should decide in advance all the fields you want to include in the table. However, if later on you realize you forgot a particular field, you can still add it to the table. Inserting a table column is also useful if you imported or inherited the data from elsewhere and you see that the data is missing a field that you require.

Insert a Table Column

1 Select a cell in the column to the left of which you want to insert the new column.

A If you want to insert the new column at end of the table, select a cell in the last table column.

2 Click the **Home** tab.

3 Click **Insert** ( ).

4 Click **Insert Table Columns to the Left**.

To insert a column at the end of the table instead, click **Insert Table Columns to the Right** (not shown).

B Excel inserts the new column.

5 Name the new field by editing the column header.

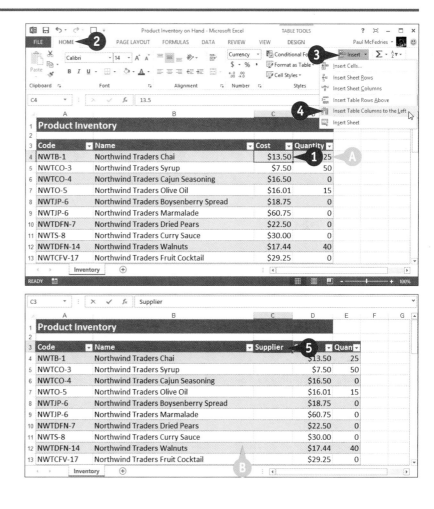

Delete a Table Row

If your table contains a record that includes inaccurate, outdated, or unnecessary data, you should delete that row to preserve your table's data integrity.

An Excel table is a repository of data that you can use as a reference source or to analyze or summarize the data. However you use the table, it is only as beneficial as its data is accurate, so you should take extra care to ensure the data you enter is correct. If you find that an entire record is inaccurate or no longer needed, Excel enables you to quickly delete that row.

Delete a Table Row

1 Select a cell in the row you want to delete.

Note: To delete multiple rows, select a cell in each row you want to delete.

2 Click the **Home** tab.

3 Click **Delete** (⌦).

4 Click **Delete Table Rows**.

A Excel deletes the row.

Delete a Table Column

I f your table contains a field that you do not require, you should delete that column to make your table easier to work with and manage.

As you see later in this chapter and in Chapter 12, you analyze and summarize your table information based on the data in one or more fields. If your table contains a field that you never look at and that you never use for analysis or summaries, consider deleting that column to reduce table clutter and make your table easier to navigate.

Delete a Table Column

1 Select a cell in the column you want to delete.

Note: To delete multiple columns, select a cell in each column you want to delete.

2 Click the **Home** tab.

3 Click **Delete** (⅗).

4 Click **Delete Table Columns**.

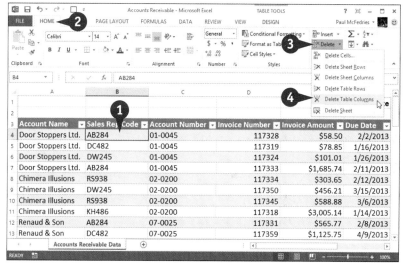

Ⓐ Excel deletes the column.

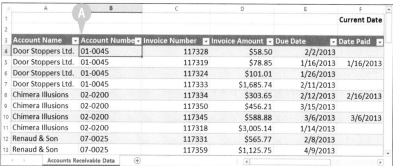

Add a Column Subtotal

You can get more out of your table data by summarizing a field with a subtotal that appears at the bottom of the column.

Although the word *subtotal* implies that you are summing the numeric values in a column, Excel uses the term more broadly. That is, a subtotal can be not only a numeric sum, but also an average, a maximum or minimum, or a count of the values in the field. You can also choose more esoteric subtotals such as a standard deviation or a variance.

Add a Column Subtotal

1 Select all the data in the column you want to total.

Note: See "Select Table Data," earlier in this chapter, to learn how to select column data.

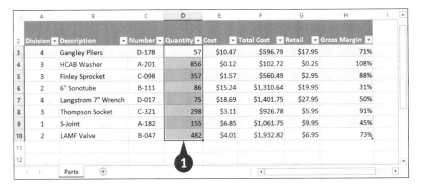

2 Click the **Quick Analysis** smart tag (🖻).

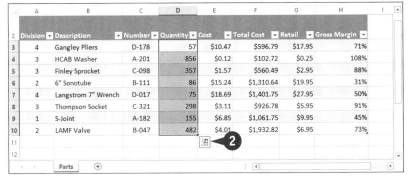

The Quick Analysis options appear.

3 Click **Totals**.

4 Click the type of calculation you want to use.

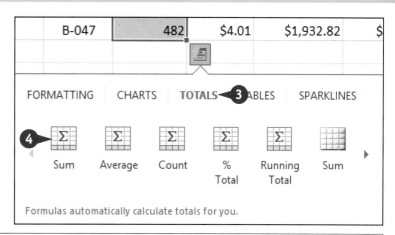

🅰 Excel adds a Total row to the bottom of the table.

🅱 Excel inserts a SUBTOTAL function to perform the calculation you chose in Step **4**.

🅲 Click the cell's ☑ to choose a different type of subtotal.

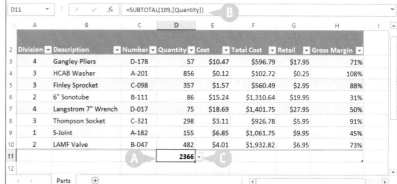

TIP

Is there a quick way to insert a total row in my table?

Yes. If the column you want to total is the last column in the table, you can add the total row and include a SUBTOTAL function for that column with just a few mouse clicks:

1 Click any cell within the table.

2 Click the **Design** tab.

3 Click the **Total Row** check box (☐ changes to ☑).

🅰 Excel automatically inserts a row named Total at the bottom of the table.

🅱 Excel adds a SUBTOTAL function below the last column.

4 Click the cell's ☑ and then click the type of subtotal you want to use.

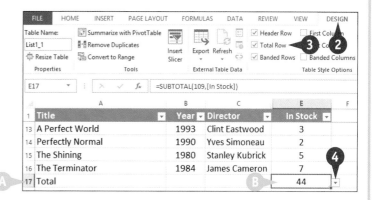

Convert a Table to a Range

I f you no longer require the Excel table tools, you can convert a table to a normal range.

Tables are extremely useful Excel features but they can occasionally be bothersome. For example, if you click a table cell, click the Design tab, and then click a cell outside the table, Excel automatically switches to the Home tab. If you then click a table cell again, Excel automatically switches back to the Design tab. If you are not using the table features in the Design tab, this behavior can be annoying, but you can prevent it from happening by converting the table to a normal range.

Convert a Table to a Range

1 Click a cell inside the table.

2 Click the **Design** tab.

3 Click **Convert to Range** (🔳).

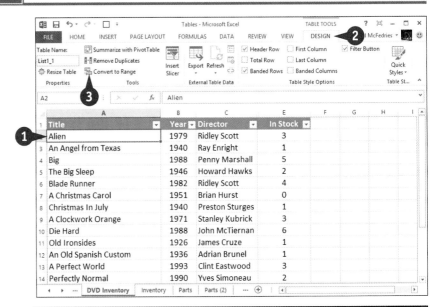

Excel asks you to confirm.

4 Click **Yes**.

Excel converts the table to a normal range.

Apply a Table Style

You can give an Excel table more visual appeal and make it easier to read by applying a table style.

A table style is a combination of formatting options that Excel applies to 13 different table elements, including the first and last column, the header row, the total row, and the entire table. For each element, Excel applies one or more of the following formatting options: the font, including the typeface, style, size, color, and text effects; the border; and the background color and fill effects.

Apply a Table Style

1 Click a cell inside the table.

2 Click the **Design** tab.

3 Click the **Table Styles** ▼ .

The Table Styles gallery appears.

4 Click the table style you want to use.

Ⓐ Excel applies the style to the table.

Build a Custom Table Style

You can make it easier to format tables the way you prefer by creating a custom table style.

Excel comes with dozens of predefined table styles, all of which vary with the document theme. If none of the predefined table styles is right for your needs, you can use the Format Cells dialog box to apply your own formatting to the various table elements. If you want to reuse this formatting in other workbooks, you can save the formatting options as a custom table style.

Build a Custom Table Style

1 Click a cell inside the table.

2 Click the **Design** tab.

3 Click the **Table Styles** ▼ (not shown).

Ⓐ The Table Styles gallery appears.

4 Click **New Table Style**.

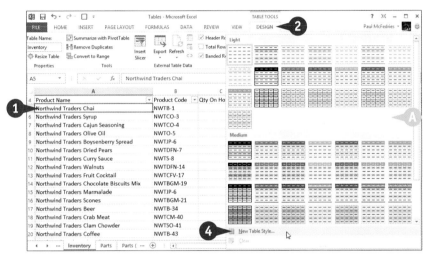

The New Table Style dialog box appears.

5 Type a name for the style.

6 Click the table element you want to format.

7 Click **Format**.

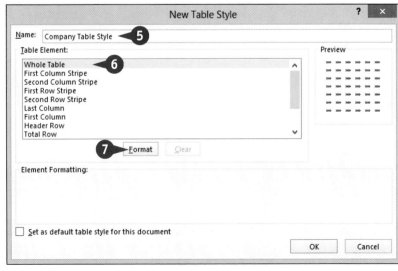

The Format Cells dialog box appears.

8 Use the tabs to select the formatting options you want in your cell style.

Note: Depending on the table element you are working with, some of the formatting options may be disabled.

9 Click **OK**.

10 Repeat Steps **5** to **8** to set the formatting for the other table elements, as needed.

11 Click **OK** in the New Table Style dialog box (not shown).

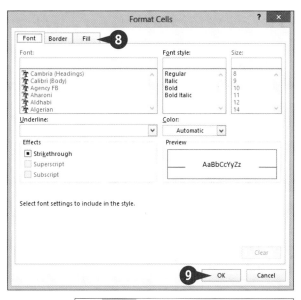

12 Click the **Table Styles** (not shown).

B Your table style appears in the Custom section of the Table Styles gallery.

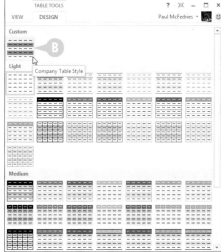

Is there an easy way to use the custom style for all the tables I create?

Yes. If you want to use your custom table style for all or most of the tables you create, you should set the custom style as the default. When you are creating a new custom table style, follow Steps **1** to **10** and then click to select the **Set as default table style for this document** check box (☐ changes to ☑). For an existing custom table style, click a table cell, click the **Design** tab, click the **Table Styles** , right-click the custom style, and then click **Set As Default**.

How do I make changes to a custom table style?

To change the formatting for a custom table style, click a table cell, click the **Design** tab, and then click the **Table Styles** to display the Table Styles gallery. Right-click the custom style, click **Modify**, and then follow Steps **6** to **11**.

Create a PivotTable

You can more easily analyze a large amount of data by creating a PivotTable from that data. A PivotTable is a powerful data analysis tool because it automatically groups large amounts of data into smaller, more manageable categories, and it displays summary calculations for each group.

You can also manipulate the layout of — or *pivot* — the PivotTable to see different views of your data. Although you can create a PivotTable from a normal range, for best results, you should convert your range to a table before creating the PivotTable (see "Convert a Range to a Table," earlier in this chapter).

Create a PivotTable

1 Click a cell within the table that you want to use as the source data.

2 Click the **Design** tab.

3 Click **Summarize with PivotTable** (⊞).

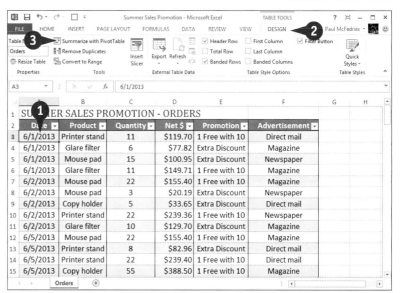

The Create PivotTable dialog box appears.

4 Click **New Worksheet** (○ changes to ◉).

A If you want to place the PivotTable in an existing location, click **Existing Worksheet** (○ changes to ◉) and then use the **Location** range box to select the worksheet and cell where you want the PivotTable to appear.

5 Click **OK**.

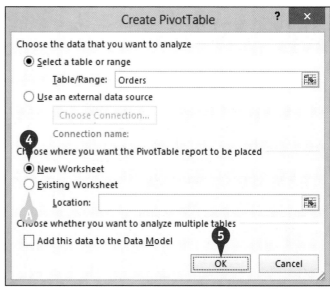

Ⓑ Excel creates a blank PivotTable.

Ⓒ Excel displays the PivotTable Fields List.

6 Click and drag a field and drop it inside the ROWS area.

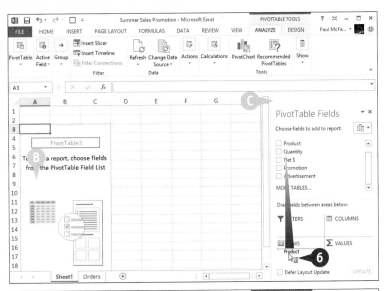

Ⓓ Excel adds the field's unique values to the PivotTable's row area.

7 Click and drag a numeric field and drop it inside the VALUES area.

Ⓔ Excel sums the numeric values based on the row values.

8 If desired, click and drag fields and drop them in the COLUMNS area and the FILTERS area.

Each time you drop a field in an area, Excel updates the PivotTable to include the new data.

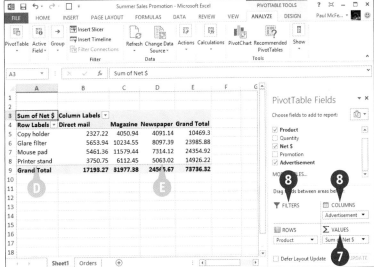

Are there faster ways to build a PivotTable?
Yes. In the PivotTable Fields list, if you click a check box for a text or date field (☐ changes to ☑), Excel adds the field to the ROWS area; if you click a check box for a numeric field (○ changes to ⦿), Excel adds the field to the VALUES area. You can also right-click a field and then click the area you want to use.

Can I add multiple fields to each area?
Yes. You can add as many fields as you like to each area. You can also move a PivotTable's fields from one area of the PivotTable to another. This enables you to view your data from different perspectives, which can greatly enhance the analysis of the data. Moving a field within a PivotTable is called *pivoting* the data. To move a field, use the PivotTable Fields list to click and drag a field from one area and drop it on another.

CHAPTER 12

Analyzing Data

You can get more out of Excel by performing *data analysis*, which is the application of tools and techniques to organize, study, and reach conclusions about a specific collection of information. In this chapter you learn data analysis techniques such as sorting and filtering a range, setting validation rules, and using subtotals and scenarios.

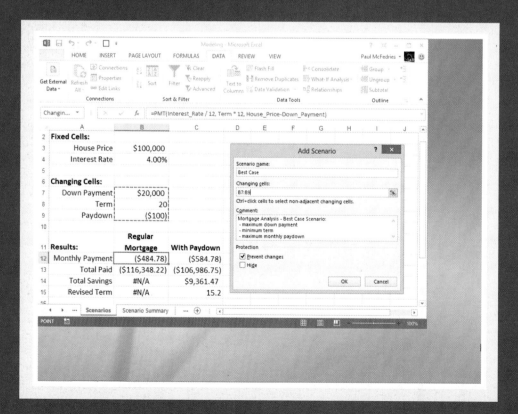

Sort a Range or Table

You can make a range easier to read and analyze by sorting the data based on the values in one or more columns.

You can sort the data in either ascending or descending order. An ascending sort arranges the values alphabetically from A to Z, or numerically from 0 to 9; a descending sort arranges the values alphabetically from Z to A, or numerically from 9 to 0.

Sort a Range or Table

1. Click any cell in the range you want to sort.
2. Click the **Data** tab.
3. Click **Sort** (⇌).

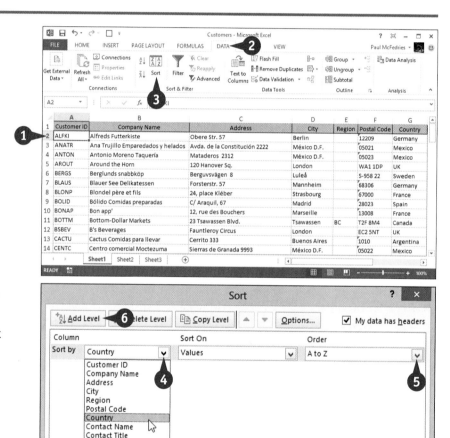

The Sort dialog box appears.

4. Click the **Sort by** ☑ and then click the field you want to use for the main sort level.
5. Click the **Order** ☑ and then click a sort order for the field.
6. To sort on another field, click **Add Level**.

A Excel adds another sort level.

7 Click the **Then by** ⌄ and then click the field you want to use for the sort level.

8 Click the **Order** ⌄ and then click a sort order for the field.

9 Repeat Steps **6** to **8** to add more sort levels as needed.

10 Click **OK**.

B Excel sorts the range.

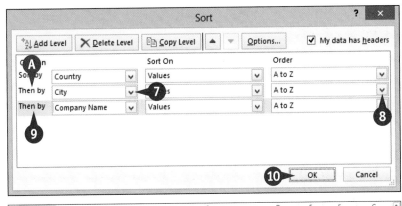

TIPS

Is there a faster way to sort a range?

Yes, as long as you only need to sort your range on a single column. First, click in any cell inside the column you want to use for the sort. Click the **Data** tab and then click one of the following buttons in the Sort & Filter group:

⌄Z↓	Click for an ascending sort.
Z↓A	Click for a descending sort.

How do I sort a range using the values in a row instead of a column?

Excel normally sorts a range from top to bottom based on the values in one or more columns. However, you can tell Excel to sort the range from left to right based on the values in one or more rows. Follow Steps **1** to **3** to display the Sort dialog box. Click **Options** to display the Sort Options dialog box, select the **Sort left to right** option (○ changes to ◉), and then click **OK**.

Filter a Range or Table

You can analyze table data much faster by only viewing those table records that you want to work with. In Excel, this is called *filtering* a range.

The easiest way to filter a range is to use the Filter buttons, each of which presents you with a list of check boxes for each unique value in a column. You filter the data by activating the check boxes for the rows you want to see. If you have converted the range to a table, as described in Chapter 11, the Filter buttons for each column are displayed automatically.

Filter a Range or Table

Display the Filter Buttons

Note: If you are filtering a table, you can skip directly to the "Filter the Data" subsection.

1 Click inside the range.

2 Click the **Data** tab.

3 Click **Filter** (▼).

Ⓐ Excel adds a Filter button (▼) to each field.

Filter the Data

1 Click ▼ for the field you want to use as the filter.

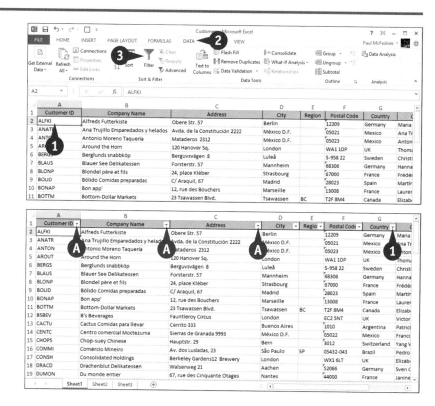

B Excel displays a list of the unique values in the field.

2 Click the check box for each value you want to see (☐ changes to ☑).

C You can toggle all the check boxes on and off by clicking **Select All**.

3 Click **OK**.

D Excel filters the table to show only those records that have the field values you selected.

E Excel displays the number of records found.

F The field's drop-down list displays a filter icon (▼).

To remove the filter, click the **Data** tab and then click **Clear** (✖; not shown).

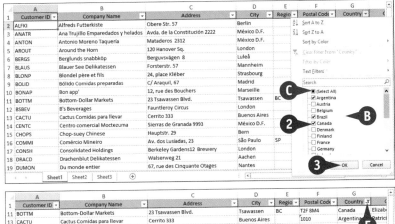

TIP

Can I create more sophisticated filters?

Yes, by using a second technique called *quick filters*, which enables you to specify criteria for a field:

1 Click ▼ for the field you want to use as the filter.

2 Click **Number Filters**.

Note: If the field is a date field, click **Date Filters**; if the field is a text field, click **Text Filters**.

3 Click the filter you want to use.

4 Enter the value you want to use.

5 Click **OK**.

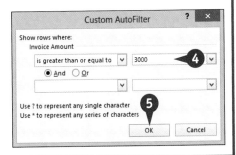

Set Data Validation Rules

You can make Excel data entry more efficient by setting up data entry cells to accept only certain values. To do this, you can set up a cell with data validation criteria that specify the allowed value or values. This is called a *data validation rule*.

Excel also lets you tell the user what to enter by defining an input message that appears when the user selects the cell. You can also configure the data validation rule to display a message when the user tries to enter an invalid value.

Set Data Validation Rules

1 Click the cell you want to restrict.

2 Click the **Data** tab.

3 Click **Data Validation** ( ).

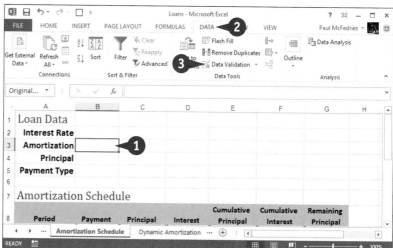

The Data Validation dialog box appears.

4 Click the **Settings** tab.

5 In the **Allow** list, click and select the type of data you want to allow in the cell.

6 In the **Data** list, click and select the operator you want to use to define the allowable data.

7 Specify the validation criteria, such as the **Maximum** and **Minimum** allowable values shown here.

Note: The criteria boxes you see depend on the operator you chose in Step **6**.

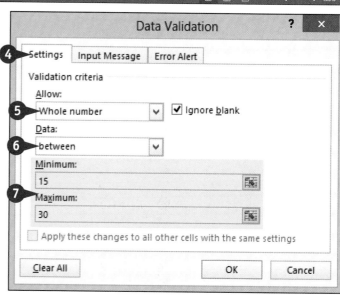

8 Click the **Input Message** tab.

9 Make sure the **Show input message when cell is selected** check box is clicked (☑).

10 Type a message title in the **Title** text box.

11 Type the message you want to display in the **Input message** text box.

12 Click **OK**.

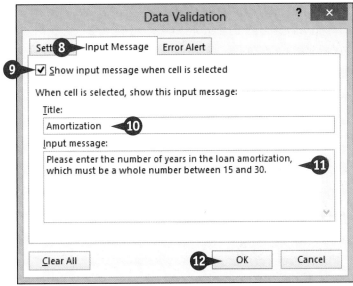

Excel configures the cell to accept only values that meet your criteria.

Ⓐ When the user selects the cell, the input message appears.

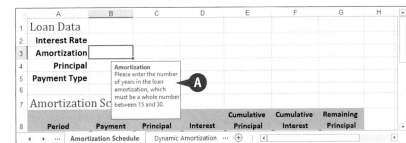

Can I configure the cell to display a message if the user tries to enter an invalid value?
Yes. Follow Steps **1** to **3** to open the Data Validation dialog box, and then click the **Error Alert** tab. Make sure the **Show error alert after invalid data is entered** check box is clicked (☑), and then specify the **Style**, **Title**, and **Error Message**. Click **OK**.

How do I remove data validation from a cell?
If you no longer need to use data validation on a cell, you should clear the settings. Follow Steps **1** to **3** to display the Data Validation dialog box and then click **Clear All**. Excel removes all the validation criteria, as well as the input message and the error alert. Click **OK**.

Create a Data Table

If you are interested in studying the effect a range of values has on the formula, you can set up a *data table*. This is a table that consists of the formula you are using, and multiple input values for that formula. Excel automatically creates a solution to the formula for each different input value.

Do not confuse data tables with the Excel tables that you learned about in Chapter 11. A data table is a special range that Excel uses to calculate multiple solutions to a formula.

Create a Data Table

1 Type the input values:

To enter the values in a column, start the column one cell down and one cell to the left of the cell containing the formula, as shown here.

To enter the values in a row, start the row one cell up and one cell to the right of the cell containing the formula.

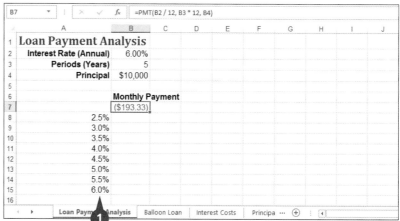

2 Select the range that includes the input values and the formula.

3 Click the **Data** tab.

4 Click **What-If Analysis** (⊞).

5 Click **Data Table**.

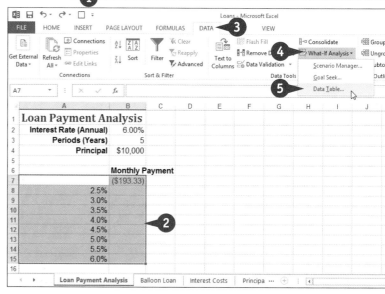

246

The Data Table dialog box appears.

6 Specify the formula cell you want to use as the data table's input cell:

If the input values are in a column, enter the input cell's address in the **Column input cell** text box.

If you entered the input values in a row, enter the input cell's address in the **Row input cell** text box.

7 Click **OK**.

A Excel displays the results.

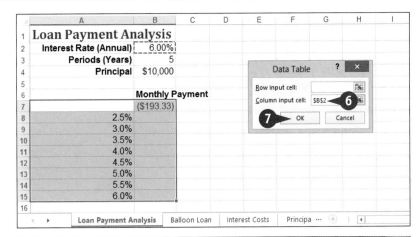

TIPS

What is what-if analysis?
The technique called *what-if analysis* is perhaps the most basic method for analyzing worksheet data. With what-if analysis, you first calculate a formula D, based on the input from variables A, B, and C. You then say, "What happens to the result if I change the value of variable A?", "What happens if I change B or C?", and so on.

When I try to delete part of the data table, I get an error. Why?
The data table results are created as an *array formula*, which is a special formula that Excel treats as a unit. This means that you cannot move or delete part of the results. If you need to work with the data table results, you must first select the entire results range.

Summarize Data with Subtotals

Although you can use formulas and worksheet functions to summarize your data in various ways, including sums, averages, counts, maximums, and minimums, if you are in a hurry, or if you just need a quick summary of your data, you can get Excel to do most of the work for you. The secret here is a feature called *automatic subtotals*, which are formulas that Excel adds to a worksheet automatically.

Summarize Data with Subtotals

1 Click a cell within the range you want to subtotal.

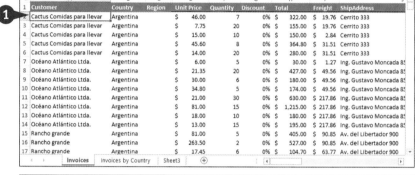

2 Click the **Data** tab.

3 Click **Subtotal** (▦).

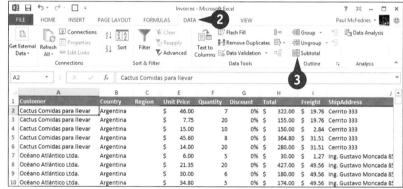

The Subtotal dialog box appears.

4 Click the **At each change in** ☑ and then click the column you want to use to group the subtotals.

5 In the **Add subtotal to** list, click the check box for the column you want to summarize (☐ changes to ☑).

6 Click **OK**.

A Excel calculates the subtotals and adds them into the range.

B Excel adds outline symbols to the range.

Note: See the following section, "Group Related Data," to learn more about outlining in Excel.

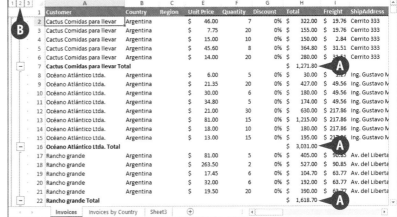

TIPS

Do I need to prepare my worksheet to use subtotals?

Yes. Excel sets up automatic subtotals based on data groupings in a selected field. For example, if you ask for subtotals based on the Customer field, Excel runs down the Customer column and creates a new subtotal each time the name changes. To get useful summaries, you need to sort the range on the field containing the data groupings you are interested in.

Can I only calculate totals?

No. The word *subtotal* here is a bit misleading because you can summarize more than just totals. You can also count values, calculate the average of the values, determine the maximum or minimum value, and more. To change the summary calculation, follow Steps **1** to **4**, click the **Use function** ☑, and then click the function you want to use for the summary.

Group Related Data

You can control a worksheet range display by grouping the data based on the worksheet formulas and data.

Grouping the data creates a worksheet outline, which you can use to "collapse" sections of the sheet to display only summary cells, or "expand" hidden sections to show the underlying detail. Note that when you add subtotals to a range as described in the previous section, "Summarize Data with Subtotals," Excel automatically groups the data and displays the outline tools.

Group Related Data

Create the Outline

1. Display the worksheet you want to outline.

2. Click the **Data** tab.

3. Click the **Group** ▾.

4. Click **Auto Outline**.

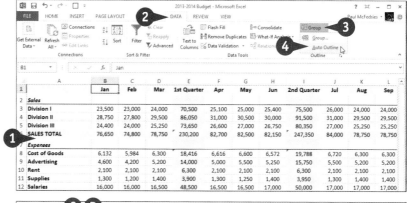

Ⓐ Excel outlines the worksheet data.

Ⓑ Excel uses level bars to indicate the grouped ranges.

Ⓒ Excel displays level symbols to indicate the various levels of the detail that are available in the outline.

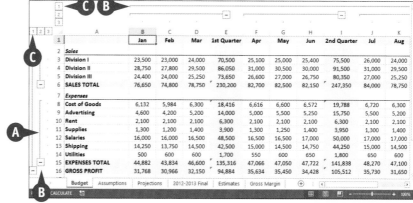

Use the Outline to Control the Range Display

1 Click a **Collapse** symbol ($\boxed{-}$) to hide the range indicated by the level bar.

D You can also collapse multiple ranges that are on the same outline level by clicking the appropriate level symbol.

E Excel collapses the range.

2 Click the **Expand** symbol ($\boxed{+}$) to view the range again.

F You can also show multiple ranges that are on the same outline level by clicking the appropriate level symbol.

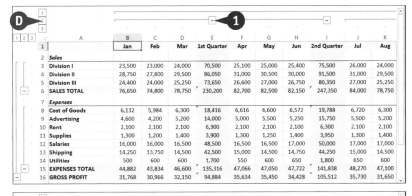

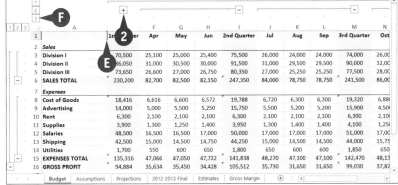

TIP

Do I have to prepare my worksheet before I can group the data?

Yes. Not all worksheets can be grouped, so you need to make sure your worksheet is a candidate for outlining. First, the worksheet must contain formulas that reference cells or ranges directly adjacent to the formula cell. Worksheets with SUM( ) functions that subtotal cells above or to the left are particularly good candidates for outlining.

Second, there must be a consistent pattern to the direction of the formula references. For example, a worksheet with formulas that always reference cells above or to the left can be outlined. Excel will not outline a worksheet with, say, SUM( ) functions that reference ranges above and below a formula cell.

Analyze Data with Goal Seek

If you already know the formula result you want, but you must find an input value that produces that result, you can use the Excel Goal Seek tool to solve the problem. You tell Goal Seek the final value you need and which variable to change, and it finds a solution for you.

For example, you might know that you want to have $50,000 saved to purchase new equipment five years from now, so you need to calculate how much to invest each year.

Analyze Data with Goal Seek

1 Set up your worksheet model.

Note: See the first Tip at the end of this section to learn more about setting up a worksheet for Goal Seek.

2 Click the **Data** tab.

3 Click **What-If Analysis** ( ).

4 Click **Goal Seek**.

The Goal Seek dialog box appears.

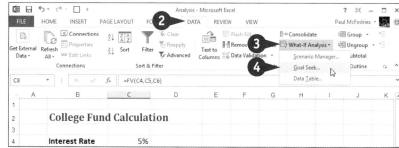

5 Click inside the **Set cell** box.

6 Click the cell that contains the formula you want Goal Seek to work with.

7 Use the **To value** text box to type the value that you want Goal Seek to find.

8 Click in the **By changing cell** box.

9 Click the cell that you want Goal Seek to modify.

10 Click **OK**.

A Goal Seek adjusts the changing cell value until it reaches a solution.

B The formula now shows the value you entered in Step **7**.

11 Click **OK**.

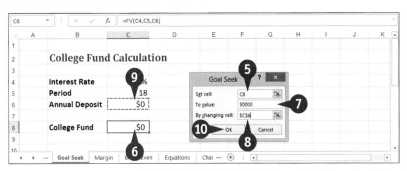

TIPS

How do I set up my worksheet to use Goal Seek?

Setting up your worksheet model for Goal Seek means doing three things. First, set up one cell as the *changing cell*, which is the value that Goal Seek will manipulate to reach the goal. Enter an initial value (such as 0) into the cell. Second, set up the other input values for the formula and give them proper initial values. Third, create a formula for Goal Seek to use to reach the goal.

What other types of problems can Goal Seek solve?

One common problem is called a *break-even analysis*, where you determine the number of units you have to sell of a product so that your total profits are 0. In this case, the changing cell is the number of units sold, and the formula is the profit calculation. You can also use Goal Seek to determine which price (the changing cell) is required to return a particular profit margin (the formula).

Analyze Data with Scenarios

You can analyze the result of a formula by creating sets of values that enable you to quickly use those values as the inputs for a formula.

For example, one set of values might represent a best-case approach, while another might represent a worst-case approach. In Excel, each of these coherent sets of input values — known as *changing cells* — is called a *scenario*. By creating multiple scenarios, you can easily apply these different value sets to analyze how the result of a formula changes under different conditions.

Analyze Data with Scenarios

Create a Scenario

1 Set up your worksheet model.

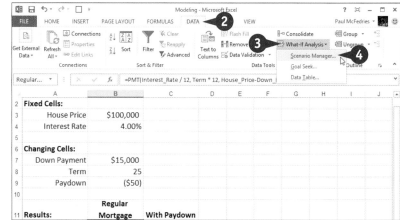

2 Click the **Data** tab.

3 Click **What-If Analysis** ( ).

4 Click **Scenario Manager**.

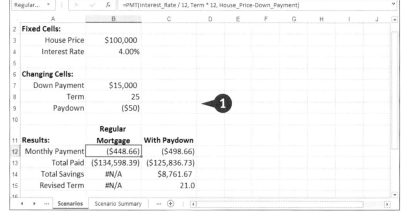

The Scenario Manager dialog box appears.

5 Click **Add**.

The Add Scenario dialog box appears.

6 Type a name for the scenario.

7 Click in the **Changing cells** box.

8 Select the cells you want to change in the scenario.

9 Type a description for the scenario.

10 Click **OK**.

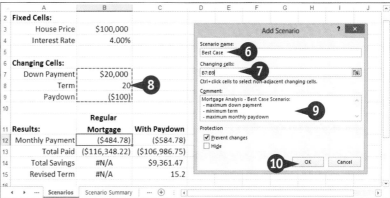

TIPS

Are there any restrictions on the changing cells?

When you are building a worksheet model for use with scenarios, make sure that each changing cell is a constant value. If you use a formula for a changing cell, Excel replaces that formula with a constant value defined in the scenario, so you lose your formula.

Do I need to add a description to each scenario?

Yes. As you see in the next section, once you have one or more scenarios defined, they appear in the Scenario Manager, and for each scenario you see its changing cells and its description. The description is often very useful, particularly if you have several scenarios defined, so be sure to write a detailed description in Step **9** to help you differentiate your scenarios later on.

continued ▶

Analyze Data with Scenarios (continued)

Excel stores your scenarios in the Scenario Manager. You can use the Scenario Manager to perform a number of scenario-related tasks. For example, you can select one of your scenarios and then click a button to display the scenario's values in your worksheet. You can also use the Scenario Manager to edit existing scenarios and to delete scenarios you no longer need.

Analyze Data with Scenarios (continued)

The Scenario Values dialog box appears.

11 Use the text boxes to specify a value for each changing cell.

Ⓐ To add more scenarios, click **Add** and then repeat Steps **6** to **11**.

12 Click **OK**.

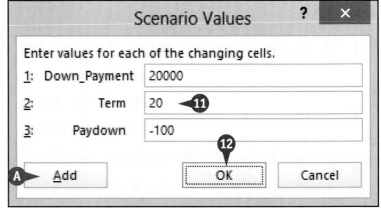

13 Click **Close**.

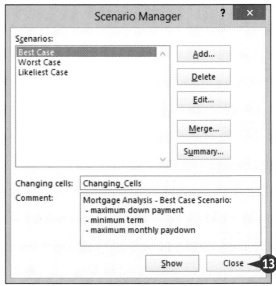

Display Scenarios

1. Click the **Data** tab.
2. Click 🖹.
3. Click **Scenario Manager**.

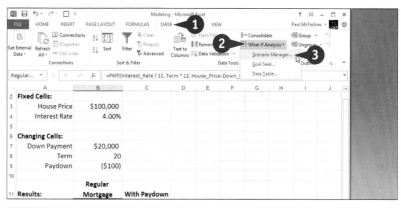

The Scenario Manager dialog box appears.

4. Click the scenario you want to display.
5. Click **Show**.
Ⓑ Excel enters the scenario values into the changing cells and displays the formula result.
6. Repeat Steps **4** and **5** to display other scenarios.
7. Click **Close**.

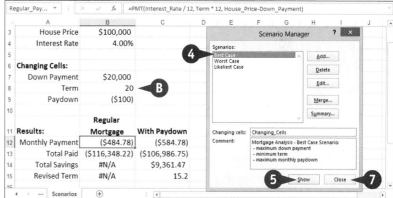

TIPS

How do I edit a scenario?

If you need to make changes to a scenario, you can edit the name, the changing cells, the description, and the scenario's input values. Click the **Data** tab, click 🖹, and then click **Scenario Manager**. In the Scenario Manager dialog box, click the scenario you want to modify, and then click **Edit**.

How do I remove a scenario?

If you have a scenario that you no longer need, you should delete it to reduce clutter in the Scenario Manager. Click the **Data** tab, click 🖹, and then click **Scenario Manager**. Click the scenario you want to delete. Note that Excel does not ask you to confirm the deletion, so double-check that you have selected the correct scenario. Click **Delete** and then click **Close**.

Remove Duplicate Values from a Range or Table

Y ou can make your Excel data more accurate for analysis by removing any duplicate records. Duplicate records throw off your calculations by including the same data two or more times. To prevent this, you should delete duplicate records. However, rather than looking for duplicates manually, you can use the Remove Duplicates command, which can quickly find and remove duplicates in even the largest ranges or tables.

Before you use the Remove Duplicates command, you must decide what defines a duplicate record in your data. That is, does every field have to be identical or is it enough that only certain fields are identical?

Remove Duplicate Values from a Range or Table

1 Click a cell inside the range or table.

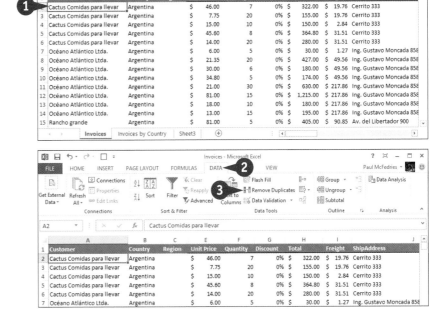

2 Click the **Data** tab.

3 Click **Remove Duplicates** ( ).

The Remove Duplicates dialog box appears.

④ Select the check box beside each field that you want Excel to check for duplication values (☐ changes to ☑).

Note: Excel does not give you a chance to confirm the deletion of the duplicate records, so be sure you want to do this before proceeding.

⑤ Click **OK**.

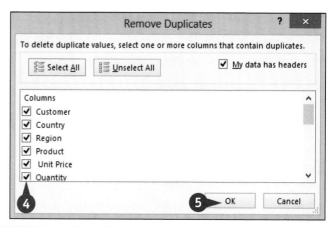

Excel deletes any duplicate records that it finds.

Ⓐ Excel tells you the number of duplicate records that it deleted.

⑥ Click **OK**.

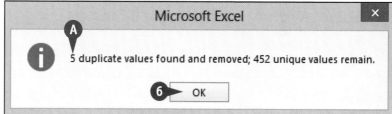

TIPS

If I have a lot of columns, is there a quick way to check for duplicates based on just a couple of those fields?

Yes. If your table has many fields, you may want Excel to use only one or two of those fields to look for duplicate records. Rather than deactivating all the other check boxes manually, first click **Unselect All** in the Remove Duplicates dialog box to clear all the check boxes (☑ changes to ☐). You can then click to activate just the check boxes you want Excel to use (☐ changes to ☑).

Can I remove duplicates even if my range does not have column headers?

Yes. Excel can still examine the column data even if there are no headers. In this case, follow Steps **1** to **3** to open the Remove Duplicates dialog box, then make sure the **My data has headers** check box is deselected (☐). Use the check boxes labeled Column A, Column B, and so on to choose the columns that you want Excel to check for duplicate values (☐ changes to ☑) and then click **OK**.

Load the Excel Analysis ToolPak

You can get access to a number of powerful statistical analysis tools by loading the Analysis ToolPak add-in. The Analysis ToolPak consists of 19 statistical tools that calculate statistical measures such as correlation, regression, rank and percentile, covariance, and moving averages.

You can also use the analysis tools to generate descriptive statistics (such as median, mode, and standard deviation), random numbers, and histograms.

Load the Excel Analysis ToolPak

1 Click the **File** tab (not shown).

2 Click **Options**.

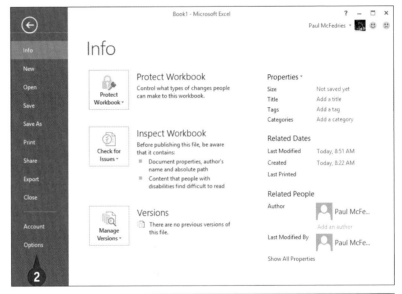

The Excel Options dialog box appears.

3 Click **Add-Ins**.

4 In the Manage list, click **Excel Add-ins**.

5 Click **Go**.

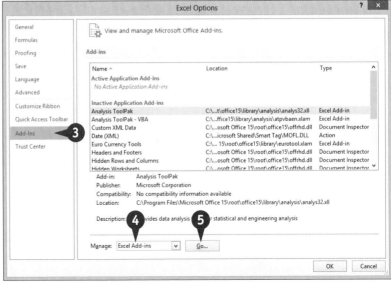

The Add-Ins dialog box appears.

6 Click the **Analysis ToolPak** check box (☐ changes to ✔).

7 Click **OK**.

Excel loads the Analysis ToolPak add-in.

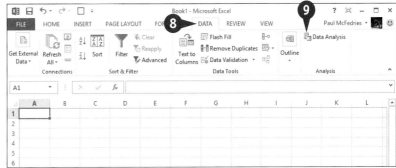

8 Click the **Data** tab.

9 Click **Data Analysis** (🖳) to access the Analysis ToolPak tools.

TIP

How do I use the statistical tools?

The specific steps you follow vary from tool to tool, but you can follow these general steps to use any of the Analysis ToolPak's statistical tools:

1 Click the **Data** tab.

2 Click 🖳.

The Data Analysis dialog box appears.

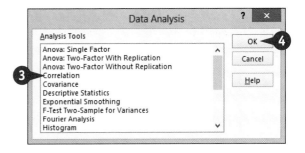

3 Click the tool you want to use.

4 Click **OK**.

Excel displays a dialog box for the tool.

5 Fill in the dialog box (the controls vary from tool to tool).

6 Click **OK**.

CHAPTER 13

Visualizing Data with Charts

You can take a worksheet full of numbers and display them as a chart. Visualizing your data in this way makes the data easier to understand and analyze. To help you see your data exactly the way you want, Excel offers a wide variety of chart types, and a large number of chart options.

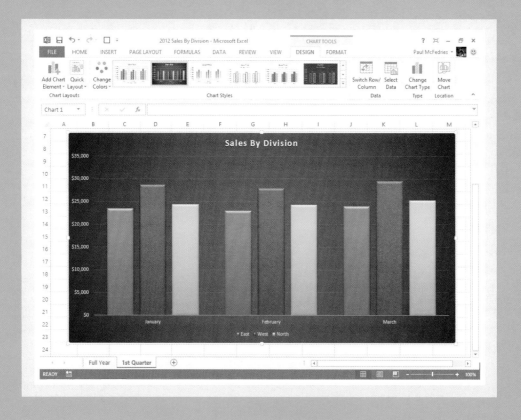

Examine Chart Elements

One of the best ways to analyze your worksheet data — or get your point across to other people — is to display your data visually in a *chart*, which is a graphic representation of spreadsheet data. As the data in the spreadsheet changes, the chart also changes to reflect the new numbers.

You have dozens of different chart formats to choose from, and if none of the built-in Excel formats is just right, you can further customize these charts to suit your needs. To get the most out of charts, you need to familiarize yourself with the basic chart elements.

Ⓐ Category Axis

The axis (usually the X axis) that contains the category groupings.

Ⓑ Chart Title

The title of the chart.

Ⓒ Data Marker

A symbol that represents a specific data value. The symbol used depends on the chart type.

Ⓓ Data Series

A collection of related data values. Normally, the marker for each value in a series has the same pattern.

Ⓔ Data Value

A single piece of data, also called a *data point*.

Ⓕ Gridlines

Optional horizontal and vertical extensions of the axis tick marks. These lines make data values easier to read.

Ⓖ Legend

A guide that shows the colors, patterns, and symbols used by the markers for each data series.

Ⓗ Plot Area

The area bounded by the category and value axes. It contains the data points and gridlines.

Ⓘ Value Axis

The axis (usually the Y axis) that contains the data values.

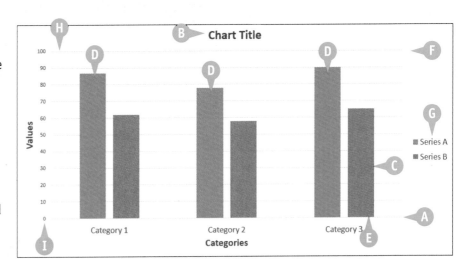

Excel offers 11 different types of charts, including column charts, bar charts, line charts, and pie charts. The chart type you use depends on the type of data and how you want to present that data visually.

Chart Types

Chart Type	Description
Area chart	A chart that shows the relative contributions over time that each data series makes to the whole picture.
Bar chart	A chart that compares distinct items or shows single items at distinct intervals. A bar chart is laid out with categories along the vertical axis and values along the horizontal axis.
Bubble chart	A chart that is similar to an XY chart, except that there are three data series, and in the third series the individual plot points are displayed as bubbles (the larger the value, the larger the bubble).
Column chart	A chart that, like a bar chart, compares distinct items or shows single items at distinct intervals. However, a column chart is laid out with categories along the horizontal axis and values along the vertical axis.
Doughnut chart	A chart that, like a pie chart, shows the proportion of the whole that is contributed by each value in a data series. The advantage of a doughnut chart is that you can plot multiple data series.
Line chart	A chart that shows how a data series changes over time. The category (X) axis usually represents a progression of even increments (such as days or months), and the series points are plotted on the value (Y) axis.
Pie chart	A chart that shows the proportion of the whole that is contributed by each value in a single data series. The whole is represented as a circle (the "pie"), and each value is displayed as a proportional "slice" of the circle.
Radar chart	A chart that makes comparisons within a data series and between data series relative to a center point. Each category is shown with a value axis extending from the center point.
Stock chart	A chart that is designed to plot stock-market prices, such as a stock's daily high, low, and closing values.
Surface chart	A chart that analyzes two sets of data and determines the optimum combination of the two.
XY chart	A chart that shows the relationship between numeric values in two different data series. It can also plot a series of data pairs in XY coordinates. (This is also called a *scatter* chart.)

Create a Chart

You can create a chart from your Excel worksheet data with just a few mouse clicks. Excel offers nearly 100 default chart configurations, so there should always be a type that best visualizes your data. If you would prefer to let Excel suggest a chart type based on your data, see the following section, "Create a Recommended Chart."

Regardless of the chart type you choose originally, you can change to a different chart type at any time. See "Select a Different Chart Type," later in this chapter.

Create a Chart

1 Select the data that you want to visualize in a chart.

A If your data includes headings, be sure to include those headings in the selection.

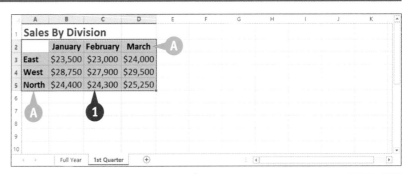

2 Click the **Insert** tab.

3 Click a chart type.

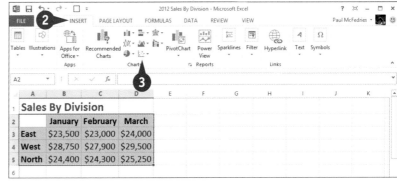

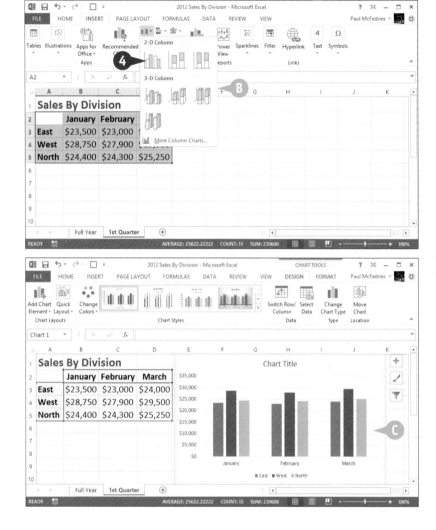

B Excel displays a gallery of configurations for the chart type.

4 Click the chart configuration you want to use.

C Excel inserts the chart.

The tasks in the rest of this chapter show you how to configure, format, and move the chart.

TIP

Is there a way to create a chart on a separate sheet?

Yes. You can use a special workbook sheet called a *chart sheet*. If you have not yet created your chart, select the worksheet data, right-click any worksheet tab, and then click **Insert** to display the Insert dialog box. Click the **General** tab, click **Chart**, and then click **OK**. Excel creates a new chart sheet and inserts the chart.

If you have already created your chart, you can move it to a separate chart sheet. See the Tip in "Move or Resize a Chart," later in this chapter.

Create a Recommended Chart

Y̶ou can make it easier and faster to create a chart by choosing from one of the chart configurations recommended by Excel.

With close to 100 possible chart configurations, the Excel chart tools are certainly comprehensive. However, that can be an overwhelming number of choices if you're not sure which type would best visualize your data. Rather than wasting a great deal of time looking at dozens of different chart configurations, the Recommended Charts command examines your data and then narrows down the possible choices to about ten configurations that would work with your data.

Create a Recommended Chart

1 Select the data that you want to visualize in a chart.

A If your data includes headings, be sure to include those headings in the selection.

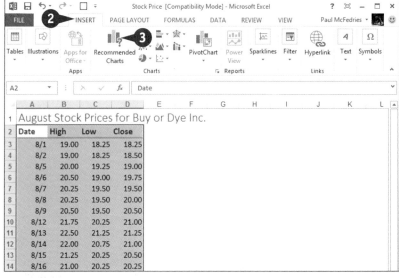

2 Click the **Insert** tab.

3 Click **Recommended Charts**.

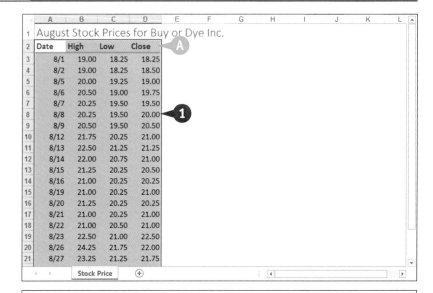

The Insert Chart dialog box appears with the Recommended Charts tab displayed.

④ Click the chart type you want to use.

Ⓑ A preview of the chart appears here.

⑤ Click **OK**.

Ⓒ Excel inserts the chart.

Is there a faster way to insert a recommended chart?

Yes, you can use the Quick Analysis feature in Excel:

① Select the data that you want to visualize in a chart, including the headings, if any.

② Click the **Quick Analysis** Smart tag (📊).

③ Click **Charts**.

Excel displays the chart types recommended for your data.

④ Click the chart type you want to use.

Excel inserts the chart.

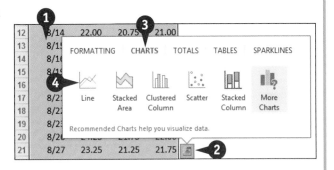

Add Chart Titles

You can make your chart easier to understand by adding chart titles, which are labels that appear in specific sections of the chart. By including descriptive titles, you make it easier for other people to see at a glance what you chart is visualizing.

There are three types of chart titles that you can add. The first type is the overall chart title, which usually appears at the top of the chart. You can also add a title for the horizontal axis to describe the chart categories, as well as a title for the vertical axis, which describes the chart values.

Add Chart Titles

1 Click the chart.

2 Click the **Design** tab.

3 Click **Add Chart Element**.

4 Click **Chart Title**.

5 Click **Above Chart**.

Ⓐ Excel adds the title box.

6 Type the title.

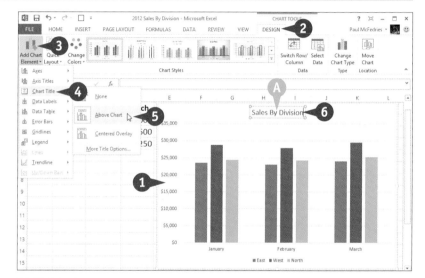

7 Click **Add Chart Element**.

8 Click **Axis Titles**.

9 Click **Primary Horizontal**.

Ⓑ Excel adds the title box.

10 Type the title.

11 Click **Add Chart Element**.

12 Click **Axis Titles**.

13 Click **Primary Vertical**.

Ⓒ Excel adds the title box.

14 Type the title.

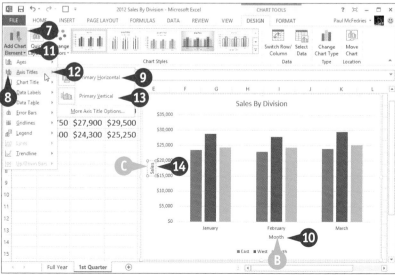

Add Data Labels

You can make your chart easier to read by adding data labels. A *data label* is a small text box that appears in or near a data marker and displays the value of that data point.

Excel offers several position options for the data labels, and these options depend on the chart type. For example, with a column chart you can place the data labels within or above each column, and for a line chart you can place the labels to the left or right, or above or below, the data marker.

Add Data Labels

1 Click the chart.

2 Click the **Design** tab.

3 Click **Add Chart Element**.

4 Click **Data Labels**.

5 Click the position you want to use for the data labels.

Note: Remember that the position options you see depend on the chart type.

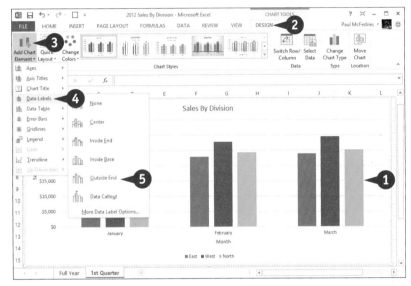

A Excel adds the labels to the chart.

Position the Chart Legend

You can change the position of the chart *legend*, which identifies the colors associated with each data series in the chart. The legend is a crucial chart element for interpreting and understanding your chart, so it is important that you place it in the best position. For example, you might find the legend easier to read if it appears to the right of the chart. Alternatively, if you want more horizontal space to display your chart, you can move the legend above or below the chart.

Position the Chart Legend

1 Click the chart.

2 Click the **Design** tab.

3 Click **Add Chart Element.**

4 Click **Legend.**

5 Click the position you want to use for the legend.

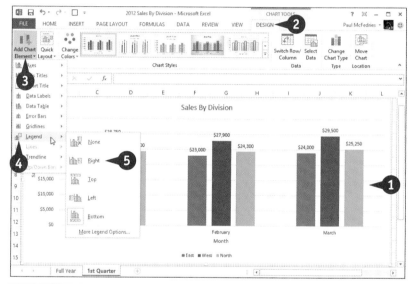

A Excel moves the legend.

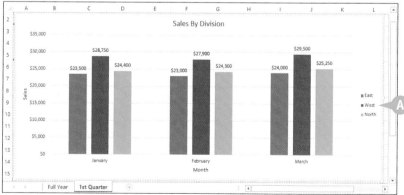

Display Chart Gridlines

Y ou can make your chart easier to read and analyze by adding gridlines. Horizontal gridlines extend from the vertical (value) axis, and are useful with area, bubble, and column charts. Vertical gridlines extend from the horizontal (category) axis and are useful with bar and line charts. *Major gridlines* are gridlines associated with the *major units* (the values you see displayed on the vertical and horizontal axes), while *minor gridlines* are gridlines associated with the *minor units* (values between each major unit).

Display Chart Gridlines

1 Click the chart.

2 Click the **Design** tab.

3 Click **Add Chart Element**.

4 Click **Gridlines**.

5 Click the horizontal gridline option you prefer.

A Excel displays the horizontal gridlines.

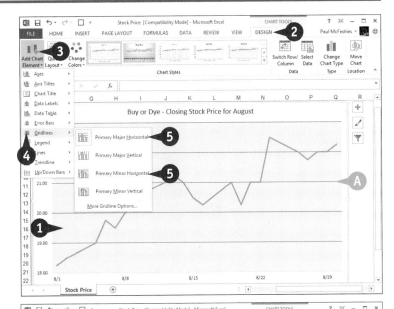

6 Click **Add Chart Element**.

7 Click **Gridlines**.

8 Click the vertical gridline option you prefer.

B Excel displays the vertical gridlines.

Display a Data Table

You can make it easier for yourself and others to interpret your chart by adding a data table. A *data table* is a tabular grid where each row is a data series from the chart, each column is a chart category, and each cell is a chart data point.

Excel gives you the option of displaying the data table with or without *legend keys*, which are markers that identify each series.

Display a Data Table

1 Click the chart.

2 Click the **Design** tab.

3 Click **Add Chart Element**.

4 Click **Data Table**.

5 Click **With Legend Keys**.

Ⓐ If you prefer not to display the legend keys, click **No Legend Keys**.

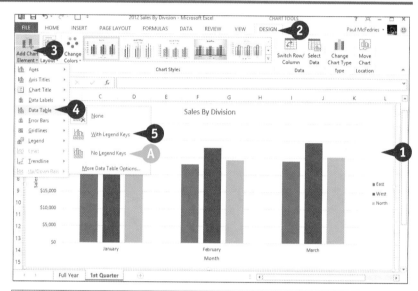

Ⓑ Excel adds the data table below the chart.

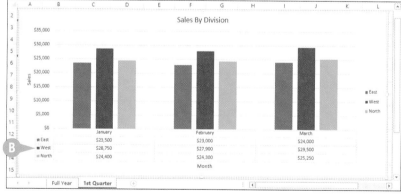

Change the Chart Layout and Style

You can quickly format your chart by applying a different chart layout and chart style. The chart layout includes elements such as the titles, data labels, legend, gridlines, and data table. The Quick Layouts feature in Excel enables you to apply these elements in different combinations with just a few mouse clicks. The chart style represents the colors used by the chart data markers and background.

Change the Chart Layout and Style

1 Click the chart.

2 Click the **Design** tab.

3 Click **Quick Layout**.

4 Click the layout you want to use.

A Excel applies the layout.

5 Click the **Chart Styles** ⊡.

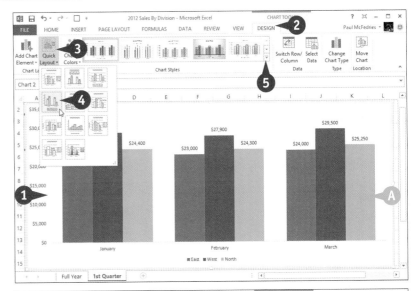

6 Click the chart style you want to use.

B Excel applies the style to the chart.

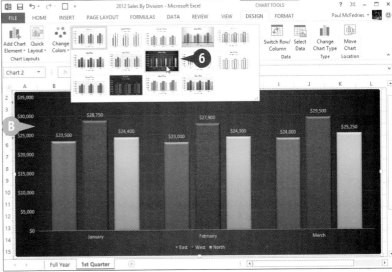

Select a Different Chart Type

If you feel that the current chart type is not showing your data in the best way, you can change the chart type. This enables you to experiment not only with the different chart types offered by Excel, but also with its nearly 100 chart type configurations.

For example, if you are graphing a stock's high, low, and closing prices, a line chart shows you each value, but a stock chart gives you a better sense of the daily price movements. Similarly, if you are using a bar chart to show percentages of some whole, you would more readily visualize the data by switching to a pie chart.

Select a Different Chart Type

1 Click the chart.

2 Click the **Design** tab.

3 Click **Change Chart Type**.

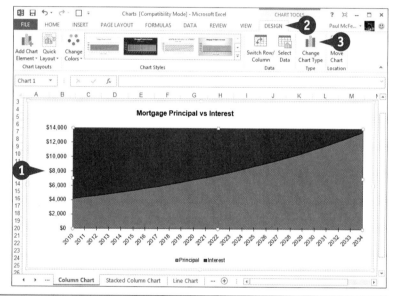

The Change Chart Type dialog box appears.

4 Click the chart type you want to use.

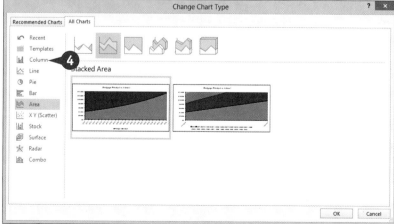

Excel displays the chart type configurations.

5 Click the configuration you want to use.

6 Click **OK**.

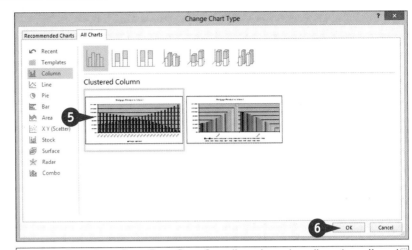

A Excel applies the new chart type.

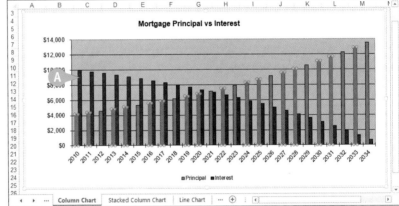

TIP

Can I save the chart type and formatting so that I can reuse it later on a different chart?
Yes. You do this by saving your work as a chart template. Follow the steps in this section and in the previous few sections of this chapter to set the chart type, titles, labels, legend position, gridlines, layout, and style. Right-click the chart's plot area or background, click **Save as Template**, type a name for the template, and then click **Save**. To reuse the template, follow Steps **1** to **3**, click **Templates**, click your template, and then click **OK**.

Change the Chart Source Data

In Excel, a chart's *source data* is the original range used to create the chart. You can keep your chart up to date and accurate by adjusting the chart when its source data changes.

You normally do this when the structure of the source data changes. For example, if the source range adds a row or column, you can adjust the chart to include the new data. However, you do not need to make any adjustments if just the data within the original range changes. In such cases, Excel automatically adjusts the chart to display the new data.

Change the Chart Source Data

1 Click the chart to select it.

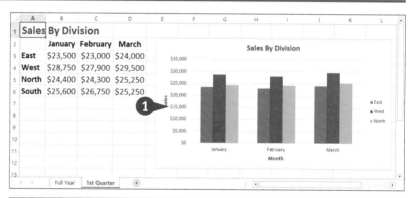

A Excel selects the chart's source data.

2 Move the Excel mouse pointer (⊕) over the lower-right corner of the range.

⊕ changes to ↔.

3 Click and drag ↔ until the selection includes all the data you want to include in the chart.

B Excel displays a blue outline to show you the new selection.

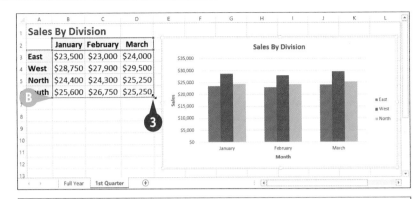

4 Release the mouse button.

C Excel redraws the chart to include the new data.

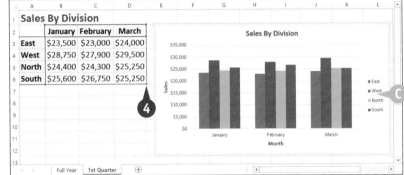

TIPS

Is there a way to swap the chart series with the chart categories without modifying the source data?

Yes. Excel has a feature that enables you to switch the row and column data, which swaps the series and categories without affecting the source data. First click the chart to select it, and then click the **Design** tab. Click **Switch Row/Column** (▦). Excel swaps the series and categories. Click ▦ again to return to the original layout.

Is there a way to remove a series from a chart without deleting the data from the source range?

Yes. You can use the Select Data Source dialog box in Excel to remove individual series. Click the chart to select it, and then click the **Design** tab. Click **Select Data** (▦) to open the Select Data Source. In the **Legend Entries (Series)** list, click the series you want to get rid of, and then click **Remove**. Click **OK**.

Move or Resize a Chart

You can move a chart to another part of the worksheet. This is useful if the chart is blocking the worksheet data or if you want the chart to appear in a particular part of the worksheet.

You can also resize a chart. For example, if you find that the chart is difficult to read, making the chart bigger often solves the problem. Similarly, if the chart takes up too much space on the worksheet, you can make it smaller.

Move or Resize a Chart

Move a Chart

1 Click the chart.

A Excel displays a border around the chart.

2 Move the mouse pointer (⬚) over the chart border.

⬚ changes to ✥.

Note: Do not position the mouse pointer over a corner or over the middle of any side of the border.

3 Click and drag the chart border to the location you want.

4 Release the mouse button.

B Excel moves the chart.

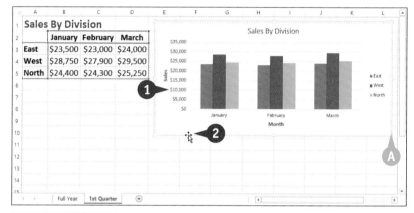

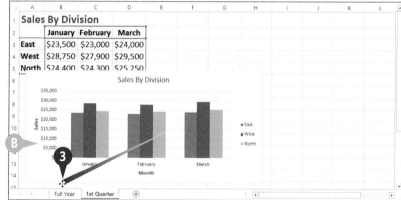

Resize a Chart

1 Click the chart.

C Excel displays a border around the chart.

D The border includes sizing handles on the corners and sides.

2 Move ▷ over a sizing handle.

▷ changes to ⟷ (left or right), ↕ (top or bottom), or ⤢ (corner).

3 Click and drag the handle.

E Excel displays a gray outline of the new chart size.

4 Release the mouse button.

F Excel resizes the chart.

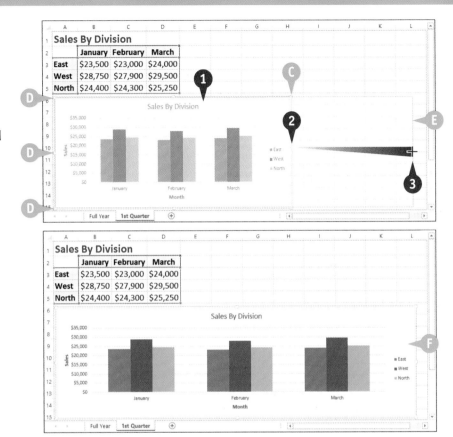

Can I move a chart to a separate sheet?
Yes. In "Create a Chart," earlier in this chapter, you learned how to create a new chart in a separate sheet. If your chart already exists on a worksheet, you can move it to a new sheet. Click the chart, click the **Design** tab, and then click **Move Chart** to open the Move Chart dialog box. Select the **New sheet** option (○ changes to ⦿). In the **New sheet** text box, type a name for the new sheet, and then click **OK**.

How do I delete a chart?
How you delete a chart depends on whether your chart exists as an object on a worksheet or in its own sheet. If the chart is on a worksheet, click the chart and then press `Delete`. If the chart exists on a separate sheet, right-click the sheet tab, click **Delete Sheet**, and then click **Delete**.

Add a Sparkline to a Cell

If you want a quick visualization of your data without having a chart take up a large amount of worksheet space, you can add a sparkline to a single cell. A *sparkline* is a small chart that visualizes a row or column of data and fits inside a single cell.

Excel offers three types of sparklines: Line (similar to a line chart), Column (similar to a column chart), and Win/Loss (for data that includes positive and negative values).

Add a Sparkline to a Cell

1 Select the row or column of data you want to visualize.

2 Click the **Insert** tab.

3 Click the type of sparkline you want to create.

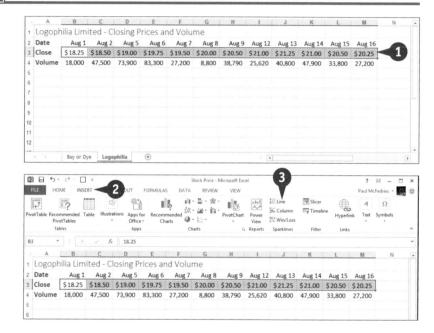

The Create Sparklines dialog box appears.

④ Click in the **Location Range** box.

⑤ Click the cell where you want the sparkline to appear.

⑥ Click **OK**.

Ⓐ Excel adds the sparkline to the cell.

Ⓑ Excel displays the Sparkline Tools tab.

Ⓒ Use the tools in the Design tab to format your sparkline.

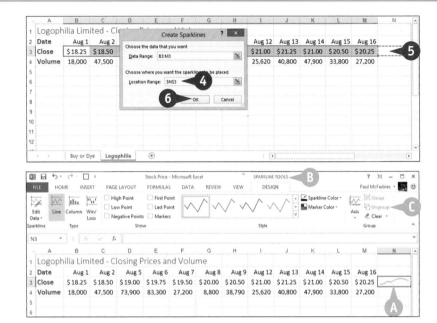

TIP

Can I add a sparkline to multiple rows or columns at once?

Yes. To do this, first select the rows or columns of data that you want to visualize. Follow Steps **2** and **3** to open the Create Sparklines dialog box and place the cursor inside the **Location Range** box. Select a single cell for each row or column that you have selected. For example, if you have selected five rows, select five cells. Click **OK**. Excel adds a sparkline for each selected row or column.

CHAPTER 14

Adding Worksheet Graphics

You can enhance the visual appeal and effectiveness of your Excel worksheets by incorporating graphic objects such as shapes, clip art, pictures, or WordArt and SmartArt images. This chapter shows you not only how to insert graphics on your worksheets, but also how to edit and format those graphics.

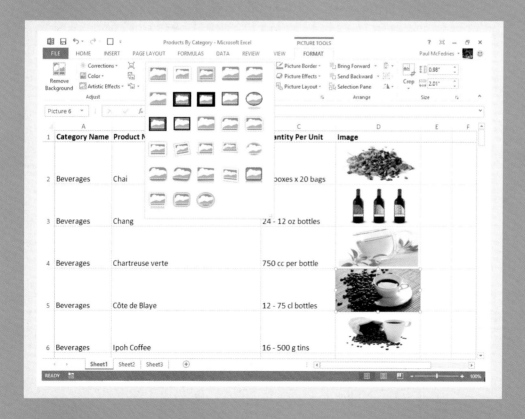

Draw a Shape

You can add visual appeal or enhance the readability of your worksheets by adding one or more shapes. The Excel Shapes gallery comes with more than 150 predefined objects called *shapes* (or sometimes *AutoShapes*) that enable you to quickly and easily draw anything from simple geometric figures such as lines, rectangles, and ovals, to more elaborate items such as starbursts, flowchart symbols, and callout boxes. You can add these shapes to a worksheet either to enhance the aesthetics of your data or to help other people read and understand your work.

Draw a Shape

1 Display the worksheet on which you want to draw the shape.

2 Click the **Insert** tab.

3 Click **Illustrations**.

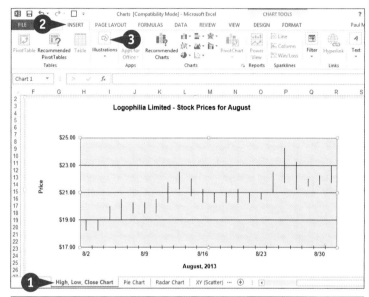

4 Click **Shapes**.

5 Click the shape you want to draw.

⬧ changes to **+**.

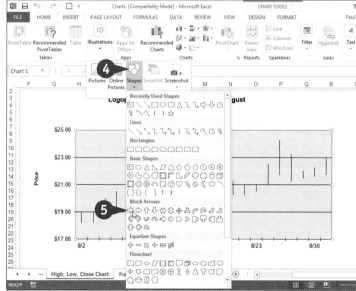

6 Click and drag the Excel mouse pointer (**+**) to draw the shape.

7 When the shape is the size you want, release the mouse button.

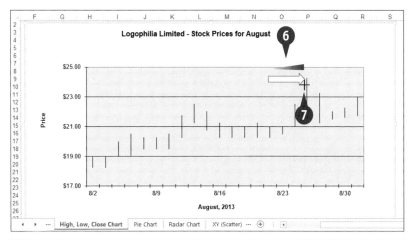

A The program draws the shape and adds edit handles around the shape's edges.

Note: If you need to move or size the shape, see "Move or Resize a Graphic," later in this chapter.

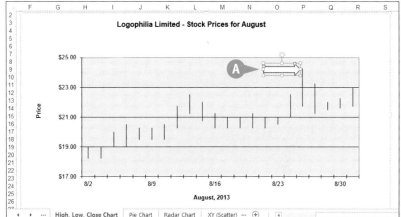

Is there an easy way to draw a perfect circle or square?

Yes, Excel offers an easy technique for drawing circles and squares. Hold down the **Shift** key as you click and drag the shape to constrain the shape into a perfect circle or square. When you finish drawing the shape, release the **Shift** key.

Can I add text to a shape?

Yes. You can add text to the interior of any 2-D shape (that is, any shape that is not a line). After you draw the shape, right-click the shape, click **Edit Text**, and then type your text inside the shape. You can use the Home tab's Font controls to format the text. When you finish, click outside of the shape.

Insert a Clip Art Image

You can improve the look of an Excel worksheet by adding a clip art image to the sheet. *Clip art* refers to small images or artwork that you can insert into your documents. Excel 2013 does not come with its own clip art, but it does give you access to the Office.com clip art collection, which contains thousands of images from various categories, such as business, people, nature, and symbols. You can use any of these clip art images without charge.

Insert a Clip Art Image

1 Display the worksheet on which you want to insert the clip art image.

2 Click the cell where you want the upper-left corner of the image to appear.

3 Click the **Insert** tab.

4 Click **Illustrations**.

5 Click **Online Pictures**.

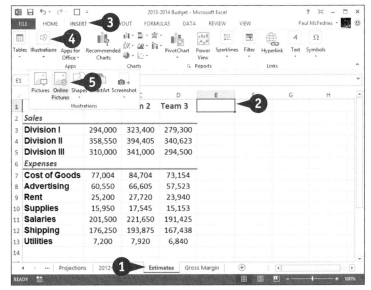

The Insert Pictures window appears.

6 Click **Office.com Clip Art**.

7 Use the **Search Office.com** text box to type a word that describes the kind of clip art image you want to insert.

8 Click **Search ( ).**

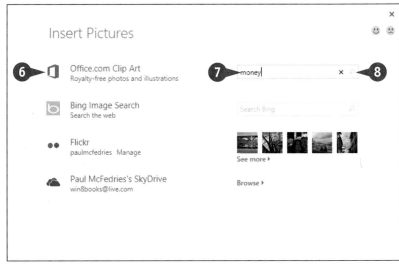

Ⓐ Excel displays a list of clip art images that match your search term.

⑨ Click the clip art image you want to use.

⑩ Click **Insert**.

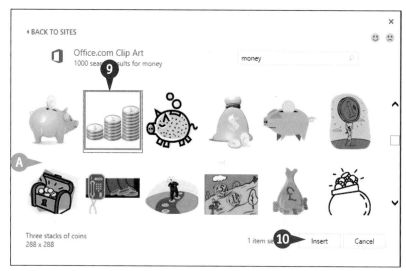

◄ BACK TO SITES

Office.com Clip Art
1000 search results for money

money

Three stacks of coins
288 x 288

1 item se ⑩ Insert   Cancel

Ⓑ Excel inserts the clip art.

Note: If you need to move or size the clip art, see "Move or Resize a Graphic," later in this chapter.

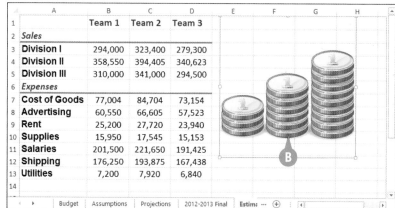

	A	B	C	D
1		Team 1	Team 2	Team 3
2	*Sales*			
3	**Division I**	294,000	323,400	279,300
4	**Division II**	358,550	394,405	340,623
5	**Division III**	310,000	341,000	294,500
6	*Expenses*			
7	**Cost of Goods**	77,004	84,704	73,154
8	**Advertising**	60,550	66,605	57,523
9	**Rent**	25,200	27,720	23,940
10	**Supplies**	15,950	17,545	15,153
11	**Salaries**	201,500	221,650	191,425
12	**Shipping**	176,250	193,875	167,438
13	**Utilities**	7,200	7,920	6,840
14				

Budget Assumptions Projections 2012-2013 Final Estima ⋯ ⊕

TIPS

Is there an easier way to locate the clip art image that I want?

Yes, you can use a web browser to locate clip art images directly using the Office.com website. Navigate to http://office.microsoft.com/en-us/images/ and then click an image category, such as Business or People. Next, filter the images by media type and image size. For clip art, you should click **Illustration** in the Media Type list and **All** in the Image Size list.

Can I insert other online images?

Yes. To search for an image on the web, follow Steps **1** to **5** to open the Insert Pictures window and then use the Bing Image Search option to search for the picture. If you have connected your Flickr account to Windows 8, you can also use the Flickr option to choose a photo. If you are using a Microsoft account with Windows 8, you can use the SkyDrive option to select an image from your SkyDrive.

Insert a Photo

You can enhance the visual appeal and strengthen the message of an Excel worksheet by adding a photo to the file.

Excel can work with the most popular picture formats, including BMP, JPEG, TIFF, PNG, and GIF. This means that you can insert almost any photo that you have stored on your computer. If you would like to insert a photo that is located online, instead, see the tips in the previous section, "Insert a Clip Art Image."

Insert a Photo

1 Open the worksheet where you want to insert the photo.

2 Click the cell where you want the upper-left corner of the photo to appear.

3 Click the **Insert** tab.

4 Click **Illustrations**.

5 Click **Pictures**.

The Insert Picture dialog box appears.

6 Open the folder that contains the photo you want to insert.

7 Click the photo.

8 Click **Insert**.

A Excel inserts the photo into the worksheet.

Note: If you need to move or size the photo, see "Move or Resize a Graphic," later in this chapter.

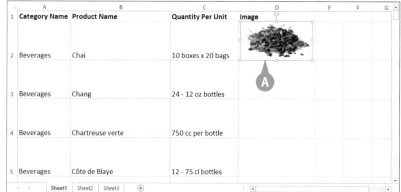

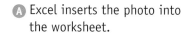

My photo has a distracting background. Can I remove it?

Yes. Excel comes with a Background Removal feature that can eliminate the background in most photos. Click the photo, click the **Format** tab, and then click **Remove Background** (🖼). If part of the foreground is in the removal color, click **Mark Areas to Keep** and then click and drag a line through the part you want to retain. When you are finished, click **Keep Changes**.

Is there a way to reduce the size of a workbook that has a lot of photos?

Yes, you can use the Compress Pictures feature to convert the photos to a smaller resolution and so reduce the size of the workbook. Click any image in the workbook, click the **Format** tab, and then click **Compress Pictures** (🖼). Click **Apply only to this picture** (☑ changes to ☐), click a **Target output** (○ changes to ◉), and then click **OK**.

Insert a WordArt Image

You can add some pizzazz to your Excel workbooks by inserting a WordArt image. A WordArt image is a graphic object that contains text stylized with shadows, outlines, reflections, and other predefined effects.

WordArt images enable you to apply sophisticated and fun effects to text with just a few mouse clicks. However, some of the more elaborate WordArt effects can make text difficult to read, so make sure that whatever WordArt image you use does not detract from your worksheet message.

Insert a WordArt Image

1 Open the worksheet in which you want to insert the WordArt image.

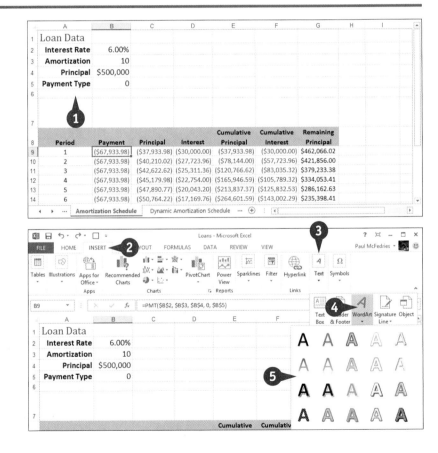

2 Click the **Insert** tab.

3 Click **Text**.

4 Click **WordArt**.

The WordArt gallery appears.

5 Click the WordArt style you want to use.

A The WordArt image appears in the worksheet.

6 Type the text that you want to appear in the WordArt image.

7 Click outside the image to set it.

Note: You will likely have to move the WordArt image into position; see "Move or Resize a Graphic," later in this chapter.

TIPS

Can I change the default WordArt formatting?
Yes. Click the WordArt image to select it, and then use the Home tab's Font controls to adjust the WordArt text font. Click the **Format** tab. In the WordArt Styles group, use the **Text Fill** (△), **Text Outline** (△), and **Text Effects** (△) galleries to format the WordArt image. You can also use the Quick Styles gallery to select a different WordArt style.

Can I make my WordArt text run vertically?
Yes. Click the WordArt image to select it. Click the **Format** tab, and then click the dialog box launcher (□) in the **WordArt Styles** group. In the Format Shape task pane, click **Text Options** and then click the **Textbox** icon (□). Click the **Text direction** (□) and then click **Stacked**. Click **Close**. Excel displays the WordArt text vertically.

Insert a SmartArt Graphic

You can add a SmartArt graphic to a workbook to help present information in a compact, visual format. A SmartArt graphic is a collection of *nodes* — shapes with some text inside — that enables you to convey information visually.

For example, you can use a SmartArt graphic to present a company organization chart, the progression of steps in a workflow, the parts that make up a whole, and much more.

Insert a SmartArt Graphic

1 Open the worksheet in which you want to insert the SmartArt image.

2 Click the **Insert** tab.

3 Click **Illustrations.**

4 Click **SmartArt**.

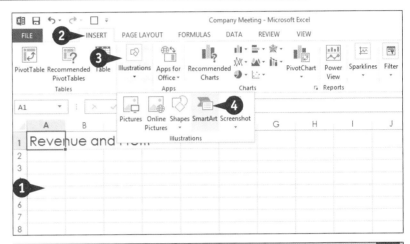

The Choose a SmartArt Graphic dialog box appears.

5 Click a SmartArt category.

6 Click the SmartArt style you want to use.

7 Click **OK**.

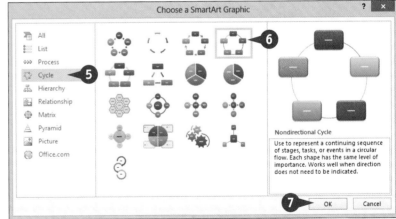

Ⓐ The SmartArt graphic appears in the document.

Ⓑ You use the Text pane to type the text for each node and to add and delete nodes.

⑧ Click a node in the Text pane.

⑨ Type the text that you want to appear in the node.

Ⓒ The text appears automatically in the associated shape.

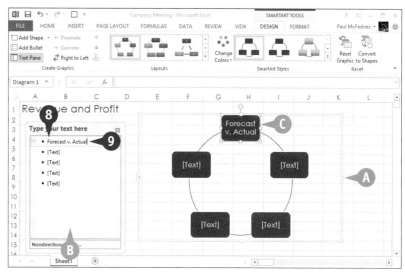

⑩ Repeat Steps **8** and **9** to fill in the other nodes in the SmartArt graphic.

Ⓓ You can click **Text Pane** (⊞) to hide the Text pane.

Note: You will likely have to move the SmartArt graphic into position; see the following section, "Move or Resize a Graphic."

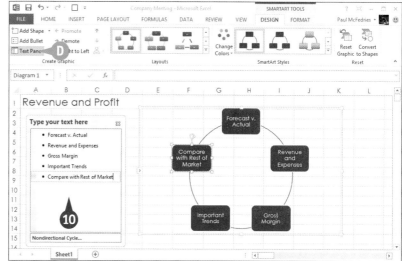

TIPS

How do I add a node to my SmartArt graphic?
To add a node to the SmartArt graphic, first decide where you want that node to appear in the current image. That is, decide which existing node you want the new node to come before or after. Click the existing node, click the **Design** tab, click the **Add Shape** ▾ , and then click **Add Shape After**. (If you want the new node to appear before the existing node, click **Add Shape Before**.)

Can I use shapes other than the ones supplied in the default SmartArt graphics?
Yes. Begin by clicking the node you want to change. Click the **Format** tab, and then click the **Change Shape** ▾ to display the Shapes gallery. Click the shape you want to use. Excel updates the SmartArt graphic node with the new shape.

Move or Resize a Graphic

To ensure that a graphic is ideally placed within an Excel worksheet, you can move the graphic to a new location or you can resize the graphic in its current location. For example, you might want to move or resize a graphic so that it does not cover existing worksheet text. Similarly, you might want to move or resize a graphic so that it is positioned near a particular worksheet element or fits within an open worksheet area. You can move or resize any graphic, including shapes, clip art, pictures, WordArt images, and SmartArt graphics.

Move or Resize a Graphic

Move a Graphic

1 Move the mouse pointer (⌖) over an edge of the graphic you want to move.

The mouse ⌖ changes to ✛.

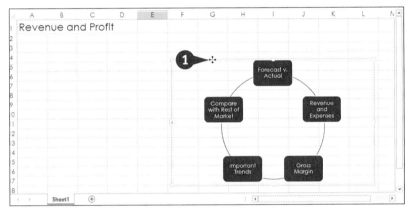

2 Drag the graphic to the location you prefer.

A Excel moves the graphic to the new location.

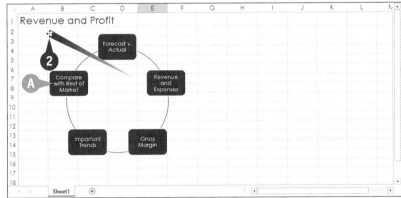

Resize a Graphic

1 Click the graphic.

B Sizing handles appear around the edges.

2 Move the mouse ⬉ over a sizing handle.

C Use a left or right handle (⬉ changes to ↔) to adjust the width.

D Use a top or bottom handle (⬉ changes to ↕) to adjust the height.

E Use a corner handle (⬉ changes to ⬈) to adjust the two sides adjacent to the corner.

3 Drag the sizing handle (the mouse pointer changes to ✛).

4 Release the mouse button when the handle is in the position you want.

F Excel resizes the graphic.

5 Repeat Steps **2** to **4** to resize other sides of the graphic, as necessary.

	A	B	C	D	E	F
1	Category Name	Product Name	Quantity Per Unit	Image		
2	Beverages	Chai	10 boxes x 20 bags			
3	Beverages	Chang	24 - 12 oz bottles			
4	Beverages	Chartreuse verte	750 cc per bottle			
5	Beverages	Côte de Blaye	12 - 75 cl bottles			

Sheet1 Sheet2 Sheet3 ⊕

	A	B	C	D	E	F
1	Category Name	Product Name	Quantity Per Unit	Image		
2	Beverages	Chai	10 boxes x 20 bags			
3	Beverages	Chang	24 - 12 oz bottles			
4	Beverages	Chartreuse verte	750 cc per bottle			
5	Beverages	Côte de Blaye	12 - 75 cl bottles			

Sheet1 Sheet2 Sheet3 ⊕

TIPS

Can I rotate a graphic?

Yes. Most graphic objects come with a rotate handle. Follow these steps:

1 Move the mouse ⬉ over the rotate handle (⬉ changes to ↻).

2 Click and drag the rotate handle clockwise or counterclockwise to rotate the graphic.

3 Release the mouse button when the graphic is in the position you want.

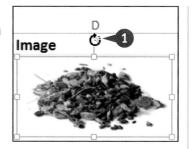

Is it possible to resize a graphic in all directions at once to keep the proportions the same?

Yes. You normally resize one side at a time by dragging a side handle, or two sides at a time by dragging a corner handle. To resize all four sides at once, hold down the **Ctrl** key and then click and drag any corner handle.

Crop a Picture

If a picture contains extraneous material near the outside edges of the image, you can often cut out those elements using a process called *cropping*. When you crop a picture, you specify a rectangular area of the image that you want to keep. Excel discards everything outside of the rectangle.

Cropping is a useful feature because it can help viewers focus on the subject of a picture. Cropping is also useful for removing extraneous elements that appear on or near the edges of a photo.

Crop a Picture

1 Click the picture you want to crop.

2 Click the **Format** tab.

3 Click the **Crop** button ( ).

A Crop handles appear around the picture.

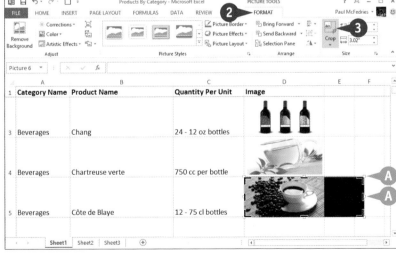

4 Click and drag a crop handle.

The mouse ⊕ changes to ✛.

B Click and drag a side handle to crop that side.

C Click and drag a corner handle to crop the two sides adjacent to the corner.

5 Release the mouse button when the handle is in the position you want.

6 Click 🖼.

Excel turns off the Crop feature.

D Excel crops the picture.

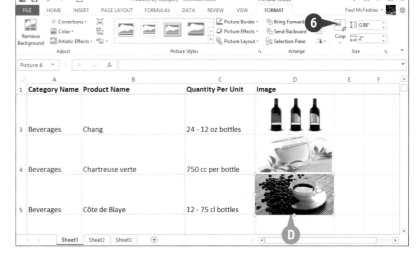

TIPS

If I have a picture with the main element in the middle, is it possible to crop in all directions at once to keep just that middle element?

Yes. You normally crop one side at a time by clicking and dragging a side crop handle, or two sides at a time by clicking and dragging a corner crop handle. To crop all four sides at once, hold down the `Ctrl` key and then click and drag any corner crop handle.

Can I crop a picture to a particular aspect ratio or shape?

Yes. Excel offers a couple of cropping options. If you know the aspect ratio (the ratio of the width to the height) you want, click the **Crop** ▼, click **Aspect Ratio**, and then click the ratio, such as 3:5 or 4:6. If you prefer to crop to a shape, such as an oval or arrow, click the **Crop** ▼, click **Crop to Shape**, and then click the shape.

Format a Picture

You can enhance your shapes, clip art, photos, WordArt images, and SmartArt graphics by formatting the images. For example, Excel offers more than two dozen picture styles, which are predefined formats that apply various combinations of shadows, reflections, borders, and layouts.

Excel also offers a dozen picture effects, which are preset combinations of special effects such as glows, soft edges, bevels, and 3-D rotations.

Format a Picture

Apply a Picture Style

1 Click the picture you want to format.

2 Click the **Format** tab.

3 Click the **Picture Styles** ⬇.

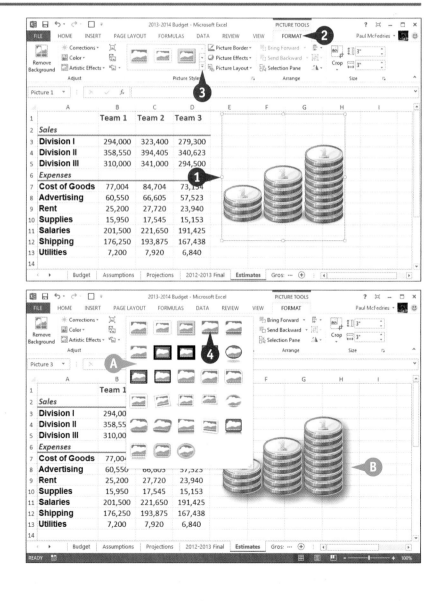

A Excel displays the Picture Styles gallery.

4 Click the picture style you want to use.

B Excel applies the style to the picture.

Apply a Picture Effect

1 Click the picture you want to format.

2 Click the **Format** tab.

3 Click the **Picture Effects** button ( ).

Note: If the image is a shape, the button is named **Shape Effects**.

4 Click **Preset**.

5 Click the effect you want to apply.

Ⓒ Excel applies the effect to the picture.

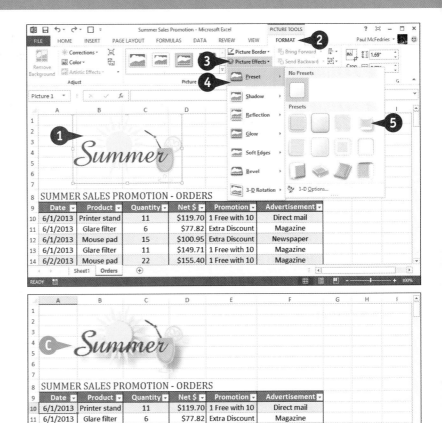

I applied a style to a picture, but now I want to change the picture to something else. Do I have to start over?

No. You can simply replace the existing picture with the other picture, and Excel preserves the style so you do not have to repeat your work. Click the existing picture, click the **Format** tab, and then click the **Change Picture** button ( ). Select the new picture you want to use and then click **Insert**.

If I do not like the formatting that I have applied to a picture, can I return the picture to its original look?

Yes. If you have not performed any other tasks since applying the formatting, click **Undo** ( ) until Excel has removed the formatting. Alternatively, click , click **Preset**, and then click the icon in the **No Presets** section. To reverse all the changes you have made to a picture since you inserted the image, click the picture, click **Format**, and then click **Reset Picture** ( ).

CHAPTER 15

Collaborating with Others

If you want to collaborate with other people on a workbook, Excel gives you several ways to do this, including adding comments, sharing a workbook, and even working on a spreadsheet online. You can also control your collaborations by protecting worksheet data and tracking the changes that others make.

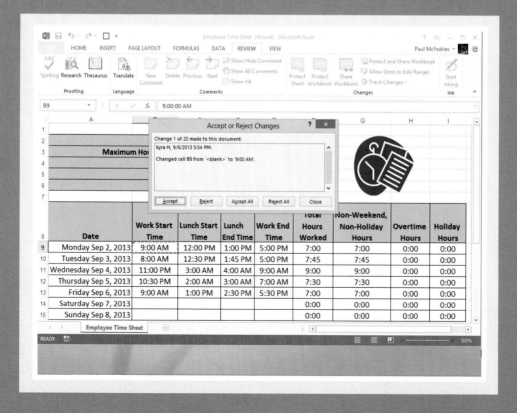

Add a Comment to a Cell

If you have received a workbook from another person, you can provide feedback to that person by adding a comment to a cell in the workbook. A comment is often the best way to provide corrections, questions, critiques, and other feedback because it does not change anything on the actual worksheet.

Each comment is attached to a particular cell and Excel uses a comment indicator to mark which cells have comments. When you view a comment, Excel displays the comment in a balloon.

Add a Comment to a Cell

Add a Comment

1 Click the cell you want to comment on.

2 Click the **Review** tab.

3 Click **New Comment** (▭).

Note: You can also right-click the cell and then click **Insert Comment**.

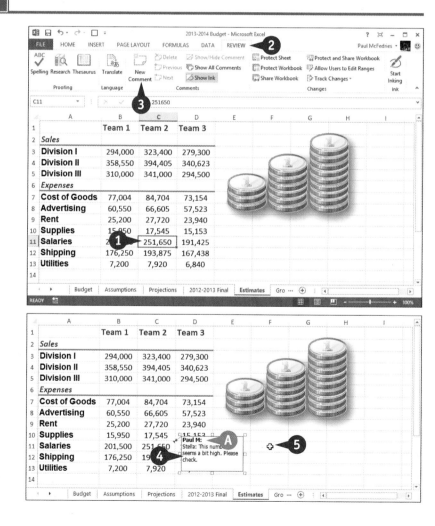

Excel displays a comment balloon.

Ⓐ Excel precedes the comment with your Excel username.

4 Type your comment.

5 Click outside the comment balloon.

B Excel adds a comment indicator ( ) to the top-right corner of the cell.

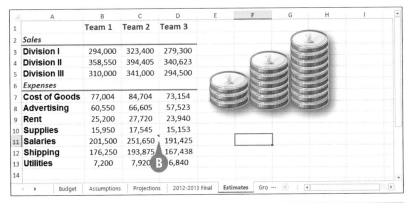

View a Comment

1 Move the Excel mouse pointer ( ) over the cell.

C Excel displays the comment in a balloon.

D In the Review tab, you can also click **Next** ( ) and **Previous** ( ) to run through the comments.

E In the Review tab, you can also click **Show All Comments** ( ) to display every comment at once.

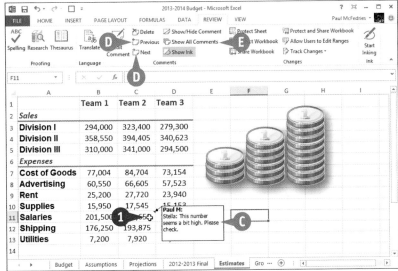

Can I edit or remove a comment?
Yes. To edit an existing comment, click the cell that contains the comment, click the **Review** tab, click **Edit Comment** ( ) to open the comment in a balloon, and then edit the balloon text. To remove a comment, click the cell that contains the comment, click the **Review** tab, and then click **Delete Comment** ( ).

How do I change my Excel username?
When collaborating, your username is important because it tells other people who added the comments. If you current username consists of only your first name or your initials, you can change it. Click **File** and then click **Options** to open the Excel Options dialog box. Click the **General** tab and then use the **User name** text box to edit the name. Click **OK**. Note, however, that this does not change your username in any existing comments.

Protect a Worksheet's Data

If you will be distributing a workbook to other people, you can enable the options in Excel for safeguarding worksheet data by activating the sheet's protection feature. You can also configure the worksheet to require a password to unprotect it.

There are two main methods you can use to safeguard worksheet data: You can unlock only those cells that users are allowed to edit and you can configure a range to require a password before it can be edited.

Protect a Worksheet's Data

1 Display the worksheet you want to protect.

2 Click the **Review** tab.

3 Click **Protect Sheet** (📖).

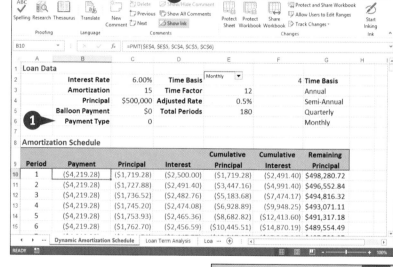

Excel displays the Protect Sheet dialog box.

4 Make sure the **Protect worksheet and contents of locked cells** check box is activated (☑).

5 Use the **Password to unprotect sheet** text box to type a password.

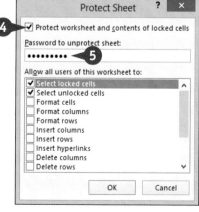

6 Click the check box beside each action that you want to allow unauthorized users to perform (☐ changes to ☑).

7 Click **OK**.

Excel asks you to confirm the password.

8 Type the password.

9 Click **OK**.

If you want to make changes to a worksheet, click the **Review** tab, click **Unprotect Sheet** (🗔), type the unprotect password, and then click **OK**.

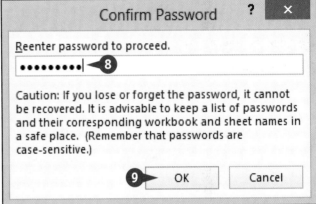

TIPS

When I protect a worksheet, no one can edit any of the cells. Is there a way to allow users to edit some of the cells?

Yes. This is useful if you have a data entry area or other range that you want other people to be able to edit but you do not want them to alter any other part of the worksheet. First, unprotect the sheet if it is currently protected. Select the range you want to unlock, click **Home**, click **Format**, and then click **Lock Cell** to turn off that option for the selected range.

When I protect a worksheet, can I configure a range to require a password before a user can edit the range?

Yes. First, unprotect the sheet if it is currently protected. Select the range you want to protect, click the **Review** tab, and then click **Allow Users to Edit Ranges**. In the Allow Users to Edit Ranges dialog box, click **New** to open the New Range dialog box. Type a title for the range, use the **Range** text box to type a password, and then click **OK**. When Excel prompts you to reenter the password, type the password and then click **OK**.

Protect a Workbook's Structure

You can prevent unwanted changes to a workbook by activating protection for the workbook's structure. You can also configure the workbook to require a password to unprotect it.

Protecting a workbook's structure means preventing users from inserting new worksheets, renaming or deleting existing worksheets, moving or copying worksheets, hiding and unhiding worksheets, and more. See the tips at the end of this section to learn which commands Excel disables when you protect a workbook's structure.

Protect a Workbook's Structure

1 Display the workbook you want to protect.

2 Click the **Review** tab.

3 Click **Protect Workbook** ( ).

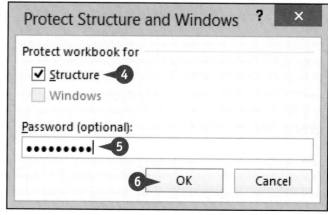

Excel displays the Protect Structure and Windows dialog box.

4 Click the **Structure** check box (☐ changes to ☑).

5 Type a password in the **Password** text box, if required.

6 Click **OK**.

If you specified a password,
Excel asks you to confirm it.

7 Type the password.

8 Click **OK**.

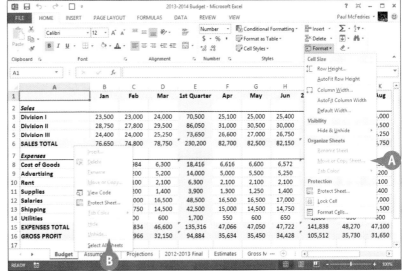

Ⓐ Excel disables most
worksheet-related commands
on the Ribbon.

Ⓑ Excel disables most
worksheet-related commands
on the worksheet shortcut
menu.

What happens when I protect a workbook's structure?

Excel disables most worksheet-related commands, including Insert Sheet, Delete Sheet, Rename Sheet, Move or Copy Sheet, Tab Color, Hide Sheet, and Unhide Sheet. Excel also prevents the Scenario Manager from creating a summary report.

How do I remove workbook structure protection?

If you no longer require your workbook structure to be protected, you can remove the protection by following Steps **1** to **3**. If you protected your workbook with a password, type the password and then click **OK**. Excel removes the workbook's structure protection.

Share a Workbook with Other Users

You can allow multiple users to modify a workbook simultaneously by sharing the workbook. Once you have shared a workbook, other users can open the workbook via a network connection and edit the file at the same time. Note that Excel cannot share a workbook that contains a table, so you need to convert any tables to ranges before performing this task. See Chapter 11 for more information.

When you share a workbook, Excel automatically begins tracking the changes made to the file. For more information on this feature, see the following section, "Track Workbook Changes."

Share a Workbook with Other Users

1 Display the workbook you want to share.

2 Click the **Review** tab.

3 Click **Share Workbook** (▭).

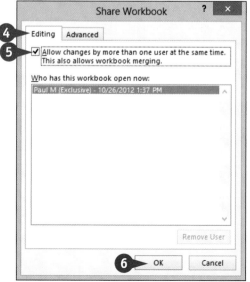

The Share Workbook dialog box appears.

4 Click the **Editing** tab.

5 Click the **Allow changes by more than one user at the same time** check box (☐ changes to ☑).

6 Click **OK**.

Excel tells you that it will now save the workbook.

7 Click **OK**.

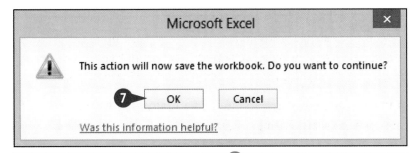

Excel saves the workbook and activates sharing.

A Excel displays [Shared] in the title bar.

You and users on your network can now edit the workbook at the same time.

TIP

How do I know if other people currently have the workbook open?
The Editing tab of the Share Workbook dialog box maintains a list of the users who have the workbook open. To see this list, follow these steps:

1 Display the shared workbook.

2 Click the **Review** tab.

3 Click 📖.

The Share Workbook dialog box appears.

4 Click the **Editing** tab.

A The **Who has this workbook open now** list displays the users who are currently editing the file.

5 Click **OK**.

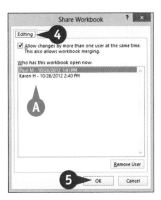

Track Workbook Changes

If you want other people to make changes to a workbook, you can keep track of those changes so you can either accept or reject them (see the following section, "Accept or Reject Workbook Changes"). The Track Changes feature in Excel enables you to do this.

When you turn on Track Changes, Excel monitors the activity of each reviewer and stores that reviewer's cell edits, row and column additions and deletions, range moves, worksheet insertions, and worksheet renames.

Track Workbook Changes

1 Display the workbook you want to track.

2 Click the **Review** tab.

3 Click **Track Changes** ( ).

4 Click **Highlight Changes**.

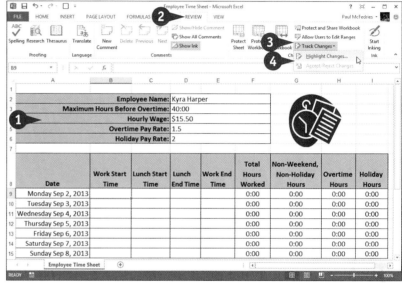

The Highlight Changes dialog box appears.

5 Click the **Track changes while editing** check box (changes to).

A Leave the **When** check box activated ( ) and leave **All** selected in the list.

B To learn more about the **Who** and **Where** options, see the tips at the end of this section.

C Leave the **Highlight changes on screen** check box activated ( ) to view the workbook changes.

6 Click **OK**.

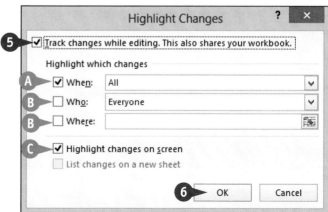

Excel tells you it will now save the workbook.

⑦ Click **OK**.

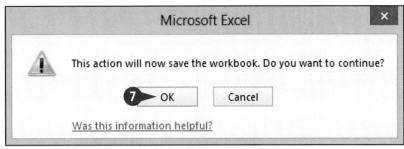

Excel activates the Track Changes feature.

Ⓓ Excel shares the workbook and indicates this by displaying [Shared] beside the workbook name.

Note: See the previous section, "Share a Workbook with Other Users," to learn more about workbook sharing.

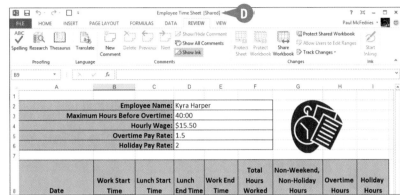

Is there a way to avoid having my own changes highlighted?

Yes, you can configure the workbook to show every user's changes but your own. Follow Steps **1** to **4** to open the Highlight Changes dialog box. Click the **Who** check box (☐ changes to ☑), click the **Who** ☑, and then click **Everyone but Me**. Click **OK** to put the new setting into effect.

Can I track changes in just part of the worksheet?

Yes, you can modify this task so that Excel only tracks changes in a specific range. Follow Steps **1** to **4** to open the Highlight Changes dialog box. Click the **Where** check box (☐ changes to ☑), click inside the **Where** range box, and then select the range you want to track. Click **OK** to put the new setting into effect.

Accept or Reject Workbook Changes

After you turn on the Track Changes features in Excel, as described in the previous section, "Track Workbook Changes," you can accept or reject the changes that other users make to the workbook. As a general rule, you should accept the changes that other users make to a workbook. The exception is when you know a change is incorrect. If you are not sure, it is best to talk to the other user before rejecting a change. If you and another user make changes to the same cell, Excel lets you resolve the conflict by accepting your edit or the other user's edit.

Accept or Reject Workbook Changes

1 Display the workbook you are tracking.

2 Click the **Review** tab.

3 Click **Track Changes** ( ).

4 Click **Accept/Reject Changes**.

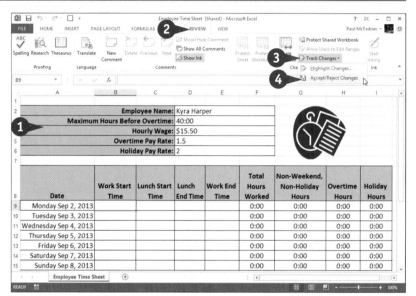

If your workbook has unsaved changes, Excel tells you it will now save the workbook.

5 Click **OK**.

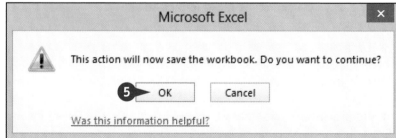

The Select Changes to Accept or Reject dialog box appears.

Ⓐ Leave the **When** check box activated (☑) and leave **Not yet reviewed** selected in the list.

Ⓑ If you only want to review changes made by a particular user, click the **Who** check box (☐ changes to ☑), click the **Who** ⌄, and then click the user's name.

6 Click **OK**.

The Accept or Reject Changes dialog box appears.

Ⓒ Excel displays the details of the current change.

7 Click an action for the change.

Ⓓ Click **Accept** to leave the change in the workbook.

Ⓔ Click **Reject** to remove the change from the workbook.

Excel displays the next change.

8 Repeat Step **7** to review all the changes.

Ⓕ You can also click **Accept All** or **Reject All** to accept or reject all changes at once.

Select Changes to Accept or Reject ? ✕

Which changes

Ⓐ ☑ Whe_n: Not yet reviewed ⌄

Ⓑ ☐ Wh_o: Everyone ⌄

☐ Whe_re:

6 OK Cancel

Accept or Reject Changes ? ✕

Change 1 of 20 made to this document:

Kyra H, 9/6/2013 5:54 PM: Ⓒ

Changed cell B9 from '<blank>' to '9:00 AM'.

Ⓓ Ⓔ Ⓕ Ⓕ

7 Accept Reject Accept All Reject All Close

		Work Start Time	Lunch Start Time	Lunch End Time	Work End Time	Total Hours Worked	Non-Weekend, Non-Holiday Hours
8	Date						
9	Monday Sep 2, 2013	9:00 AM	12:00 PM	1:00 PM	5:00 PM	7:00	7:00
10	Tuesday Sep 3, 2013	8:00 AM	12:30 PM	1:45 PM	5:00 PM	7:45	7:45
11	Wednesday Sep 4, 2013	11:00 PM	3:00 AM	4:00 AM	9:00 AM	9:00	9:00
12	Thursday Sep 5, 2013	10:30 PM	2:00 AM	3:00 AM	7:00 AM	7:30	7:30
13	Friday Sep 6, 2013	9:00 AM	1:00 PM	2:30 PM	5:30 PM	7:00	7:00
14	Saturday Sep 7, 2013					0:00	0:00
15	Sunday Sep 8, 2013					0:00	0:00

Employee Time Sheet

TIPS

What happens if I and another user make changes that affect the same cell?

In this situation, when you save the workbook, Excel displays the Accept or Reject Changes dialog box, which shows the change you made as well as the change the other user made. Click whatever change is the correct one and then click **Accept**. If there are multiple conflicts, you can save time by clicking your change or the other user's change and then clicking either **Accept All** or **Reject All**.

When I complete my review, should I turn off the tracking feature?

Unless you know that other people still require access to the workbook, you should turn off the tracking feature when your review is complete. To do this, click the **Review** tab, click 📝, and then click **Highlight Changes** to open the Highlight Changes dialog box. Click the **Track changes while editing** check box (☑ changes to ☐), and then click **OK**.

Save a Workbook to Your SkyDrive

I f you are using Windows 8 under a Microsoft account, then as part of that account you get a free online storage area called *SkyDrive*. You can use Excel to add any of your workbooks to your SkyDrive. This is useful if you are going to be away from your computer but still require access to a workbook. Because the SkyDrive is accessible anywhere you have web access, you can view and work with your spreadsheet without using your computer.

Save a Workbook to Your SkyDrive

1 Open the workbook you want to save to your SkyDrive.

2 Click the **File** tab.

3 Click **Save As**.

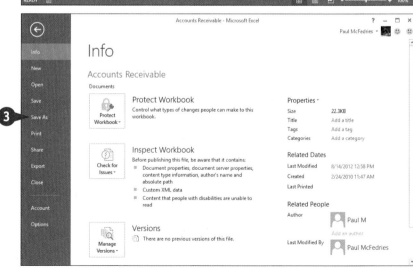

The Save As tab appears.

4 Click your SkyDrive.

A If you see the SkyDrive folder you want to use to store the workbook, click it and skip to Step **8**.

5 Click **Browse**.

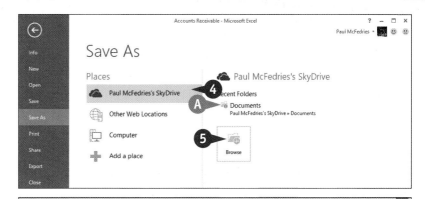

The Save As dialog box appears.

6 Click **SkyDrive**.

Note: The first time you save a file to your SkyDrive, you might see a folder that uses a series of letters and numbers as its name instead of the SkyDrive folder.

7 Double-click the subfolder you want to use to store the workbook.

8 Click **Save**.

Excel saves the workbook to your SkyDrive.

How do I open a workbook that has been saved to my SkyDrive?

Follow these steps:

1 Click the **File** tab.

2 Click **Open**.

3 Click your SkyDrive.

4 Click **Browse**.

The Open dialog box appears.

5 Open the SkyDrive folder that contains the workbook.

6 Click the workbook.

7 Click **Open**.

Excel opens the SkyDrive workbook.

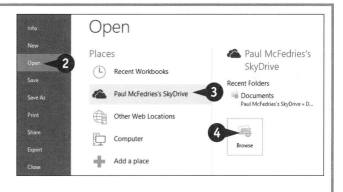

Send a Workbook as an E-Mail Attachment

If you want to send an Excel workbook to another person, you can attach the workbook to an e-mail message and send it to that person's e-mail address.

A typical e-mail message is fine for short notes but you may have something more complex to communicate, such as budget numbers or a loan amortization. Instead of trying to copy that information to an e-mail message, it would be better to send the recipient a workbook that contains the data. That way, the other person can then open the workbook in Excel after receiving your message.

Send a Workbook as an E-Mail Attachment

1. Open the workbook you want to send.

2. Click the **File** tab.

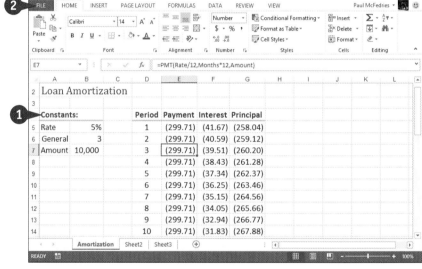

3. Click **Share**.

4. Click **Email**.

Excel displays the Email commands.

5. Click **Send as Attachment**.

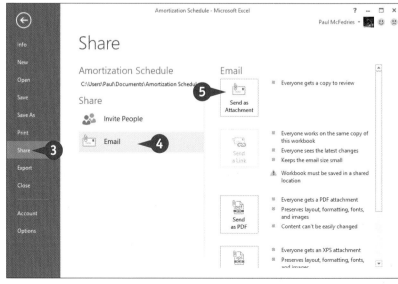

Outlook creates a new e-mail message.

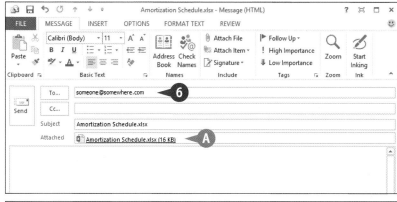

Ⓐ Outlook attaches the workbook to the message.

⑥ Type the address of the recipient.

⑦ Type your message text.

⑧ Click **Send**.

Outlook sends the message.

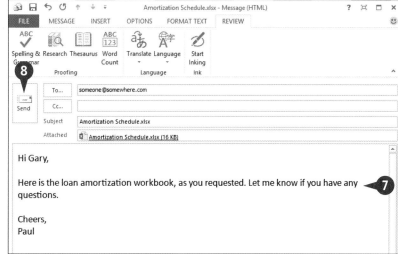

TIPS

Are there any restrictions related to sending file attachments?

There is no practical limit to the number of workbooks you can attach to a message. However, you should be careful with the total size of the files you send. If you or the recipient has a slow Internet connection, sending or receiving the message can take an extremely long time. Also, many Internet service providers (ISPs) place a limit on the size of a message's attachments, which is usually between 2 and 10MB.

What can I do if the recipient does not have Excel?

If the other person does not use Excel, you can send the workbook in a different format. One possibility would be to save the workbook as a web page (see the following section, "Save Excel Data as a Web Page"). Alternatively, if your recipient can view PDF (Portable Document Format) files, follow Steps **1** to **4** to display the Email commands, and then click **Send as PDF**.

Save Excel Data as a Web Page

If you have an Excel range, worksheet, or workbook that you want to share on the web, you can save that data as a web page that you can then upload to your website.

When you save a document as a web page, you can also specify the title text that appears in the browser's title bar and the keywords that search engines use to index the page. You can also choose whether you want to publish the entire workbook to the web, just a single worksheet, or just a range of cells.

Save Excel Data as a Web Page

1 Open the workbook that contains the data you want to save as a web page.

Ⓐ If you want to save a worksheet as a web page, click the worksheet tab.

Ⓑ If you want to save a range as a web page, select the range.

2 Click the **File** tab.

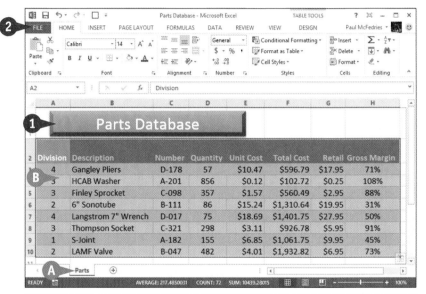

3 Click **Save As**.

4 Click **Computer**.

5 Click **Browse**.

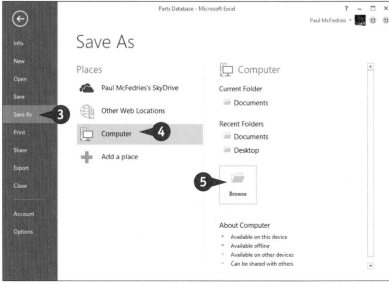

The Save As dialog box appears.

6 Click the **Save as type** ☑ and then click **Web Page**.

7 Select the folder where you want to store the web page file.

8 Click **Change Title**.

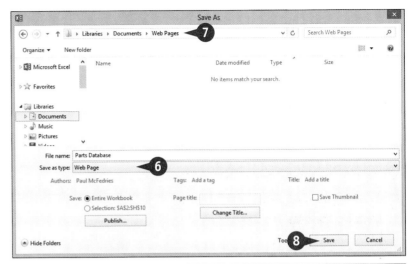

The Enter Text dialog box appears.

9 Type the page title in the **Page title** text box.

10 Click **OK**.

11 Click **Tags** and then type one or more keywords, separated by semicolons.

12 Choose which part of the file you want to save as a web page (○ changes to ●):

C Click **Entire Workbook** to save the whole workbook.

D Click **Selection** to save either the current worksheet or the selected cells.

13 Click **Save**.

Excel saves the data as a web page.

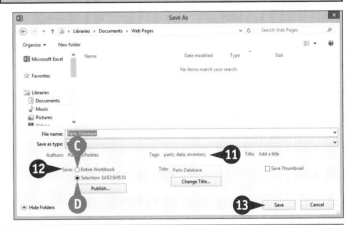

TIP

If I make frequent changes to the workbook, do I have to go through this procedure after every change?
No, you can configure the workbook to automatically save your changes to the web page file. This is called AutoRepublish. To set it up, follow Steps **1** to **12** to get the workbook ready for the web and then click **Publish**. In the Publish as Web Page dialog box, click **AutoRepublish every time this workbook is saved** (☐ changes to ☑). Click **Publish**. Excel saves the workbook as a web page and will now update the web page file each time you save the workbook.

Make a Workbook Compatible with Earlier Versions of Excel

You can save an Excel workbook in a special format that makes it compatible with earlier versions of Excel. This enables you to share your workbook with other Excel users.

If you have another computer that uses a version of Excel prior to Excel 2007, or if the people you work with use earlier Excel versions, those programs cannot read documents in the standard format used by Excel 2013, Excel 2010, and Excel 2007. By saving a workbook using the Excel 97-2003 Workbook file format, you make that file compatible with earlier Excel versions.

Make a Workbook Compatible with Earlier Versions of Excel

1 Open the workbook you want to make compatible.

2 Click **File**.

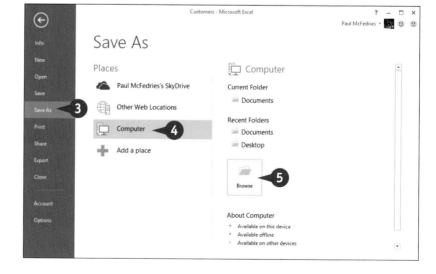

3 Click **Save As**.

4 Click **Computer**.

5 Click **Browse**.

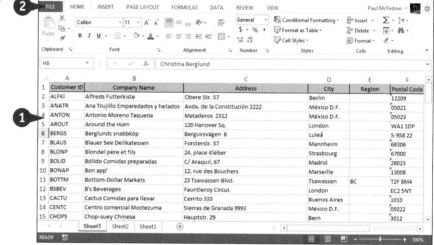

The Save As dialog box appears.

6 Select the folder in which you want to store the new workbook.

7 Click in the **File name** text box and type the name that you want to use for the new workbook.

8 Click the **Save as type** ⌄.

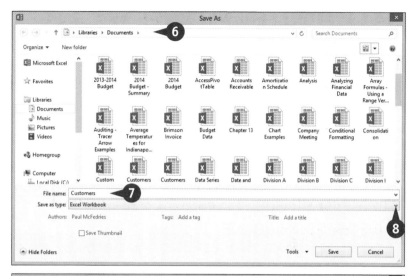

9 Click the **Excel 97-2003 Workbook** file format.

10 Click **Save**.

Excel saves the file using the Excel 97-2003 Workbook format.

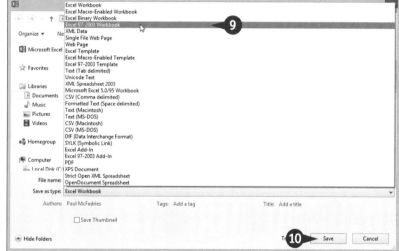

TIPS

Can people using Excel 2010 and Excel 2007 open my Excel 2013 workbooks?
Yes. The default file format used by both Excel 2010 and Excel 2007 is the same as the one used by Excel 2013.

Which versions of Excel are compatible with the Excel 97-2003 Workbook file format?
For Windows, the Excel 97-2003 Workbook file format is compatible with Excel 97, Excel 2000, Excel XP, and Excel 2003. For the Mac, the Excel 97-2003 Workbook file format is compatible with Excel 98, Excel 2001, and Office 2004. In the unlikely event that you need to share a document with someone using either Excel 5.0 or Excel 95, use the Microsoft Excel 5.0/95 Workbook file format instead.

Mark Up a Worksheet with a Digital Pen

Excel comes with a digital ink feature that enables you to give feedback by marking up a worksheet with pen marks and highlights. This is often easier than adding comments or cell text.

To use digital ink on a worksheet, you must have either a tablet PC or a graphics tablet, each of which comes with a pressure-sensitive screen. You can then use a digital pen — or sometimes your finger — to draw directly on the screen, a technique known as *digital inking*.

Mark Up a Worksheet with a Digital Pen

Activate Digital Inking

1 Click the **Review** tab.

2 Click **Start Inking** (✐).

Excel enables digital inking.

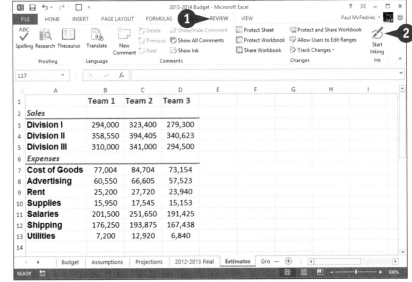

Mark Up with a Pen

1 Tap the **Pens** tab.

2 Tap **Pen** (✐).

3 Use the **Pens** gallery to select a pen color and thickness.

Ⓐ You can also use the **Color** (✐) and **Thickness** (≡) buttons to customize the pen.

4 Use your digital pen (or finger) to write your marks or text on the worksheet.

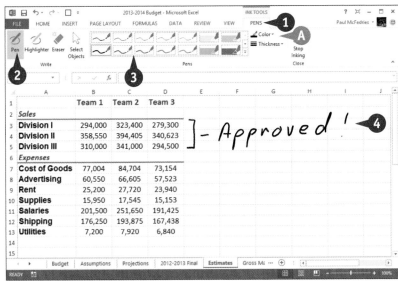

Mark Up with a Highlighter

1 Tap the **Pens** tab.

2 Tap **Highlighter** (⟋).

3 Use the **Pens** gallery to select a highlighter color and thickness.

Ⓑ You can also use ⟋ and ☰ to customize the highlighter.

4 Use your digital pen (or finger) to highlight the worksheet text.

Erase Digital Ink

1 Tap the **Pens** tab.

2 Tap **Eraser** (⟋).

3 Use your digital pen (or finger) to tap the ink you want to remove.

Excel erases the ink.

Ⓒ When you no longer need to mark up the worksheet with digital ink, tap **Stop Inking** (☒).

TIP

Is there a way to hide a worksheet's digital ink without deleting that ink?

Yes. This is a good idea if you want to show the worksheet to other people but you do not want them to see the digital ink, either because it contains sensitive information or because it makes the worksheet harder to read. To toggle your digital ink off and on, click the **Review** tab and then click **Show Ink** (⟋).

Collaborate on a Workbook Online

If you have a Microsoft account, you can use the SkyDrive feature to store an Excel workbook in an online folder (see "Save a Workbook to Your SkyDrive," earlier in this chapter) and then allow other users to collaborate on that workbook using the Excel Web App.

Collaboration here means that you and the other users can edit the workbook online at the same time. To allow another person to collaborate with you on your online workbook, it is not necessary that the person have a Microsoft account. However, you can make your online workbooks more secure by requiring collaborators to have a Microsoft account.

Collaborate on a Workbook Online

1 Use a Web browser to navigate to http://skydrive.live.com.

Note: If you are not already logged in, you are prompted to log on to your Microsoft account.

Your SkyDrive appears.

2 Click the folder that contains the workbooks you want to share.

3 Click **Share folder**.

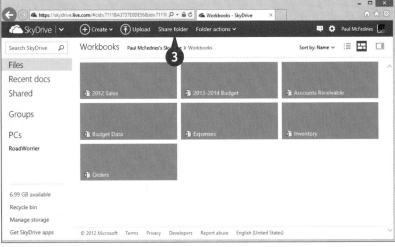

The folder's sharing options appear.

4 Click **Send email**.

5 Type the e-mail address of the person you want to collaborate with.

Note: To add multiple addresses, press `Tab` after each one.

6 Type a message to the user.

7 Click **Recipients can edit** (☐ changes to ☑).

8 If you want to require users to sign in with a Microsoft account, click **Require everyone who accesses this to sign in** (☐ changes to ☑).

9 Click **Share**.

SkyDrive sends an e-mail message to the user. The user clicks the link in that message, optionally logs on with a Microsoft account, and can then edit a workbook in the shared folder.

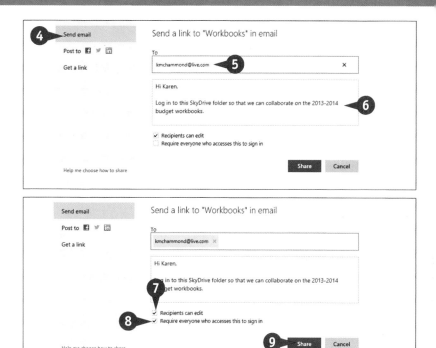

TIP

How do I know when other people are also using a workbook online?

When you open a workbook using the Excel Web App, examine the lower-right corner of the Excel screen. If you see **1 person editing**, it means you are the only user who is working on the file. However, if you see **2 people editing**, then it means another person is collaborating on the workbook with you. To see who it is, click the **2 people editing** message (**A**), as shown here.

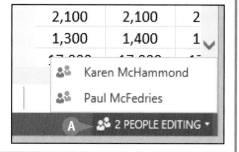

Index

Index

FLEXIBLE. FAST. FUN.

At DigitalClassroom.com, you choose your way to learn!

DigitalClassroom.com lets you choose when, where, and how to learn new skills. This subscription-based online learning environment is accessible anytime from your desktop, laptop, or smartphone.

Learn to design with Photoshop, InDesign, or Dreamweaver. Sharpen your computer skills on Windows or Mac. Conquer HTML programming. Master Excel. Explore these and many more technologies in this collaborative, social media-enabled environment — anytime!

- Learn online with video tutorials and supplemental e-books
- Access video lessons 24/7 from any Internet-connected device
- Study Photoshop, Dreamweaver, HTML, Office, Windows, and many other technologies in classes taught by industry experts and trusted trainers
- Interact with other students in DigitalClassroom.com forums and on Facebook, Twitter, Pinterest, YouTube, and LinkedIn

Learn more! Sample www.DigitalClassroom.com for free, now!

DIGITAL CLASSROOM